The Gold Seekers!

Don Miguel Peralta discovered gold near Superstition Mountain, but lost it when the Apaches wreaked vengeance upon those who had defiled the sacred dwelling place of their Thunder God.

Jacob Walz, "The Dutchman," was told where to find gold by his Indian bride but died in agony for revealing the secret of her people.

Dr. Abraham D. Thorne, ministered to the Apaches, earning their gratitude and a blindfolded trip into the sacred highlands for three bags of gold.

Dr. John D. Walker, organized the Pima Indians to fight the Apaches, won a beautiful and talented Pima wife and discovered that gold was not the only wealth.

Meet these men and scores more—from wild-eyed dreamers to wild-eyed murderers—in Robert Joseph Allen's personally researched chronicle of Arizona's "evil, terrible mountain."

The Story of Superstition Mountain and the Lost Dutchman Gold Mine is an original POCKET BOOK edition.

The Story of Superstition Mountain and the Lost Dutchman Gold Mine

by Robert Joseph Allen

PUBLISHED BY POCKET BOOKS NEW YORK

THE STORY OF SUPERSTITION MOUNTAIN AND THE LOST
DUTCHMAN GOLD MINE

POCKET BOOK edition published November, 1971
4th printing..........March, 1972

This original POCKET BOOK edition is printed from
brand-new plates made from newly set, clear, easy-to-read type.
POCKET BOOK editions are published by POCKET BOOKS, a division of
Simon & Schuster, Inc., 630 Fifth Avenue, New York, N.Y. 10020.
Trademarks registered in the United States and other countries.

L

To

my adored wife, Eadie, whose
faith caused this book to be
undertaken, and who contributed
so much intelligence,
ability and work to its completion.

Also
my deepest appreciation and
gratitude to those three pretty,
talented and tenacious
secretary-researchers, Linda
Johannpeter, Darrin Stanley
and Mary Tarr.

R.J.A.

INTRODUCTION

This is a book in which a mountain, Superstition Mountain, an evil, terrible mountain, is the protagonist.

A prodigious effort was expended to make this story as accurate as years of study and research could accomplish. All dates mentioned are accurate, or approximately so, and the names used are of people who became famous or infamous due to the Mountain. They shared at one time or another the experience of having the often fatal fascination of the Mountain draw them to its vicinity.

Some march gloriously through the pages of this book; others repulsively—those men and women who were attracted to Superstition Mountain by the lure of sudden riches, and who collectively left behind them a record of adventure, love, greed, murder, honor, mystery, romance, tragedy, intrigue, treachery, revenge, madness, kindness, malignant jealousy, courage, meanness, sacrifice, intolerance and viciousness, as well as bleached bones, numerous beheaded bodies, raging gold fever, and lost treasure.

The story of one of them, John D. Walker and his beautiful and extraordinarily talented Pima wife, Chur-ga, is the most fascinating the history of Arizona has produced. Reading the old records that reveal the ingratitude, bigotry and greed that this family endured is shattering, even for a hardened reporter.

The factual material as well as the rich legends that constitute the story of the Old Dutchman, Jacob Walz, full of the romance, adventure, murders, and mystery that featured his extraordinary career in and around the Mountain could not have been improved upon or added to by even the most imaginative writer.

The majority of the characters mentioned in this book who were attracted to the Mountain were outstanding in morals and honesty, but many who came balked at no crime or ruthless action that suited their purposes. They lived, lusted, murdered, cheated and robbed with such abandon that the pain they caused reaches vicariously to the present despite the years that intervene. Thousands of others, with characters of every shade of gray, were beguiled by the Mountain.

And still they come. They are there as you read this, prowling the Mountain, and the deaths are continuing.

All of them find something of value there. Perhaps not riches or happiness, but Pedro de Castenada, the Spanish historian who traveled with Francisco Vasquez de Coronado during his explorations of the New World, put their case well in describing the adventures of Coronado and his men while seeking the Seven Golden Cities of Cibola: *"Granted that they did not find the riches of which they had been told; they did find the next best thing—a place in which to search for them."*

The Story of
Superstition
Mountain
and
the Lost
Dutchman
Gold Mine

Chapter 1

There have always been lost mines and lost treasures galore and millions of people who search for them and dream about them and use the thought of them to give meaning and purpose to their lives. But none have been so dedicated in their purpose, or so heedless of danger when they move from dreaming to actively searching, as the aficionados who have steadily come from literally all over the world to comb Superstition Mountain, the most fabled mountain in the world, hard by Apache Junction, Arizona, about thirty-five miles from the city of Phoenix.

It was formed eons ago when the earth's gradually cooling crust developed a crevice that let surface water rush into the molten interior, creating an instant steam pressure of unimaginable power. This pressure caused an atomizer-like reaction, forcing a squirt of the molten mass that fills the heart of the earth back up the crevice to the surface, creating a mass of volcanic material rearing thousands of feet into the air.

When the mass cooled it hardened into a stupefying contour featured by thousands of cliffs, peaks, and mesas, known collectively as Superstition Mountain. The collection rests on a plateau held high, as bearers carry a catafalque, above the surrounding terrain and bears such striking names as Geronimo's Head, Three Red Hills, Picacho Butte, Fish Creek, Tortilla, Black Mountain, Miner's Needle, and Bluff Springs. The Spanish explorers called them *Sierra de la Espuma*—"Mountains of the Foam." Viewed from the southwest is a facade that makes all appear to be simply one high mountain and to the Apaches that vantage point was all that counted, hence the term Superstition Mountain in the singular sense. Very few people, even today, really understand the difference. All the books and magazine articles about this range of mountains refer to them in the singular as Superstition Mountain. In this book, therefore, the writer will follow long-established custom and refer to the mass as Superstition Mountain, singular.

I

The unusually severe thunderstorms that its formation, or evil genius, causes, deluge the vast sawtooth-surfaced plateau, creating torrents that rush down in various directions, cutting additional barrancas and accentuate the general tortuousness. To add to the Mountain's ferocity, something in the matter that was ejected from the world's center, coupled with the climate of Arizona, has proved ideal for the growth of cacti and nearly every variety of thorn-bearing plant imaginable grows all over it—the most dreadful of plants to make one's way through.

It is not the world's highest mountain—there are much higher ones. But it is the most rugged and treacherous of all and has earned an unequaled infamy as a killer of men, and women too, by causing a madness in them that moved them to kill each other—the ones who came to search its wilderness of volcanic upheaval in tortured shapes for the rose quartz vein, or lode, reputed to be rich beyond the dreams of avarice in free gold. The lode is now known as the "Lost Dutchman Gold Mine." And the greatest killer of all has been the terrain of the Mountain itself.

Charlatans, con men, and mentally disturbed persons have told stories that many times caused stampedes to the general area where they said they had found the fabulous "rose quartz vein heavy with gold," only to have their stories of finding the lode invariably proved dishonest, self-seeking, or self-delusionary.

The peculiar characters attracted by the legend caused the question of whether or not the lode *actually* exists, or ever existed, to become a matter of heated pro and con. Those who have business interests near the Mountain, especially of the kind that benefits from its status as a tourist attraction, argue passionately with those who seem to have an even more powerful involvement—a sentimental interest in the mine, either as an entity or a legend, and some of them don't seem to care particularly which it is.

Superstition's ramparts can only be gained by traversing canyons that gash its western and eastern ends, and then only by expensively and elaborately equipped pack trains of mules and extraordinarily well-trained horses. The favorite location of the lode in the calculations of most of its aficionados has put it near Weaver's Needle, known to Mexicans as the Finger of God. A strange, phallic finger of smooth, black basalt rock, Weaver's Needle emerges perpendicularly from the plateau and towers hundreds of feet into the air. Incredibly deep crevices, sheer cliffs, and ravines choked with catclaw, prickly pear, paloverde, saguaro, and ocotillo guard its base.

The Apaches were probably the first people to set eyes on Superstition Mountain centuries before the Spanish conquistadors saw its awesome cliffs and crags. The first of these Spanish conquistadors came north with Francisco Vasquez de Coronado from Mexico, in 1540, seeking the town of Quivira, one of the legendary Seven Golden Cities of Cibola. The cities had been described by Cabeza de Vaca, a Spanish explorer who came to the New World in 1528 as royal treasurer of the expedition of Panfilo de Narvaez to colonize Florida. Of the large number on this expedition who landed at Tampa Bay and started inland, only Cabeza de Vaca and three companions were ever heard of again. They turned up eight years later in Mexico after having crossed the continent in one of the most remarkable journeys on record. They had spent much of the time as slaves of the Indians, from whom de Vaca heard of the "golden cities." When he returned to Spain he wrote of the many wonders he had seen, which included the first known account of herds of buffalo.

When news of de Vaca's report reached Coronado, who was then commander of a Spanish exploring expedition based in Mexico, he immediately organized a select group and headed north. After crossing the Rio Grande he was told by Indians he steadily encountered from then on of a mountain where there was much gold. It was also the abode of their Thunder God and his staff of lesser gods, they said, and his voice was the thunder that rolled among its spires. When Coronado and his men came to the Mountain they were frustrated by its towering crags and almost impassable terrain—as were many thousands of others who came after them during the following four centuries. And the Indians would not help Coronado explore back of the Mountain, even after torture, because they feared that their Thunder God would not like them to, and would punish them for it. Their medicine men had indicated as much to them.

They not only believed that His voice from high on the Mountain spoke to them, but that their medicine men could understand Him and interpret for them just what He wanted them to know. Following a blinding flash of lightning, His voice thundered forth with an ear-splitting crash to hammer home a point, or, appeased, faded away to a rolling rumble that echoed hauntingly around the peaks crowning the Mountain. The medicine men strained with all their senses and will-power to grasp His meaning, because only when His message was clear to them did He cause the sun to come out again and shine as a benediction to all.

When the Spaniards tried to explore the Mountain on their own, their numbers were steadily decimated by mysterious disappearances. If one of them so much as strayed a few feet from his companions, he was never seen alive again. The few bodies of those that they recovered had had their heads cut off and carted away by someone or something.

The terrified survivors finally refused outright to go up and behind the Mountain again, so Coronado dubbed it *Monte Superstition*, the origin of its now infamous name, and moved north for several leagues until he discovered the most stupendous of the Seven Wonders of the World, the Grand Canyon of Arizona.

From there he swung left to California, then southeast to the source of the Rio Grande which he followed to the sea and then northward again into what is now Kansas. From there, Coronado headed back to Spain where Castenada helped him describe in glowing terms the many wonders they had seen in the New World and to warn of the frightful Mountain where swift and cruel death waited for those who violated its sanctity.

Whether or not angry gods have ever destroyed invaders of the Mountain, it is a known fact that the Apaches *have* dedicated themselves to wreaking vengeance on anyone who violates the sanctity of their Thunder God's abode. It is as sacred to them as St. Peter's to a Catholic, or Mecca to a Moslem.

Chapter 2

Don Miguel Peralta, a member of a Mexican family that owned a rancho in Sonora, Mexico, as big as some small states, was the first white man to discover gold near Superstition Mountain while searching in 1845 for the vein of almost pure gold described to Coronado by the Apache Indians.

Before returning to Mexico for men, equipment, and supplies with which to explore his discovery, he memorized various salient points of the topography that would guide him back to the towering Mountain. To make sure that he could find his mine again, he used the Mountain's most outstanding landmark, a peculiarly shaped peak, which he described as "looking like a sombrero," to use as a sighting point for a compass course to his mine. "I am calling the mine 'Sombrero Mine,'" he wrote in a letter he sent by carrier to relatives in Sonora shortly after he discovered it.

To his reverent peons, however, the peak, or spire, looked more like a finger pointing skyward, and ever afterwards, they called it the "Finger of God." But to Pauline Weaver, a hard-bitten, early white explorer, it was just another landmark on which to etch his name with a bowie knife when he came upon it sometime during the 1850s. Subsequent trappers and prospectors found his name carved there, and it made its way forever onto the maps of the new territory of Arizona as Weaver's Needle. Strangely enough, from a certain vantage point, it does resemble a weaver's needle.

After returning from Mexico with a force of several hundred peons he had recruited to work his dazzling gold discovery, Peralta shipped millions of pesos worth of almost pure gold concentrate taken from his Sombrero Mine during the following three years.

The Apaches were naturally enraged at the defiling of the abode of their Thunder God by Peralta and his men. Even worse, the miners were making merry with the lissome Apache maidens, who had been attracted by the gay, singing,

5

guitar-strumming men from south of the Rio Grande, and especially by their clean smell—they often changed into fresh clothes and had a habit of taking occasional baths, particularly in anticipation of festive occasions.

The braves of all Apache tribes in Arizona found this state of affairs intolerable. In 1848 they raised a large force of warriors which was placed under the command of Mangas Coloradas. This great chieftold brought his contingent of warriors from their stronghold in the Chiricahua Mountains and joined with Cochise, an even more famous chief of the Chiricahuas, to drive the Spanish intruders from their land.

Peralta got wind of the Apache plan and immediately stopped operations at the mine and withdrew all the men, equipment, and livestock to the sanctuary on the mesa high on Superstition. Then, in order to make a run for it to his hacienda in Mexico, he began loading his available burros and mules with all they could carry of the gold concentrate that he and his miners had accumulated since the last shipment to Sonora. In anticipation of returning some day, he took elaborate precautions to conceal the entrance to his mine, and to smooth away all signs that anyone had ever worked within miles of the vicinity.

But the Apaches learned of Peralta's intended flight from a peon whom they captured in *flagrante delicto* with one of their girls. Consequently, Coloradas and Cochise were able to move their braves quietly into strategic positions during the night that Peralta had scheduled for his takeoff. The Mexicans came down from their aerie before dawn, filing through canyons and clefts which they thought would screen their movements. When they assembled at the foot of the three-thousand-foot-high sheer cliffs on the northwest end of the Mountain to start the long trek to Sonora, they unwittingly moved into the open end of an Apache U-formation. The place is now known as Massacre Ground (according to U.S. Department of the Army, Corps of Engineers maps).

The Mexicans never had a chance. They were taken utterly by surprise and at a disadvantage with their heavily laden mules and burros. The pack animals promptly stampeded, demoralizing the horses of Peralta's armed guard. These mounts of the leaders and guards and their riders rapidly fell victims to a withering hail of arrows, for the Apaches were among the world's deadliest with bow and arrow. As for the unarmed, unmounted, almost helpless peons, they were cut down by the stone axes of the red men. None of these peons, who were little better than slaves for hundreds of years in Spanish-ruled Mexico had been armed. (Naturally no Spanish nobleman would have trusted them with weapons, knowing well the ultimate use to which slaves would likely put them.)

The mules that toted the equipment of the miners and their guards, and the burros that carried the concentrate, many of them maddened by arrows in their flanks, scattered amid the hundreds of wild, deep ravines and washes that slice up the area slanting away from the foot of Superstition on its north and west parapets. These animals were hunted down by the Apaches at their leisure because Indians prized them greatly as food.

It was reported—accurately, as later events were to prove —that the Apaches dumped the concentrate-filled packsaddles on the ground after capturing the burros. From its appearance they deemed the concentrate to be some sort of stone rubble that the Mexicans inexplicably valued. Apaches of that period only knew of gold in its refined form, and then only in the form of Spanish ornaments they'd seen. Gold-bearing concentrate, no matter how rich, must have looked like mere rubble to them, although there were other Indian tribes, especially in Mexico and Peru, who knew about gold and how to refine it.

A couple of years after the Massacre, a contingent of the U.S. Army came across the macabre scene and gathered up what was left of the bodies of the peons who had died there and gave them burial in a huge common grave. Peralta's body was not found. It was the custom of Spanish noblemen to be richly dressed, and it is likely the Apaches carried off his body as a trophy. The records do not indicate whether the army men found any of the gold concentrate. Later discoveries were to show that such of the gold-laden burros as escaped the Apaches sought the sanctuary of the many deep washes in the immediate area. Both concealment and good browsing were to be found there, with usually a spring, or at least seepage of water at the foot of the Mountain. There they eventually perished.

Among the wonderful tales of Sinbad the Sailor is one about a magic mountain that stood by a narrow strait connecting two seas. In the center of the mountain was a huge magnet, which exerted so strong an attraction on the metal parts of passing sailing vessels that the ships were drawn helplessly ashore to the foot of the mountain.

The story of Superstition Mountain and the tale of the gold-laden burros and mules spread for years all over the world. It was a story to which men of every description listened eagerly, and for the *adventuresome* men among them it had as irresistible an appeal as Sinbad's magnet had for metal.

Most of the men, and women too, who listened and noted were honest and well-intentioned enough, but a percentage were criminals on the run including robbers and murderers of the bold variety to whom crime was a chosen way of life. They and those robbers and killers who are less bold—assassination or bushwhacker types, who always follow the stand-up killers, in a manner of speaking, as jackals do the lion for their leavings—preyed on the good people who came to Arizona to look for the lost mine, and are still doing so.

In time these rapacious, amoral human jackals made it extremely dangerous even to be in the vicinity of Superstition Mountain. They were men and women who unhesitatingly shot prospectors in the back for the grub in their packs; what little money they might have, or anything of value. But the macabre touch came from the psychotic or sadistic killers who killed just to see blood flow, or who could not resist torturing and killing anybody or anything helpless. They were like hunters who kill game for the sheer joy of seeing something die—something they have no desire to eat, or even take back for others to eat or profit from. This type perpetrated the murders that have made the area more infamous for cold-blooded killings and bushwhacking than any other scene of lost treasure the world has ever known.

From time to time there would be reports that the mouldering remains of a packsaddle and its burden of rich gold concentrate had been found. As the years went on the area came to be known as Goldfield.

In the early 1850s, two Mexican War veterans, Aloysious Hurley and Sean O'Connor, who were prospecting near Superstition, found the skeleton of a burro and the golden treasure in its disintegrated packsaddle. Riches beyond their wildest dreams lay before their eyes. They must have known that this windfall came from the Peralta Massacre, because, according to the stories they told after they had settled down in Idaho as rich and respected old men, they set themselves to searching the entire length of the draw, or barranca, in which they had found the dead burro. This barranca gradually deepened as it approached the foot of the Mountain, where it ended up against a precipice. It was easy to see, they said, that the burro kept going up the barranca until he found himself faced by the cliff and then didn't have sense enough to retrace his steps. During the following weeks they found another burro skeleton and two packsaddles of concentrate heavy with the metal that is bright and yellow, hard and cold, but nevertheless can make reality of the stuff of dreams.

By laboriously breaking up the concentrate with a crude pestle and mortar and panning out the bulk of the waste material, they condensed their rich find into a small, heavy quantity, which they poured into canvas sacks and concealed in the camping outfit on their pack mule. They knew only too well that the West of those days swarmed with men who, if they suspected what the mule was carrying, would unhesitatingly bushwhack them for it, or for even a fraction of it. Also, they didn't want to attract competitors to their gold-strewn area.

They left their field of golden harvest late in the summer because they had a long way to go; they wanted to sell their gold at the U.S. mint in San Francisco before the fall and winter snowstorms blocked the Mountain passes, and they didn't want to go by the southern route and risk crossing the nearly five hundred miles of the deserts of Arizona and California.

After having the almost pure gold concentrate smelted by a mill near Sutter Creek, California, they sold the gold at the mint, each one taking half of the proceeds five days apart to attract as little attention as possible. They emerged with a total of $37,000 in U.S. gold specie. Gold at that time was worth about $200 per pound.

They went back the next year and for several years thereafter, to comb the area of the Massacre and each year added to the fortune they were building up through finding Peralta's scattered treasure. Each year the pickings grew leaner, and despite their precautions, word of their find leaked out so that more and more adventurers of all sorts came to the vicinity to hunt the concentrate-laden packsaddles the Apaches had scorned.

Finally, after several close shaves with outlaws who would have thought nothing of killing them for no more than their camping outfit, especially the pack mules, Hurley and O'Connor became so busy on their last trip avoiding the unsavory characters who were fairly infesting the place by this time and also seeking the Peralta treasure, that they failed to find any more gold. More than once they came across dead bodies of obvious prospectors, practically all of whom had been bush-whacked. Some were plainly the victims of white men, and many others bore even more plainly the trademark of Apache customs.

The last known case of anyone finding the bones of one of Peralta's gold-laden burros was C. H. Silverlocke, who turned up in Phoenix one day in 1914 with some bits of badly de-composed leather, some pieces of metal wrought Spanish-fashion into corner braces for a packsaddle, and $18,000 worth of gold concentrate.

Tom Daly who, with his partner Phil Kent, once owned the Superstition Mountain Pack Outfit, which was organized to take thrill-seekers as far behind the Mountain as they cared to venture, found and explored the camp where Peralta and his peon miners lived during the years they worked the mine. The original *arrastres* in which they separated the gold from the ore, and the remains of forges where they sharpened and tempered their tools, can still be seen there, as well as traces of a small racetrack where they evidently held holiday horse and mule races.

"About every time I make a trip up onto the main plateau," Tom says, "I pass the general area where Peralta and his men lived on a mesa atop a small inner mountain, one perfectly designed by nature to help them fend off Apache attacks that were such a grim feature of living in the Arizona of those days. I can see traces of now-dim trails that rendezvous there. And an old well is in the area; also, we've found and collected bones of mules, burros, and horses, traces of old packsaddles and Spanish-type mule shoes and pits where they made char-coal to sharpen and temper the steel of their tools, such as drills, hammers, and picks. As a matter of fact, there are still traces of charcoal in those old pits."

Tom has lived in the vicinity of Superstition Mountain for over forty years, and during all that time he has been either a working cowboy or a guide packing dudes into the Mountain, as well as to all the other hinterlands of Arizona. For many years Phil and he made a specialty of guiding people into and out of Superstition, and they sometimes helped search for bodies or for prospectors lost there. Both are considered by sheriffs and lawmen to be among the top experts on the topography of the Mountain. They are experts, too, on the subject of the specialized equipment and know-how needed up there to get through the cactus, ironwood, catclaw brush, and paloverde trees choking the ravines and crevices, and how to skirt the many sheer cliffs. The old-time blacksmith shop which the partners maintain to shoe their many horses, mules and burros and to repair their rolling equipment, is decorated with those numerous relics they picked up around the scene of the old mining camp, such as Spanish-type harness buckles, forged iron burro shoes, hard-rock drilling bits, and digging implements.

A tough, astonishingly muscular man for one of his age ("I'm somewhere past fifty," he admits) and as flat in the stomach and lean in the hips as one of Remington's cowboys, Tom was once a guide and trail companion for Zane Grey. He has also worked for the U.S. Forest Service Geographical Survey, and for the Army Engineers on various expeditions. He has often been hired because of his famed riding ability (at one time he busted broncos for a living) to impersonate movie stars, over thirty in all, in long shots when spectacular, dangerous riding was called for in the scripts. Among the movies involved were: *Broken Arrow, The Fight at the O. K. Corral, Partners,* and *Three Valiant People.* He has also worked for some of the biggest cattle outfits in Arizona, the Lee Doyle Quarter Circle D-Bar spread near Flagstaff, the Bernard Hughes Double S spread, and the legendary Barkley Ranch.

Phil Kent has almost the same history as Tom, of cowboying, bronco busting, and stunt man in western movies. One night Phil and the writer were sitting around a little campfire near a makeshift corral in the shadow of Superstition, with the moon bright on Weaver's Needle, which may have had something to do with Phil, looking for all the world like the Marlboro Man, being in a rarely talkative mood. At dawn he was scheduled to pack a party on a week's trek into one of the wildest areas up back of the Mountain. "The location of the Peralta camp does little," he said that night, "to indicate where the mine might have been. The intense prospecting that has been done by literally thousands of prospectors, both amateur and professional, in the vicinity of that Spanish camping ground on the mesa that Tom and I first stumbled on, without discovering their mine, makes it seem to me that the mine is some distance off. The Spaniards probably transported the ore to their *arrastres* on the mesa by burros, where part of their work force then reduced it to manageable concentrate while the rest of the men worked at the mine miles away, getting it out, thereby making the exact location of the mine about the biggest will o' the wisp the world has ever known, and costing hundreds of lives in the years since."

Chapter 3

The story of those who searched Superstition Mountain for the Peralta Mine is dominated by the names of three remarkable men. In order of their appearance on the scene, they were: Dr. Abraham D. Thorne, Dr. John D. Walker, and Jacob Walz. They truly were "remarkable men," as history shows.

From all the evidence, and especially judging from their actions at the time of the Peralta Massacre, it is true that the Apaches did not appreciate the value of the gold ore concentrate that Peralta and his men were so desperately trying to carry back to Mexico even to the extent of taking a calculated risk on their lives, but as time went on and the Apaches learned more of the ways of the white men, it is equally clear from subsequent events that they caught on fairly soon to the value of the Peralta concentrate. Their actions in the case of Dr. Abraham D. Thorne, of Lemitar, New Mexico, conclusively establishes this, even without other proof, of which there is plenty.

Rancher Barney Barnard (whom the Apaches made a blood brother shortly after he returned from World War I because he saved the life of an Apache soldier in France) told the writer of several instances he knew about personally, where the White Mountain Tribe of Apaches in later years, after having learned how to smelt concentrate into gold bullion sufficiently pure to be cashed at U.S. mints, went back and gathered as much as they could find of the concentrate left behind after the Massacre, and used the proceeds to buy blooded bulls and other stock for their reservation. Barney told the writer he was a partner with them in many of these enterprises. He also owned a large ranch on the slope of Superstition Mountain.

Dr. Thorne was born in East St. Louis, Illinois, and from earliest childhood dreamed of being a doctor. He was always trying to get other children to play "doctor" with him. After they got tired of playing "plainsmen" and "Indians" he would convince them they were full of Indian arrows from the battle and needed his professional services to help extract the arrows, staunch the flow of blood, and bandage up the holes that the arrows had made.

"In imagination I must have restored hundreds of scalps," Dr. Thorne related years later while writing about this part of his childhood, "and repaired about every kind of wound there was. I longed only to patch up wounds that had been received in battle, particularly with Indians. Of course, I know it is usual for children to dream of battles and of playing glorious parts in these sanguinary 'extensions of politics,' but with me it went deep, so deep that I never changed. I went to an approved medical school in Philadelphia, and when I graduated from this well-regarded college, with honors, I immediately decided to find some means of becoming a surgeon with the troops in the Civil War, which was then raging full blast."

The famous frontier figure, Colonel Christopher Carson, colonel of cavalry in the volunteer forces of the Territory of New Mexico, better known as "Kit" Carson, was visiting some relatives in East St. Louis when Thorne came back from medical school with his brand new diploma. Thorne wangled an introduction to this fabulous frontiersman, and then found an opportunity to ask if there was anything Carson could or would do to get him appointed an army doctor.

"He assured me that he would do everything he could to further this aim of mine," said Thorne, "and after a while began telling me about the exciting opportunities there might be for me in the war with the Apaches on the New Mexico-Arizona frontier where he was not only a colonel of cavalry, but an Indian agent."

At that time in Arizona things were going very badly for

the settlers in the sanguinary struggle against the Apaches; miners, ranchers, and townspeople were nearly at their mercy. The townspeople were mostly older men and their wives, as well as the wives, sisters, and children of younger men who were back East fighting in the Civil War on one side or the other.

General James H. Carleton, a sort of National Guard type of general who commanded the 3,000 California irregulars, called the California Column, who were enlisted to defend the Territory of Arizona, decided to mount an intensive campaign of virtual extermination with his motley command against any Apaches who refused to knuckle under.

In an official order to his "command" of October 12, 1862 (which Kit Carson told his men to ignore, or disobey if they were forced to a choice), the general said, "All Indian men of that tribe [Apaches] are to be killed wherever you find them; the women and children will not be harmed, but you will take them prisoners. . . . If the Indians send a truce flag and desire to treat for peace, say to the bearer that your hands are now untied and you have been sent to punish them for their treachery and their crimes; that you have no power to make peace; that you are there to kill them whenever you find them . . . that we have no faith in their promises. . . . I trust that this severity, in the long run, will be the most *humane* course that could be pursued toward these Indians."

Thereupon the general marched his men up the hills and down the hills again, but their forays were almost barren of results. The Apaches were far too versed in hit-and-run, and too much at home in the thousands of canyons and mountain hideouts that feature Arizona, to be seriously threatened by such tactics and, anyway, the soldiers by and large had little heart for killing Apaches on their own ground. Yet it was this very "ground" that those arrayed against the Indians were determined to possess.

In his message delivered to the First Legislative Assembly of the Territory of Arizona at Prescott, September 26, 1864, Governor John N. Goodwin said: "The principal causes of the failure of the campaign to accomplish its purposes are ignorance of the country and lack of competent guides.

"But for them [the Apaches]," he went on to say, "mines would be worked, innumerable sheep and cattle would cover these plains, and some of the bravest and most energetic men that were ever the pioneers of a new country, and who now fill bloody and unmarked graves, would be living to see their brightest anticipations realized. *It is useless to speculate on . . . which party is in the right or wrong. . . .* It is enough to know that [this feeling] is relentless and unchangeable . . . one policy only can be adopted: a war must be prosecuted until they are compelled to submit and go upon a reservation."

When Fort McDowell was established in September, 1865 (about thirty miles northeast of Phoenix on the west bank of the Rio Verde, about eight miles from its junction with the Salt River), it was for the purpose of protecting white settlers and peaceful Indians against hostile Indians of the neighboring mountains. The Fort was mostly garrisoned by five companies of a force called the California Column, a somewhat haphazard aggregation of volunteers from southern California, Arizona, and New Mexico. Colonel Carson saw the new Fort as an opportunity for Dr. Thorne and had him appointed as an army doctor with officer's rank.

By the time Thorne arrived at Fort McDowell in 1865 the situation was indeed desperate. The Apaches, fighting not only for their lands, but against their own extermination as well, were trying in turn to kill or run off all the whites in the Territory. It was an appalling situation for both sides.

There were, however, Apaches known to detest fighting and killing and who only wanted to live in peace. Some cooler heads prevailed on the high command in Washington to offer these a five-mile-long, one-mile-wide strip along the bank of the Verde River in front of the Fort, as a sanctuary. President Abraham Lincoln promised all Apaches who would come and live there and *stay* there with peaceable intentions would be protected by the army. Lincoln also ordered Colonel Carson to give them adequate amounts of food and clothing. Because even the Apache had heard that Abe Lincoln did not speak with a forked tongue, several hundred showed up. The spot had been selected as an easy place for the army to defend, because of the river in front, the Fort in back, and the Fort's big guns to fend off flanking attacks. In time it came to be unofficially known as The Strip.

Thorne found several groups of Indians from other tribes also living on The Strip.

The conditions of sanitation and preparation of food were deplorable. Disease ran rampant; between epidemics and unnecessary malnutrition in their immediate past, the Indians were indeed in a pitiful condition. They had never known doctors in the proper meaning of the term.

Young Thorne had until then been paid by fee as a doctor for the troops and other personnel attached to army activities, but Colonel Carson arranged a commission for him. The rank gave dignity to his dealings with others and made things a lot easier for him.

Trouble was brewing among the Indians down along the banks of the river on The Strip when Thorne first arrived, but the troops at the Fort didn't care a hoot how resentful the Indians became. Indeed they did more than their share—if that was possible—of adding to the growing resentment of the Indians there.

A big factor in making Dr. Thorne's experiences on The Strip one of the great legends of the maturing West, as well as playing a part in the story of what was to become known as the Lost Dutchman Mine, was the doctor's natural ear for languages. Once he had settled in at the Fort and had the medical affairs of the white soldiers and their dependents in fairly good shape, he began visiting the Indians in their encampment by the river. "Mere words," he said afterwards, "could never describe my heartsickness at what I saw, particularly from the viewpoint of a doctor who knew that so very, very much of these distressing conditions could be easily changed with a little knowledge, good will and understanding on both sides."

The Indians even on The Strip where they were supposed to be fed, clothed, and protected by the army, regarded the white soldiers and the pioneers with an inward boiling fury that was all the more corrosive because it had to be repressed. Their rage centered around the same old fact that the settlers had taken, without so much as a by-your-leave, most of their best land. Not only this, but they had been able to brand the Indians as naturally murderous savages and troublemakers so that they were never credited with clean hands, as lawyers put it, when they sought redress in court.

When they had sought to right their wrongs by force of arms, the soldiers slaughtered them a a rate of ten to one on the average.

There are many stories about the origin of the Apache Indians, the most powerful, feared, hated, and difficult of all the Indian tribes the settlers of North America ever had to deal with. They had a high level of basic intelligence which no doubt had something to do with their intractability, probably because it made them suffer deeply over being despoiled of the land on which they had lived for many centuries and from which the whites were bent on removing them with superior fire power, and then justifying this robbing with sophistry, cant, and hypocrisy.

It is hardly a question as to who were the greater aggressors in that dark and bloody period of American history: the Indians who had many fertile acres upon which they had lived and prospered, or the white settlers streaming west, and coveting these lands, and seizing them by force—this being rather easy for them, as they all had guns, and they never had any hesitancy about claiming God was on their side in order to quiet their consciences to some degree, though there must have been a rather considerable number of less callous ones who suffered from guilt feelings just the same.

The Apaches are thought to be descended from Athapascan Indians who are supposed to have come from somewhere in the north, and before that across the Bering Straits, and even before that to have bridged the gap between South Pacific islands and the North American continent, using canoes for transportation. They then kept drifting southward until they finally came to southern Arizona, that has a climate that for warmth approximated the South Pacific climate where they are believed to have lived for thousands of years before becoming nomadic. Their name, Apache, comes from the Zuni word "Apachu," or enemy.

The Apaches' normal stamping grounds at the time Christopher Columbus discovered America were northern Mexico and many parts of what is now Arizona and New Mexico. They lived in mud-plastered brush shelters known as "wickiups," built by the women of the tribe. Even beavers build better shelters than those wickiups were. But they were efficient when it came to shielding off the burning sun of the desert climate, and they were easy for the women to build, which suited the nonwork attitude of the male Apaches as a whole, who were among the bravest of the brave in battle, but who hated all forms of plain work with a passion.

Though many of the Apaches may have been devious and cruel—and they largely were, even among themselves—they more than met their match when the Spanish settlers arrived in their area during the first half of the sixteenth century. Those first Spanish Conquistadors were the most cruel, ruthless pillagers the world has ever known. They worked on a share-and-share-alike split of the loot with the Spanish crown and the Catholic Church (then practically partners in the government of the Spanish Empire) and were licensed by both to practice armed robbery on all natives in the New World within reach. They were not only given carte blanche by their government to do this but were showered with honors and other rewards for sending back spoils. Also, they were blessed by priests and given honorary titles in the Church for such of these spoils as found their way into the possession of the Church officials.

In many cases, priests came with them to convert the Indians to the Catholic way of life, not so much, apparently, for the salvation of their souls, though this was the announced purpose. Their true aim, seemingly, was to instill in the Indians a docility to make it easier to enslave them. Indians by the thousands were put to work in the land and mines for the glory and profit of the Spanish crown and the Catholic Church of that time.

But the Apache Indian alone among all the other tribes never really gave in to the Conquistadors. Rather than bend their necks to the yoke, they broke up into small bands or clans in order to be able to hide themselves more easily in the numerous mountains and canyons of the southwestern desert area, and became the first known guerrillas. They continued to fight for their independence during the more than two centuries the Spaniards ran the rest of their part of the world.

Thorne decided at the very outset that if he was to help these benighted, smoldering human beings, he must be able to communicate perfectly with them. The sure road to this was to learn their language, and this is where his quick ear was invaluable. He got along at first with a sort of crude sign language.

Almost his first move was to persuade them to heat water and wash their babies as often as possible—preferably every day—particularly their eyes, because there was a veritable plague of sore eyes among the young children, which in a deplorable number of cases had already resulted in blindness.

Next he concentrated on persuading the women to wash not only the babies' clothes regularly, but to wash their own clothes in hot water, and themselves more frequently. He found means to get them a little laundry soap, and by means somewhat unpopular with the soldiery at the Fort he procured tubs and buckets and other containers from the Fort's stores in which water could be heated.

While he battled for progress in the cleanliness campaign, he was also making steady progress at getting a grasp of the language—amazing progress when the difficulties of mastering any of the Indian tongues is considered.

One of the hardest things he attempted was to persuade the Indians to burn or bury their trash and garbage. They had been accustomed for centuries to throwing bones and other refuse from their eating out into the path in front, or onto an area in back of their tepees, wickiups, or hogans. They used the path or, at best, the small area in back of the wickiup to powder their noses, so to speak, and really didn't seem to mind the awful stench. A tolerance of it had no doubt been building up from a period reaching way back into antiquity.

Thorne soon learned that persuasion, or almost any other means available to him at the time, was a frustratingly slow way to put a dent in these customs. It was only when he resorted to the device of cutting down, or increasing, the food supply from the Fort's commissary to influence the solution of any problem of the moment, that he began to have a means of bargaining with them. The poor devils were always hungry —it was almost a way of life with the Apaches.

When he first began by trying to persuade, and then insisting on his sanitary policy, the Indians argued with him, no doubt quite reasonably from their viewpoint, that it was ridiculous to spend a part of each day cleaning up the areas in front of their homes and walking some distance away to latrines to answer calls of nature—Thorne had insisted on this "distance." It was much simpler to throw the garbage out the opening of their tepees where it would be handy for the camp's dogs, of which, like all savages of those times, there were many hundreds in the camp, and all practically starving. And *why not* answer calls of nature in the handiest spot when the urge was on them? What was wrong with that? If the stench became too overpowering even for the Indians themselves, then wasn't it more logical to move their lodgings a short distance along the bank of the river, or further up the slope, than to take all that other trouble several times a day, *every* day?

Then, too, they were very suspicious of most "foibles" of the white man because they had often learned to their sorrow that when the white man began insisting on something or other from the Indians, it was too often in his own self-interest and usually wound up bad for the Indians. It can be easily understood, therefore, why it was so difficult for the Apaches and a sprinkling of other Indians in The Strip to accept as a fact that Dr. Thorne had no angle whatsoever, as we say these days, but was motivated wholly and unselfishly in behalf of the Indians' welfare.

However, the gifts of extra food turned the trick despite the opposition of the medicine men. Food can make friends with anyone or anything, and soon it began to turn the camp into a shining place. Helping out also was the fact that they began to *like* clean clothes, particularly the women, and especially the mothers, both on their babies *and* themselves. Soon the braves found that they were much more popular around the boudoir if they weren't an olfactory horror.

Most of the aged Indians had nothing left of their teeth but some rotting stubs which was much worse than no teeth at all, and Dr. Thorne could hardly bear to contemplate the years of agony they had endured as one tooth after another slowly decayed day-by-day, month-by-month through the years until they got to the condition he often saw.

He early determined to have as many of those teeth out as he could get around to. Though as yet he had only a sketchy knowledge of Indian nature and tribal status symbols, he was nevertheless certain that having, or pretending to have, absolute courage was one of them, and that they would stoically endure whatever agony was necessary to have them pulled out if he told them publicly they should. Notwithstanding, he felt that if some means could be found to get those teeth out painlessly it would be a wonderful thing for all concerned.

He had a small supply of ether for emergency operations at the Fort, but he knew he would need a great deal more, and he began to figure how he could get an additional supply, not only to use on their teeth but for the other surgery so many of them needed. They were always having accidents, especially from reckless horseback riding. More stunt riding was done in that five-mile strip by braves trying to show other braves who had the most courage and dash than for the usual reason of getting from one place to another on the back of a horse.

Thorne knew he had to prepare a very persuasive requisition if he was to get any considerable amount of ether, because at that time ether was one of the scarcest necessities of the entire Civil War effort. In the East where hundreds, sometimes thousands, of men were being grievously wounded almost every month, the demand for ether during surgery to repair their wounds or amputate shattered members as efficiently as possible, was very great, especially to guard against the shock of surgery, which in the pre-anesthetic days killed the patient more often than not.

After some thinking on the subject he hit on a plan: he asked Kit Carson—who by this time had been promoted to brigadier general—the next time he came through on an inspection visit to send a requisition for a large jug of ether, and to set forth as a reason that perhaps a not inconsiderable share of the peace and welfare of the whole Southwest depended on this ether being used humanely for the benefit of the showpiece Indians on The Strip to keep them in a friendly and peaceable frame of mind that would, hopefully, cause them to influence other Indians to emulate their examples.

General Carson used his magic and on a red-letter day for the friendly Apaches in The Strip, the huge flagon of ether arrived by overland supply train from Taos, forwarded from the East via St. Louis.

By this time the medicine men had become covertly threatening as Thorne continued to heal and comfort the sick and the injured, but he did not try to meet them head-on, which he might very well have done with the power of the Fort and the vast majority of the Indians on The Strip behind him. For one thing, he was fairly certain that they would find some obscure way to kill him if he did. Instead he set unobtrusively about devising means to lessen their hostility, and, if possible, win them over to his side.

After the ether arrived he saw in it a wonderful opportunity to win over those hocus-pocus artists. After selecting an old medicine man with the usual mouthful of dreadfully decayed teeth, Thorne told him on a suitable occasion that the Great Spirit of all Indians had appeared in a vision and asked Thorne to help Him temporarily remove the old man's spirit from his body and take it to a far place where the Great Spirit could talk to it. After he had persuaded the medicine man to stretch out on his pallet of blankets and hay, Thorne began muttering over him what he hoped sounded like incantations, meanwhile waving turkey feathers soaked in ether under his nose, just enough to put him partially under. Then, using sepulchral tones, he gave the old boy quite a harangue, interspersed every now and then with a sufficient whiff of ether. The medicine man, now nearly out from the ether, heard a weird voice saying to him as from a very far distance, "I am the Great Spirit, father of all Indians, and you have long been one of my favorites. Therefore, listen well to what I have to say to you. I will now cause you to sleep deeply, and while you slumber your teeth that have been hurting you for so long will leave your mouth and you will not know when they depart. When you wake you will have a great thirst and I command you to then drink the bitter waters that I will prepare for you and leave with the young white man whose hair is the color of corn kernels when they are ripe. You will do all things he tells you to and as a reward your health will become greatly improved. The bitter waters will cause you to be freed of all bad things that are in you, and you will find yourself refreshed both in body and in spirit, and the pain from your teeth will be gone. In return for these things I ask that you tell all of your people what has happened to you, and encourage them to also seek the removal of their bad teeth and other bad things and to allow the young white medicine man to treat and cure them of all ills in my name."

At this point Thorne stepped up the ether dosage until the patient was completely under; then he pulled those awful teeth. When the old boy came to he could instantly feel that his teeth had departed, and so had much of the continual pain that he had lived with for many years, and, sure enough, he had a raging thirst, which, of course, is a feature of having been under the influence of ether. Also, as the Great Spirit had promised, Thorne was waiting with the bitter nostrum which the old boy quickly swallowed. Sure enough, he soon felt much, much better—happier, really, and was thoroughly cleansed of body. This was to be expected because the "bitter waters" was a large draught of Missouri White Mule liberally laced with epsom salts.

He also felt that he had been cleansed in spirit, because he now wanted to act more honest not only toward Thorne, but all the other Indians of his clan. He became the greatest disciple that any doctor could wish for when it came to spreading never-ceasing praise of Thorne's powers and skills. His system, once it was freed of the constant poisoning it had been receiving from his rotten teeth, became almost buoyant and the contrast gave him a sort of permanent euphoria. His tales of his audience with the Great Spirit found eager and credulous listeners in The Strip, practically all of whom believed already that Thorne could perform miracles with their bodies.

Of course it wasn't easy to persuade the Indians to take deep whiffs from the pungent smelling stuff that Dr. Thorne poured on a soft cotton cloth and held to their mouth and nostrils, but there are always those hardy souls who are willing to be pioneers. After the other Indians saw how these courageous ones had had a terrifying looking carbuncle lanced without feeling it in the slightest, or numerous bad teeth extracted and were infinitely more comfortable even from the moment they woke up than they had been for years, they were pretty well persuaded that the "sleep from smell" was a boon for all who must face severe pain.

Broken bones had always been a particular problem with primitive people. Skilled doctors or surgeons were, of course, unknown to them. A few individuals acquired a certain amount of skill in setting bones or in midwifery, but the skeletons unearthed dating back for many centuries show that they must have suffered terribly from poor treatment, or none at all. When they had a broken bone in some part of the body where it could be put back end-to-end by pulling on one end while the victim was pulled in the other direction, their primitive doctors, i.e., medicine men, could manage the trick. But when they had a fracture, such as broken bones in the complex structure of the foot, face, or hand, or any of the bones in the region of the chest cavity or pelvis, the native doctors were practically helpless. As a result, if the patient survived he was usually a cripple for the rest of his life.

Naturally, Thorne himself was far from as skilled or proficient as doctors today. But from all accounts he did have a marvelous natural ability for treating common ills and repairing accidents, and in the eyes of the Apaches he came to be regarded as the medicine man of medicine men and fully entitled to sit some day on the right hand of their Thunder God.

The facility he had to make them physically better off in many ways, and to work wonders for the health of their children made it possible for him to finally get the entire camp completely cleared of all refuse and obnoxious substances, and the people trotting to relieve themselves at the latrines he had them dig and outfit on the outer perimeter of the living area. These things alone improved their health greatly.

Teaching the mothers to wash the eyes of their children daily with a mild antiseptic solution, which he prepared by the gallon and distributed to them, produced an immediate improvement—a precious one this time—in their children's eyes. Before he departed his post at Fort McDowell a few years later there was practically no eye trouble left among the children.

Many of the elders of the tribe had a certain amount of poor vision that could be easily corrected by the crude eyeglasses available in those days, and the astonishment of the Indians when they looked for the first time through the glasses Thorne procured and fitted them with, was a heart-stirring thing. Most eye doctors in those times fitted glasses (there were no optometrists as we know them now) by simply taking around a large basket of lenses with various strengths and having the patient keep trying them on first one eye and then the other, until by the process of trial and elimination the pair of glasses was found in the basket that most improved their vision.

Thorne was afterwards to say that the time he spent healing the bodies and lifting the morale of the Indians in the vicinity of Fort McDowell was the best and most satisfactory period of his life. "It was such a fulfilling thing to start absolutely at the very beginning of their experience with medicine and surgery and go on from there," he said. "I cannot describe the feeling it gave me. Also I have no doubt that, being human, the godlike status to which they elevated me in their minds and demonstrated fervently in their actions, had its effect on me. It was a very exalting thing, believe me.

"The skills I was able to impart to their midwives was of great immediate benefit to them with enormous possibilities for the future, and when they taught other women to be midwives by using my medical skills to deliver babies, then I felt I had accomplished right there alone enough to satisfy any true doctor.

"In obstetrics, as in any other craft, you learn things of great value from experience, but it is best to be taught, at first, by an expert the preponderance of the skills involved. Many things can happen during birth that require someone in attendance who has been taught the accumulated experience of centuries, if the baby's life, and often the mother's, is to be saved. Most midwives in the old days learned simply by delivering babies, and few of them ever managed to grasp the necessary physiology involved, such as how the bones are arranged and the muscles work and what can be done to assist both in the process of birth. The percentage of fatalities that attended the birth of babies before the science of obstetrics was well developed was absolutely appalling. It certainly had been among Indians.

"The Apache midwives knew nothing of forceps, for instance, which do so much to aid in the delivery of babies in many cases and are absolutely necessary in certain cases if damage to the baby and permanent injury to the mother is to be avoided. Episiotomies (the incision that is sometimes made just before the baby is born to prevent stretching and tearing) were not only totally unknown to the midwives among the Apaches, but the first time they saw me making an incision in the case of a young Indian girl about to give birth, with the female relatives of the girl clustered thickly around her from age-old habit, they were pretty hard to control. It hadn't been easy for them to reconcile to the affront to tribal custom of a man being present, let alone a white man, while one of their own was having a baby. But after the baby had been born in this case, they watched me sew up the incision with what obviously was a great air of relief. They, and especially the brave who was her husband, had probably been worrying that I would leave the young girl with a permanent enlargement.

"After a while the midwives adapted themselves to use without question all the things I taught them, and displayed gratitude for the obvious lack of pain the mothers suffered when they'd had a few whiffs of ether during the delivery. Before that the screaming that rolled over the camp and echoed from the hills during childbirth was a natural part of the process to them. Though they accepted it as inevitable it must always have been extremely distressing especially to the folks of the prospective mother who loved her—and make no mistake about it: love for each other, despite their stoic demeanor, was as poignantly present among those Apaches as ever existed among the most cultured whites.

"When they saw what judicious whiffs of ether could do for a prospective mother when she had reached a bad period of labor, they simply thought it was one of the most wonderful things that could happen to women.

"The Indian women adapted themselves so well to what I taught them and had such gratitude for this knowledge, that I felt I should also teach the medicine men some of the things I knew about medicine and the practice of surgery, for in this way I could strike a great lick for the future of the Apache tribes throughout Arizona. Aside from the immeasurable good they could do inside their own tribes if they put this learning into practice, word about it was bound to increase their prestige so greatly that the medicine men in other tribes would hear about it and come to see and learn. So that is what I did. I taught them to set bones; to fashion and use proper splints; to lance boils and other infected parts; to take care of infected eyes; to wash wounds and keep them washed regularly with plain soap and water, which is very effective in the antisepticizing of wounds. I taught them how to clamp and sew arteries in cases of severe cuts or wounds, and how to then sew up or suture these wounds themselves—a thing that they scarcely knew how to do before I arrived on the scene. I also showed them how to reduce pain with cold compresses; how to recognize the signs of severe constipation—a debilitating condition that was much prevalent among them at that time— and how to obtain from the white men the plain drugs, especially epsom salts, for the relief of this condition. There were so many things I *could* teach them, that I found myself spending many hours, including all of my off days, at it."

One day Thorne was approached by a fierce-looking Apache brave who had the air of one used to authority. Speaking in the Apache tongue he said that his youngest wife had been unfortunate with two babies; they had not lived to cry after birth and now she was soon to have another. If Thorne could help her produce a warrior son alive and in good health he would call down on him the blessings of the Thunder God of the Apaches. This obvious chieftain looked to be about six feet two inches and had thick straight black hair, which he combed back and caught with a red ribbon near the collar of his softly tanned and richly ornamented deerskin jacket. His face was distinguished by wide cheekbones, a high-bridged nose, and eyes that were clear, bright, and bold. His body was lean and, despite his age obviously being on the shady side of fifty, was extraordinarily well-muscled with broad shoulders.

It suddenly came to Thorne from the many descriptions he had heard, that this was the mighty Cochise, who was and had been defeating, or outwitting, in battle the best the whites could field against him. "You are Cochise," he said to him.

"Call me Brother!" he replied, laying his hand on Thorne's shoulder.

Thorne asked to examine his wife and was immediately taken to a large tepee constructed of superbly tanned skins, situated some distance off by itself from the other dwellings in The Strip. By the number of braves who were guarding it, Thorne now knew for certain that the man striding at his side was indeed the legendary Cochise, a name that means "Hickory Wood" in Apache. The tepee was the portable dwelling used by Cochise when he traveled.

Thorne's examination revealed that Cochise's beautiful young wife was narrow-hipped and restricted as to pelvic space. She didn't look to be more than thirteen years old. There might be a little difficulty, he told the Chief, but assured him he would do the best he could. He arranged for a series of massages for her, after showing some of the women how to do it, a thing they quickly learned. In due course she arrived at her time; Thorne had left word that he was to be notified at the first sign of labor and he got there promptly. The women had everything arranged so that she would be comfortable and could do all in her power to assist in the birth under his directions. In due course, and using forceps and a bit of ether now and then, he almost painlessly delivered her of a fine, healthy baby boy. Cochise, though he already had fine sons by earlier wives, was simply beside himself with joy.

Thorne's fame spread faster than ever after this, and the braves visualized healthy boys and girls arriving like corn popping in a pan—the girls growing up to be the mothers of many strong sons, and the sons becoming mighty warriors who would kill many traditional enemies of the Apache, and perhaps drive the white man back off the fertile land which they had taken from the Indians within a space of no more years than encompassed the lifetime of a young child.

In a few days, Cochise, now very much the proud father, asked Thorne to stop by his resplendent tepee after he had finished his doctoring calls. There Thorne found the mother all smiles and brightness and already up doing the chores and cooking the evening meal, while the new born son chortled nearby. Cochise motioned Thorne over to a corner where strung upon a cord of rawhide were some repulsive scalps, two with thick black hair, and three only too obviously the scalps of white people. Taking the string of scalps and pressing them into Thorne's hands, he said, "These are scalps I take with my own hands; I want you to have them."

Though revolted, Thorne knew how the Indians felt about a gift refused, especially one that was so tremendously precious to them as the scalps they took. The first scalp an Apache got was his real entrance into being a man among men in the tribe and when he had taken three or more he was from then on thought of as a full fledged warrior. Therefore, not knowing what else to do, Thorne accepted the scalps with what he imagined were suitable expressions of gratitude and carried them back to the Fort concealed in one of his saddle bags, wondering how he could dispose of them.

The next day he asked a Maricopa friend of his, who lived with his tribe farther southwest on the Gila (pronounced Hee-la) River what he ought to do about the scalps. The Maricopa's eyes lit up with an unholy light. "I buy them from you," he said excitedly. "Perhaps you like much hides; much grain; much good things to eat. We have plenty this year from our farms to trade."

His words gave Thorne an inspiration. "I should be glad to sell them to my great friend, the Maricopa," he told him and marching over to his tethered horse, he gingerly lifted the scalps out of the saddle bag and handed them over to the Maricopa, who by this time was fairly slavering with anticipation. "These scalps," said the Maricopa, "will take him who has them straight to where Elder Brother [the God of the Maricopas, Papagos, and Pimas] resides in the sky, and he who take them from other Indians, and from our friends the white people, and did not keep them for himself, has offended Him and when he die he must go forever to where there are no women or papoose or food or soft skins upon which to sleep, and which to shelter him. He go, like white men say, to hell."

True to his word, in a few days the Maricopa arrived at Fort McDowell with several ponies dragging Indian-type sleds loaded with hides and food and other things precious to the Indians. Thorne accepted them with many expressions of thanks, and as soon as they were well out of sight on the way back to their settlement, he had a team of horses hitched to one of the Fort's trail wagons to lug the whole shooting match down to The Strip where he distributed it all to those most in need.

Needless to say, he did not tell them where the windfall came from but instead impressed upon them that their Thunder God was taking care of those whom he especially favored.

As time went on, Cochise, now at war with the white men, would slip back to The Strip every now and then. On these trips he had to exercise the greatest of care, for while he and the other Apaches were guaranteed sanctuary *on* The Strip, he traveled to and from it at his own risk, and there were many white men who would have killed him if they could, even on The Strip, for what they would have considered the honor of it.

One night while they were smoking a pipe around a fire, as Thorne told it afterwards, Cochise tried to explain the origin of the implacable hatred he'd had for white people. "Once," he said, "I heard that a band of U.S. soldiers were looking for a young boy by the name of Mickey Free, who had been stolen. I was camped near the Overland Mail Station at Apache Pass at the time. Some soldiers came to the station, and one of my scouts told me that they thought I had stolen the boy. I was friendly to the white people then, and I was doing everything I could to look after their safety as well as my own. This was [and he held up three fingers] about that many summers and winters ago. So the next day [January 30, 1861, according to official historical records] I went down to offer to help find the boy and the young chief in charge [Second Lieutenant George N. Bascom, Seventh Infantry according to these same records] asked me to step into his tent for some hospitality. Suddenly, I heard soldiers surrounding the tent, and then the young white chief jumped up and said they were going to hold me and my men, but I was too quick for them and with my hunting knife I slashed a big slit in the tent behind me and ran through the soldiers to my horse. They fired many shots at me before I could get on my horse, and three of the bullets hit me, but I managed to get away. I was many moons getting well, and you can see the bad scars that I still have. Some of my men were killed—others captured, and later they hanged six of them. Only a few escaped. I promised myself that when I was able to ride again I would, with the help of the Great Spirit, make the white men pay for what they did, and we have.

"I'm not the only one of our people who has suffered treachery at the hands of your people; there have been many, many such affairs," Cochise went on to say. "Our greatest chief, Mangas Coloradas, was murdered by your soldiers one summer and a winter ago in the most treacherous way of all: shot dead by guards after he had voluntarily approached another of your army chieftains [Captain E. D. Shirland on January 14, 1863, at Apache Pass]. They said he tried to escape. The fact that he was seized despite the circumstances was treachery enough in itself to illustrate the characters of his assassins."

Thorne already knew the shameful details of the murder. Coloradas had been twenty years older than Cochise, and the two were blood brothers. Coloradas was also a very striking physical specimen. He had bulky arms, a huge body, broad legs, and an enormous head. His eyes were widely spaced and his nose was slender, almost delicate. His name meant "Red Sleeves" in Spanish. In a knife battle with several Mexicans, he killed them all, after which his arms were red with blood from fingertips to shoulders, and hence the name.

The way in which Mangas got his name was typical of the way Apaches acquired their permanent names. At birth they were usually given some short, handy name but this was only designed to serve them until the Thunder God would bring about an incident that would reveal what their permanent name should be. Sometimes a marked trait of character, or an unusual conformation of the body would indicate to the medicine man what the person's name should be, and he would then give it to them. Until this happened the youth was called ish-kay-nay, or boy.

Sometimes one of the women was given a distinctive name, but not often, being deemed altogether inferior. Many were left without a name of their own, and were simply spoken to as ish-tia-nay, or woman.

The names of some of the more eminent warriors on The Strip reflected this practice. There was Gian-nah-tah, which means "always ready" and it came to him because he was known as a sort of Don Juan. The Mexicans called him "Muy-macho." Then there was Nah-tanh, or the "corn flower," so called from having on one occasion, while on a raid in Sonora, escaped capture by hiding in a field of corn. Nah-kah-yen meant "keen sighted," and was so named because of his extraordinary power of vision. Too-ah-yay-say, the "strong swimmer," got his title from his swimming speed, which was very great, and so it went.

On February 7, 1866, General Irwin McDowell, in response to persistent urging on the part of Dr. Thorne, issued a special order establishing a huge government farm at Fort McDowell. The farm would relieve the enormous and dangerous amount of wagon-train hauling that had provided farm produce for the garrison and for the ever-increasing number of Indians on The Strip. Lieutenant Colonel Bennett was put in charge. The order also authorized the employment of three men at fifty dollars per month, and twenty men at forty dollars per month and rations, to build ditches, drain the soil, cultivate crops, and train a considerable number of the Indians on The Strip to learn how to do these things.

Chapter 4

Before Fort McDowell came into being, Governor Goodwin, Arizona's first territorial governor, had to face the fact that the war with the Apaches in Arizona was going badly because of the failure of General Carleton and his "army" to subdue the Apaches. From his capital at Prescott, Goodwin had recommended to Washington that a special force of Arizonians be organized to end the Apache version of a holy war being waged against the settlers "before this whole territory is lost to civilization."

He had not exaggerated the menace of the situation. The Apaches were mercilessly and continually eliminating outlying ranchers and miners until virtually all those still alive had abandoned their mines and ranches, and were huddling in Tucson or Prescott, or in forts, or in small settlements scattered around the territory, and it was the Stars and Bars of the Confederacy that were flying over Tucson. In 1862 the town had been occupied by an irregular company of Confederates from Texas under Captain Miles Hunter, and he was suspected of encouraging the Apaches to harass all other settlements to the north and east that were under nominal federal control.

The governor also recommended that a contingent of army drill masters be sent to train such recruits at Fort McDowell, newly established near Phoenix, as could be raised, with the Fort supplying the arms and other equipment needed. By the following April, this recommendation was approved by the U.S. War Department.

But when it came to raising the recruits to serve in this regiment, Governor Goodwin found himself somewhat in the position of the man who stoked up the fire in his stove, laid out condiments, vegetables, and a pot of suitable size for cooking rabbit stew, and then remembered that he hadn't yet caught his rabbit.

It was truly remarkable, as the governor soon learned, how many young men in the territory who had always been considered able-bodied, now described themselves as ravaged by a horrifying variety of diseases. Fight the Apaches? Why of course; nothing in this world would suit them better, they said, if it wasn't for their "trick knee," or the "crick in their necks," and some of them had both, and maybe a lame back to boot. A goodly portion of them were married, or hastened to be. "You couldn't expect a feller to risk getting himself killed—could you—who had a wife and, maybe, a baby on the way?"

Those whose courage had blazed most awesomely out of their words turned out to have the worst diseases and other debilities and handicaps. They had spoken in the deadly tones that are assumed to be the hallmark of born killers: "Show those Apaches cold steel—the bayonet, and they'll run like thieves." "Don't compromise with the varmints—I'd give them no mercy." "The only good Injun is a dead Injun." "This is white man's land; it is time we taught those Injuns their place." Yet they had the most pregnant wives, the most pressing things to do, and the most urgent necessities to be someplace else—in a hurry. They also suffered from faint hearts and cold feet.

Things were about the same nationally, too. President Lincoln had had to issue a conscription proclamation in May of 1863. This draft had at first provoked a flurry of protests, even riots, notably in New York City. The poor people and the foreign-born were outraged by a provision that allowed the rich to hire substitutes in the draft for their sons. But the protests soon died down, and the eligibles were hauled off to training camps. Their working parents, who were used to getting the worst of things, shrugged resignedly and from then on went numbly to scan the heavy casualty lists posted every few days in prominent public places, which was the custom then, to see if their sons had been killed, or, hopefully, only wounded.

By 1865 most of those in Arizona without well-to-do parents, or influence, and who possessed courage and patriotism, had already joined up, and the pool of "willing" manpower was nearly dry. The draft had not helped produce boys to fill Arizona's military needs during 1863 and '64, not having been made operative there, most probably because Arizona was not accepted by the Union as a Territory until 1864.

Governor Goodwin finally appealed to the well-off parents to encourage their sons to join up. These parents had been declaring in almost one voice that they too were all for the war against the Apaches being pressed to a victorious conclusion. Much as they would like to respond to the governor's appeal, however, and nothing would make them more proud than to see their sons fighting for Arizona, they said, these sons were being schooled to be the leaders of the future, a role for which their parents knew they were naturally fitted. "There are still plenty of young men who haven't the advantages we plan for our sons," they pointed out, "who are more suited for fighting Apaches."

Very often, too, those sons of well-off parents were married, or hastening to be and, in either case, were industriously and pleasurably engaged in progenitive activities.

When a certain cynical agnostic, Dr. John D. Walker, heard about all this, he said: "None of the governor's troubles in rais-

ing a regiment to defend the homes and people of Arizona
surprises me; rather I am reminded of the parable in the Bible
[St. Luke, Chapter 14, verses 17 to 23 inclusive] about the once-
generous man who had helped many in his time but had now
fallen upon hard times and hit upon the idea of giving a supper for all his relatives and friends in order to gather them together to call upon them for help. But instead of appearing
personally, they sent excuses."

This needling quote of Walker's went from person to person like a brushfire climbing a sidehill with the wind. It evoked
many hearty laughs and some indignant remarks, too. When
Walker heard about the latter, he chuckled and said: "If you
throw a stone over a high fence into a yard with several dogs
in it, and you hear a yelp, you'll know the yelp came from the
dog that was hit."

The fire-eaters were stung in direct ratio to how loudly they
had been calling for prompt, hard-line action against the
Apaches. They were not worried about their own personal
safety of course. They were only concerned about the future
of the Territory, the purity of its womanhood, and the right of
its children to grow up in freedom, peace, and prosperity.
While it was clear that they themselves had never offered to
fight the Apaches for these things, this did not cause them to
softpedal their demands that those "other fellows," whose traditional job it is and always has been, to get out there and
fight, and die if need be, be forthwith summoned to fulfill
their immemorial role.

At this juncture, Governor Goodwin hit upon the scheme
of finding some redoubtable character, preferably one who
had had a lot of experience with Indians, to act as a commander of the proposed force, or "special regiment," and then
to have this fellow recruit the rest of the needed personnel—a
scheme that was one of purely passing the buck if there ever
was one. But the trouble was, he soon learned, practically all
the *adequately* courageous and *decently* patriotic men of military age and of the required health standards had already left
the Territory to fight in the Civil War.

Finally the governor settled upon a man, J. Ross Browne,
who claimed many years of experience among the Indians. He
had made a name for himself as a writer about these sanguinary experiences, and had drawn many sketches that supposed-

ly illustrated this life. Browne eagerly accepted the honor, but when he became thoroughly acquainted with the projected objective of this special regiment, which so far was only a paper tiger, he cooled to a point where it was obvious he was going to be ineffective.

By this time it had occurred to quite a number of Arizonians, among them the governor, that there was a tribe of Indians, the Pimas (pronounced Pee-mahs), which the Apaches had been raiding for centuries in order to capture maidens and plunder, who might be persuaded to help them out of their dilemma, because the Pimas, though ordinarily one of the most peaceful of tribes, always made it an invariable practice to raid right back with the objective of making the Apaches pay at least double for these raids. It naturally followed, then, that the governor and his advisors began to ponder about who had the most influence with the Pimas, and might be able to recruit a force among them that would fight the Apaches, and help remove the very real threat of extinction that hung over the fledgeling Territory of Arizona. The name that instantly leaped to everyone's mind was the selfsame John D. Walker, who was then living in a Pima village.

The governor was still smarting, of course, over the now-famous crack about the parable that fitted his predicament, but nevertheless he sent for Walker.

Back came a reply from Walker that if the governor wanted to talk to him he d--- well knew where to find him.

The governor had to knuckle under, of course; *any* hesitation over whether he should go to the mountain if the mountain wouldn't come to him, might have been disastrous, as time had certainly become of the essence.

Because of its outcome, the meeting that occurred between the governor and Walker in the Pima village has become historic. The governor pleaded that for the sake of the white community Walker should raise a force of Pimas strong enough to control or defeat the Apaches. Walker said he would put the governor's request before the Pima chiefs and leading medicine men, *provided* the governor and all those with whom he shared authority, including the local U.S. Army Command, agreed that he, Walker, would be in sole command to train them as he saw fit, and further, that the U.S. Army would completely arm and outfit them, with the arms, horses, and mules to be retained by the Pimas and their allies at the successful end of the hostilities.

Educated as a physician and surgeon, John D. Walker was born in Nauvoo, Illinois, about the year 1840, with a strain of Wyandot blood in his veins, enough to give him the warm skin, the high-bridged nose, the prominent cheekbones, and the piercing dark eyes that made him a standout in any company. A very tall and strong man, who laughed a lot and liked horseplay and gazing on the wine when it was at its peak, and on the girls when they were equally and obviously as ready, made him greet each new day with eager enthusiasm.

Visiting California at the time the California Column was organized, he was among the first to volunteer for it, and was assigned to the Fifth Regiment, California Infantry. It was designed as sort of a reserve outfit with volunteers from various places in the West, to come to Arizona and New Mexico and take the place of U.S. Army regulars that were transferred East during the latter part of the Civil War. He joined up as a commissioned doctor, of course, but his natural qualities as a leader soon had him heading a wagon train to bring food supplies to posts in eastern Arizona and New Mexico, gathered from the Pima farms along the Gila River.

After serving with distinction for a considerable period, he was the victim of a wholly unexpected change of mind by a beautiful young belle, who literally left him waiting at a San Diego church. His vigil was ended when a messenger arrived bearing a note from her that said that by the time he read it she would be the "bride of Jesus Christ"—she was becoming a Catholic nun.

In his grief and shock he "took to drink" as the saying goes, and finally, after a spell of prolonged drunkenness, woke up one morning lying on a pallet in a Pima Indian wickiup—a physical wreck. He had been dreadfully ill for many days. He was also long absent-without-leave from his command. Broken spiritually as well as physically, he resigned his army commission and decided to make his home among the Pimas, as a sort of refuge from life as he had known it. He had become friendly with them and learned to speak their language while heading the wagon train and buying their farm produce for the army.

At that time there were seven such Pima villages strung

along the Gila River, with a total population of about four thousand, and known as Pimeria. Some twenty miles farther down the river were the Maricopa Indians, a group much akin to the Pimas. The Pimas were by preference a peaceful agricultural people, who were extraordinarily adept at scrounging food in the desert and had learned how to irrigate the land along the Gila for raising crops. They are *still* living there and modern scientific tests show they have lived there for over nine thousand years!

Blackwater, the Pima village where Walker returned to consciousness, was located a little south of the present town of Chandler, Arizona.

Among the Pima girls who ministered to him during his illness was the young maiden named Chur-ga, whose great beauty, sweetness, and kindness gradually began to penetrate the numbness that now overlaid much of his feelings and dreams of the past. She tempted his sluggish appetite with little tidbits and brought him cool drinks from the olla (the water jar that hung from its tripod in the shade nearby). Her many delightful feminine ways, which came so naturally to her that she seemed totally unaware of them, soon made her very special to him.

He fully recovered his health and from that point on he not only never took another drink of liquor, but came to hate strong drink in all its forms. There also remained with him an intense antipathy for any specific religious belief. It was not a feeling against his Creator, whom he believed in—it was more a feeling against the professionals in religion, and church *buildings* in particular; probably a mark left on him by his terrible experience at the church awaiting the bride who never came.

He never laughed or joked any more, but as the days while he was recovering lengthened into weeks, some of his feelings began to tiptoe back soft and easy as a cat walking over dewy grass to take up residence again in his healing consciousness, where in the old days they had dwelt noisily, selfishly, and confidently. For a long time he hardly noticed their return until one day he realized that the instinct which had always called his attention to the way a girl walked, was directing his eyes to Chur-ga's easy grace; then the part of him which had once made him laugh so much, began again to tickle him every now and then, and his old laugh rang out, withal sounding rather strange to him at first.

Chur-ga proved the salvation of Walker. She laughed and teased when his moods tortured him, and finally made love to him with wild abandon—the appetite for which was as natural to her as the one she had for eating. She brought an art to lovemaking that was rooted deep in the pure sensuousness she reveled in and was her birthright, handed down to her through centuries from ardent forebears who never thought for an instant of depriving themselves in any way of something they found good. The endless stultifying shibboleths that usually crippled the white man's pleasures, particularly the one that is most compelling, and should be the loveliest relationship between the sexes, and that certainly was designed by the Deity to be the most pleasurable, when its meanings and purpose have not been distorted by ugly interpretations, disturbed and puzzled the Pimas whenever they encountered them.

The meeting between Governor Goodwin and Dr. Walker at the Pima village was short and to the point. After the governor had assured Walker all his terms would be met, he agreed to try to raise and command a company of Pimas and Maricopas. They attempted to saddle Walker with J. Ross Browne as his second in command, but before long he got rid of him.

A percentage of the whites in the Territory immediately and vociferously protested the plan of dignifying and legitimizing Indian warriors in the service of the United States, and also raised a stiff argument about the wisdom of training *any* Indians to be experts in the use of modern military tactics.

But the urgency of the situation dictated the outcome. The Apaches were growing bolder and bolder. From their strongholds in the Superstition and Chiricahua Mountains they were attacking even the outlying precincts of Phoenix and Tucson, bringing steadily increasing pressure of the "something must be done" variety. Soon Governor Goodwin, with the consent of the army command, ordered the mustering and equipping of four companies, to be designated A, B, C and D, gave Dr. Walker the rank of captain, placed him in command of C Company, and gave him the formal authorization he had asked for to recruit, equip, and train as large as possible a force of Indians to man C Company.

Captain Walker then—and not until then—went formally before the leaders of the seven Pima villages though, of course, rumor had been rife among them for days. After he had given them the details, the spokesman they had agreed upon, Antonio Azul, the leading chief of the Pima villages, said they would smoke upon it and let him know before sunup. The big inducement where they were concerned was the fact that they would be fighting Apaches, whose marauding ways had been making life miserable and dangerous for the more peaceful Pimas for centuries.

They brought Walker their favorable decision at dawn, and before the day was over he had as many volunteers as he figured he could use. He selected Antonio Azul as his second in command. Thereupon things began to shape up.

At Fort McDowell the Pima volunteers, and some Maricopas, too, were completely equipped with rifles and uniforms, and training began daily with the help of regular army noncoms, though strictly according to Walker's own system of preparing his Indian soldiers for the task at hand—a system that was readily accepted by the army officers, for they soon saw its value.

His method of training stressed one point above all others: how to keep under cover as much as possible while advancing to the attack—a type of fighting for which the U.S. Marines were to become world famous in later years.

The Pimas and Maricopas were already adept at concealment for the purposes of stalking game, but Walker took them much further. He showed them how with a sprinkling of one kind of desert residue, they could make themselves resemble a gray boulder, and when around greenery, to lie on the ground and toss grass over themselves for almost perfect concealment. He taught them to hide behind ordinary desert bushes, such as yucca plants, or behind brown shrubs. He also made sure that only gray blankets were issued to them because, when wrapped in one, they blended into the desert so perfectly that it was difficult to detect them, even from a short distance. It was often said afterwards that Walker had so drilled those Indians in taking advantage of every concealment that any one of them could disappear behind a bush half his own size, or even a twig if nothing better was available. While this was an exaggeration, of course, their camouflage proficiency was the subject of so much written comment in after years that it cannot be doubted.

Soon Walker had a hard core company of some two hundred sixty volunteer Pimas, and forty men from Company B all supplied with rifles and uniforms, trained to be excellent marksmen, letter-perfect in the attack procedures he had designed, and ready to follow him anywhere. According to Major J. D. Doran, a noted Indian fighter of the time, "You could not tell him from the other Indians in the field. He dressed exactly like they did, with nothing on but a breechclout, and whooped and yelled like his Indian comrades."

He then marched them southeastward toward the Apache strongholds in the Chiricahua and Dragoon Mountains. Apprised of his mission, the marauding bands of Apache braves at first scoffed at the scientific fighting methods Walker had taught the Pimas and Maricopas. But what they overlooked, as many other people had in days gone by, was that ordinarily peaceable people take to military training like ducks to water, when necessity forces them to, and are deadly adversaries when forced into war on the just side.

When the campaign began in earnest, Walker and his Pimas were stalking a foe, wily, courageous, and proficient for centuries at guerrilla fighting. Cochise, Victorio, Geronimo, and other Apache chiefs, through their spies among the Apaches on The Strip had, of course, been carefully watching Walker's preparations and training methods. They had quickly decided that an all-out frontal battle would not be their best strategy. For one thing, though they had managed to secure about as many modern guns as they needed by raiding ranches, mines, and small communities, and ambushing wagon trains, they were still very short of ammunition, and they could see that Walker's warriors would have all the ammunition they needed—and more, too. Therefore, the Apache chiefs decided to break up into small groups, each one selecting a particular hiding place from among the thousands of deep defiles and hidden valleys that could be reached by horses and where water and grass were plentiful. Their strategy was to continue their raiding and pillaging by sallying forth from these strongholds and retreating back to them as quickly as possible after the raid.

But Walker, too, had his spies and his scouts out. Nothing

could have suited his plans better than the Apache tactic of splitting into small groups as a means of evading his Pimas. He realized that in almost every case the Apaches would probably have superior defensive positions in their high mountain valley hideouts. By the same token, they couldn't fight their way *out* of them without exposing themselves to merciless fire from besiegers, who would have plenty of concealed vantage points overlooking the valleys and defiles from which they could fire *down* on the besieged.

Walker's first general move was to train a corps of "mountain watchers" from among his best trackers, runners, and hunters. They were already adept in the art of smoke signals of universal meaning, but these could be read as easily by the Apaches as by his own men, so Walker devised an entirely new code in smoke puffs for his mountain watchers to send from their high vantage points to other watchers set up where one or more of them would always be able to signal Walker's main force. Three puffs straight up meant Apaches were in sight on the plain directly in front of the watcher sending the signal; two puffs straight up and then the third puff deflected to the right meant the Apaches were on the plain but to the right of the signaler; two puffs and a third puff to the left meant Apaches on the plain and to the left. There was almost no movement of the Apaches that these signalers couldn't convey by the time they completed the course Walker had devised.

A straight continuous upward column for more than three minutes was the one they found most useful. It meant for all hands to immediately assemble at whichever one of the various points that had been selected in advance was nearest to the smoke column. After assembling they would ride straight for the band of Apaches the mountain watcher would point out. No matter how the Apaches dodged to throw their pursuers off the trail, they could rarely succeed. If they sought refuge in their stronghold, they were then immobilized and could be besieged and picked off by the Pima sharpshooters.

As soon as one band was disposed of, Walker and his men concentrated on another. After a short experience with this strategy, the Apache chiefs realized that the rate of attrition was fatally decimating their numbers. Finally they decided to hole up on a perpendicular bluff on Big Picacho, a rocky spire of a mountain south of Pinal. On this high cliff were many caves and crevasses. They figured it as an ideal place to sell their lives dearly, if they had to, and they were no doubt hoping that Walker might not be able to induce his Pimas to face up to the price in lives for dislodging them with a frontal attack.

But Walker and his staff of Indian leaders decided to change their strategy somewhat from the one they had used in regard to the smaller strongholds they had reduced. They had their Pimas creep forward, firing at every puff of smoke that came from an Apache gun. It was then that the refinements of the art of concealment that Walker had taught them became priceless, for it saved the lives of many of them.

Soon the Apaches were abandoning the lower positions and taking refuge in the caves that dotted the steep incline, an incline that rose until it peaked off thousands of feet high. Pima volunteers climbed step-by-step after them and, while their best marksmen covered them, they threw charges of explosives into the mouths of the caves.

The surviving Apaches then abandoned the caves and began climbing steadily upwards again, pausing only to fire back at their relentless pursuers and taking a toll, though more and more of them were running out of ammunition, and there was no possibility of their getting more. Soon all of those who survived were on the top. Walker's force then halted just below the summit for a strategy conference. Some of the chiefs were for starving the Apaches on the peak into surrender, but Walker pointed out that in time most of them could creep back down through the tortuous clefts and crevices that abounded on the side of the mountain where the Pimas were, and scatter to the four winds—and become a problem all over again.

"We've got to break their effective power once and for all, and right here and now," he told his staff. "This is the time and this is the place."

As was their custom, they smoked on it for a while, but long before sunup they gave him their decision to go all the way with him when he gave the command.

On the brink of the approaching showdown battle, Walker crept from vantage point to vantage point on the face of the mountain, encouraging his warriors wherever he found them. "Before the sun goes to sleep this day," he told them, "the power of the Apaches to make big war will be forever broken." He again emphasized to them the vital necessity of their not jerking the trigger, but in gradually increasing the pressure on it to get the shot off smoothly while the sights were held steadily on the target. They also were to hold their fire after sighting the Apaches until he gave a signal by firing his .44 Colt. Above all, they were not to revert to the old Indian way of trying to prove how brave they were by creeping quietly up and then undoing these precautions by leaping to their feet and rushing upright on their enemies with what were designed to be bloodcurdling whoops!

It fell to the Apaches to commit precisely this particular foolish tactic later that day, and also give the signal for the battle to begin, when they tried to rattle the Pimas at the last moment with fierce yells and grimaces and making a desperate final charge. Walker's well-trained warriors, waiting quietly and in good order behind whatever concealment was at hand, simply took careful aim when they were at point-blank range and mowed them down. Then began a mopping-up operation against those remaining. Those Apaches to whom surrender in any case was unthinkable, and capture by the Pimas particularly repulsive, retreated to the edge of the precipice back of them, contesting every inch of the way. The last step they took was when they leaped into eternity.

For many years afterwards, according to the official eight-volume History of Arizona by Thomas E. Farish (printed and published by direction of the Second Legislature of the State of Arizona, 1915), "You could find on this battlefield the skeletons of Apaches in the crevices. Today the scene is marked 'Apache Leap.' "

Only a handful surrendered. The Pimas, after centuries of death, torture, and robbery suffered at Apache hands, were looking forward, naturally, to the "fun" of dealing with these prisoners of war according to their notions of retribution. But Captain Walker had them taken instead to Fort McDowell and handed to the U.S. Army commandant. None of the leading Apache chieftains were among this contingent. They had taken off with their sub-chiefs for their various strongholds in the Chiricahua Mountains.

Thus ended forever the formal war with the outlaw Apaches. From then on the Apaches who preferred marauding for a living operated only in small bands, mostly led by Geronimo. Cochise merely made a few sporadic raids for a year or so, and then he signed a treaty of peace and kept it honestly according to his own lights until his death from old age in 1874, of which more later. Geronimo surrendered finally to army authorities in 1886 and was confined with the few remainders of his band at Fort Sill, Oklahoma, where he died on February 17, 1909, leaving a widow and several sons, the last one of which died on the San Carlos Reservation in 1966.

Cochise's sons, Natchez and Taza, sired several children, each and both lived to a ripe old age—Natchez until 1921. Their children were also fecund and today Cochise has grandchildren and great-grandchildren on the White Mountain and San Carlos Indian Reservations.

Grandsons of the warriors who fought under Captain Walker at Apache Leap made some of the finest soldiers in World War I, winning more than their share of decorations. In World War II *their* sons flocked to the U.S. Marine Corps because, steeped in the traditions of Walker's fabled braves, marine training appealed to them. During the battle for the Solomon Islands, the marines used the Indians from various Arizona tribes for battlefront communications without resort to code when they learned that the Japanese could break regular U.S. codes but could not decipher the normal language of the Pimas, Papagos, Maricopas, Navajos, and Apaches, thinking it some sort of unearthly jargon or code devised by marine strategists.

There was a great ceremony at Fort McDowell honoring Captain Walker's Pimas and Maricopas when he marched his C Company in to be mustered out and have their names and records made secure in the archives of the army forever. They were allowed to keep *all* their guns, uniforms, remaining ammunition, and camping equipment (such as wagons, most of the horses, tents, and odds and ends) in accordance with the agreement made with Walker prior to their embarking on the expedition.

After several days of feasting and hearing speeches praising them by dignitaries such as Governor Goodwin and General Kit Carson, Captain Walker announced that the final chore for his men would be to march in full panoply and good order to a point central to their various villages where another ceremony would be held, after which they could return to their homes and families.

But a hitch threatened this plan when Walker was approached with a request for a powwow by the medicine men who had accompanied the expedition.

It was the inviolable custom of centuries, they said, that Pima warriors who killed in battle must spend fifteen days in seclusion to purify themselves from the possible wrath of Elder Brother for having killed a fellowman, even though they had been utterly justified in doing so.

For example, they went on to explain, when Walker's Pimas marched back to their villages, the "killers" would have to march behind the rest of the party, paint their faces black and eat very little. The whole party was to camp near enough on the last night so that the nonkillers (mostly priests, medicine men, and assorted functionaries) could enter the village at dawn, leaving the killers—the real heroes —to wait at this last camp. A fast runner would be sent ahead to shout the news of victory and to mention the names of the killers, because the wives of the killers also would have to go away from the rest of the village and purify themselves by fasting and remaining in seclusion.

The nonkillers would then march into the village, carrying the battle trophies on a pole, where they would be met by the womenfolk of the nonkillers who could seize the trophies and dance with them. The party would then go into the council chamber where the functionaries would tell the tale of their expedition to the rest of the men of the village. Then would come dancing around the poles with the women, and at a certain point the children would be allowed to join in. For sixteen nights they would dance every night, singing their ancient songs, while all this time the combat warriors would be sitting alone in the desert waiting until they could join the others.

Listening to this, Captain Walker thought that under this custom the warriors who had done a public duty and done it well, perhaps against their natures in the first place, received what amounted to a punishment instead of honors. It seemed to him that the ones who had fought a "smart war," i.e., one where they were in rear echelons, got the most prizes and honors.

It was strange, he reflected, that through the centuries the combat warriors did not think about this unfair custom and become rebellious toward those who had arranged these customs—delightful customs of course for the arrangers. Instead, the actual warriors had accepted it.

But it is a long lane that has no turning; nothing that man can see, or hear, or know, or feel is eternal; few things are certain, but change is one of them.

After the delegation had finished telling him that these things had always been handled this way since the time Elder Brother, who made the earth and all the things and people in it, had in the beginning decreed it, Walker replied that no one could have more reverence for Elder Brother than he had. Therefore he felt that he must tell them that he had had a dream on the eve of the Battle of Apache Leap, in which a huge ravening mountain lion had appeared before him. Then a great light dazzled him and obscured the lion; out of this light a voice like thunder, that could only have been Elder Brother's, said that if the great Pima warriors triumphed on the 'morrow, it was His counsel that those who actually fought and survived were to be given every honor other men could award them, and furthermore, *they* were to march at the head of the procession when their outfit returned to their villages.

"Elder Brother spoke well," Walker said, summoning his most sonorous tones. "He who arranged that the warriors of other Indian tribes who win honors in war are elevated in the eyes of their fellows, now wants the Pimas to enjoy the fruits of victory in the same way. He who holds the lightning in one hand and the wind in the other and Whose voice is thunder, ever seeks to right injustice."

The admonition of Elder Brother, as transmitted by Walker, carried the day, of course. The medicine men, however, must have found it a rather hard dose to pretend to swallow, but his "seance" was an old, tried and true device of their own for keeping the fee-payers in line, or to put over anything that suited their purpose, so they could see only too clearly that their Captain had hoisted them by their own petard. Also, the *real* warriors fairly worshipped their captain; to them he was all-wise. It would have been impossible for the medicine men to put him down at this juncture.

There was much feasting and rejoicing when they marched home, with the combat veterans leading the way, just as Elder Brother had seemingly wished it to be. Over and around them, and their womenfolk, too, like an aura was the knowledge and the certainty that by the grace of Elder Brother they had this time won through to final victory over the warriors of darkness who had scourged them through the centuries, and now they would be able to live out the fullness of their years with their loved ones by their side. And for Arizona Indians during the past one hundred years and more it has remained so.

For a short while after hostilities ceased, time drifted pleasantly by for Captain Walker, and life with Chur-ga and the other Pimas gradually took on more of an air of reality than all the years of his life that had gone before, but one day a disquieting thought came to him that he had been taking Chur-ga's love and devotion too much as a matter of course, and this line of thought soon brought the conviction that this, though not deliberate, needed to be corrected.

He never knew when the idea he ought to marry her first came to him, but he recognized at once that it was nothing short of an inspiration, because purely for his own sake it was something he should have done long ago. Always a man of action once he saw his course clearly, he immediately set about getting her consent, and then helping her with preparations for the marriage.

A law against marriages between Indian girls and white men had been passed in 1865 by Arizona's territorial legislature. It was, of course, an insuperable obstacle to his marriage being solemnized locally according to what had once been Walker's own religious beliefs. But even if he saw a reason to combat such a law, he would never have made any reference to it whatsoever in connection with his own coming marriage, because he realized that to do so would have brought out things that would have hurt and outraged Chur-ga and her people.

Although he felt that the law was a travesty on even the barest minimum of fairness and justice, especially in view of the fact that the Indians were first in Arizona by many centuries, and not to split very fine legal hairs, it was more their country than the white man's, he nevertheless could see no way of getting around hurting Chur-ga if he fought it.

He was also convinced that this ugly law which obviously would create unnatural conditions, not prevent them, would not stand on its own feet if brought before a U.S. Supreme Court, if comprised in the main of men who respected the Constitution and the Bill of Rights and the principle that attracted most of the immigrants to this country.

Also, he despised the pros among the Territory's forms of organized religion, whom he felt had stood shoulder-to-shoulder with the racists and helped them pass the law—or at least he despised them too much to give them the satisfaction of thinking he placed that much value on *their* marriage ceremony.

He wanted the best of everything for Chur-ga and didn't want her feelings hurt, ever, or for her to be placed in a position where the people who were responsible for the 1865 law, and hoped to benefit from it, both financially and in a bigoted way, could slight her, or make her conscious that they regarded her as inferior. Therefore he decided to have a Pima wedding, to which he would make sure that those who might snub her would not be invited, and in this way pull the teeth, blunt the claws, and neutralize the venom of the white women who fancied themselves as the social leaders of this still raw and largely primitive Territory, and frustrate the bigots of both sexes.

He made plans to have a Pima ceremony that would be the biggest and fanciest wedding in Pima history, and to have it right on their reservation, too, and in accordance with their laws and customs. He had no fear that any final legal determination of a marriage under Pima law, regardless of the color of skin, ethnic group or religion involved, would not in the end be in accordance with any United States law that would stand the test of constitutionality. And he took comfort from his conviction that in any event, it would receive the sanction of the Creator.

Many of the great figures of the West came to the wedding, quite a few of them staying for the festivities for various lengths of time up to several days. But few of their womenfolk came with them.

One guest who came, and attracted more attention by his very presence than all save the bride, was Jacob Walz, a handsome fifty-five-year-old miner who was already attracting attention in the Territory because of the beauty of his teen-aged Apache sweetheart, Ken-tee. For a wedding present he brought a buckskin tobacco sack of gold nuggets which he shyly presented to Chur-ga. "This will ward off practically all of the evil spirits you're ever likely to encounter in this world," he told her.

After the wedding ceremony, Walker was formally inducted into the Pima tribe with the traditional flowing together of blood to seal the relationship. Joseph Azul, son of Antonio, was now one of the leading chiefs, and he participated with his blood in the ceremony.

Chapter 5

Shortly after the close of the Civil War, Dr. Thorne received orders to report back to army headquarters in New Mexico to be under the direct command of General Carson.

His first thought after these orders arrived was, what about his Indian friends down on The Strip now that he would no longer be there to take care of them and continue his instructions. However, he could take comfort in the fact that the medicine men were progressing well with perfecting and enforcing camp and personal hygiene, and teaching it to new arrivals. They were also progressing amazingly well with the various treatments involving the use of medicine and surgery which he had been teaching them.

On hearing that he was leaving, the Apaches were very disturbed. He had been one of the few whites in their experience who had learned their language and their ways to do what he could to help them.

A few days before he was due to leave, Thorne was told by the old medicine man that Cochise and some other Apache chiefs wished to do something for him to show their great and everlasting gratitude for his many kindnesses to the women and children as well as the braves of the Apache settlement on the Verde River. "We have learned," said the medicine man, "that gold is the most desirable of things to the white man; that it has the power to bring him what he wants. He can, for instance, use it to win beautiful women for wives, and to destroy his enemies. We know where there is much of the stuff from which that gold comes—it is in little rocks that Mexicans dig from a hole in the ground; my people killed them all over there (waving his arm in the direction of Superstition

Mountain Range). We do not yet know how to get gold out of rocks, but white men know and our chiefs want to give a pile of the little rocks to you. But you must promise not to tell where it came from."

Thorne didn't have much faith in what the medicine man told him about the "little rocks" being gold. He had seen Indians with various colored jewels, such as amethysts and bloodstones and other semiprecious stones that Indians prize so dearly to wear as necklaces and bracelets, and he assumed that the little rocks would turn out to be something similar.

That afternoon there was a great gathering of the mightiest chiefs of the Apaches at The Strip. When Thorne came by on his regular round, they were waiting to greet him. For the first time he saw the squat, ugly Geronimo, and Coloradas' successor, Victorio. Juh and Eskiminzin were also there. Cochise and Victorio seemed to be the co-leaders for the meeting. "After one night and one sun," said Victorio solemnly, "we will take you to much gold. It is the wish of our people."

Thorne couldn't see where he had anything to lose by going along, and he thought that in any event it would be a most interesting experience, so he told them he would be most grateful to come along. One night and one sun meant the next night. When the time set for their departure came, the party, all on horses, traveled southeastward for a few miles to a bend in the trail. There the column halted and Cochise told Thorne they would have to blindfold him for his own protection because he did not want him to know where they were going. "If bad white men were to learn that you know where the Spanish gold-rocks had been gathered, they might think you also know where the mine is and torture you to make you tell them where, but you no know where mine is, so you would be in bad trouble," he said. Having gone this far, Thorne decided he might as well go the whole route, "in for a penny, in for a pound" as the saying went, so he made no objections while a blindfold was wrapped around his eyes and tied back of his head.

After a few hours they began wading through a body of water which according to Thorne's calculation of the lapse of time would be the Salt River, and when the horses were in the water they were moved back and forth in various directions, obviously, Thorne thought, according to a planned tactic on the part of Cochise to confuse him as to where they were crossing. After a rather slow-paced ride during the rest of the night he began to feel the sun on him and knew that morning had arrived. About this time the Apaches halted and removed his blindfold and he saw they were in the bottom of a very deep canyon with unusually steep sides which went almost straight up to where he could see a ribbon of sky not much wider than the green strip at the bottom of the canyon. He figured they had deliberately picked this spot because nothing much could be seen that would reveal their location because of the steepness of the canyon walls.

Just then Victorio indicated, with a grand wave of his hand, a spot directly in front of Thorne's horse and there he saw a conical pile of rocks about two feet high and of a curious color. He dismounted and after picking up a small piece he quickly realized that he was holding a chunk of gold ore of great richness. He had often seen pure gold weighed at the Fort's commissary where it was used to buy goods or was bartered for money, and he knew just about how much gold in dust or tiny nuggets was worth. He figured that the small chunk of ore, or rich concentrate, he was holding in his hand had enough gold to bring at least twenty-five dollars, perhaps more.

One of the Apaches approached with three buckskin sacks into which he scooped the pile of concentrate and then hung them on the pommel of Thorne's saddle, and they began the return journey, with Thorne again blindfolded. Sometime later they removed the blindfold and he saw that he was still in a canyon, one much larger and not nearly so blind as the other had been. Off to his right the Indians were kneeling to drink from a spring near the foot of a cliff. They motioned him to do likewise and after he drank his fill he looked up the canyon, which he judged from the position of the sun ran roughly north and south and saw an immense, very sharp perpendicular spire of rock rising against the sky almost due eastward. It was the most unusual peak he had ever seen, but before he had a chance to speculate on it much or ask any questions of Cochise concerning it, they put back his blindfold and resumed their journey.

When they got back to the river where they had moved around in circles and in other confusing maneuvers the night before, ostensibly to keep him from knowing what stream he was crossing, his horse stumbled and went in to its knees, pitching him off into the water. They quickly helped him to his feet, but as they lifted him up the blindfold, soaked and heavy with water, slipped down on his nose and he saw that he was at the mouth of a canyon that debouched on a stream he was now certain was the Salt River and again looking up the canyon he studied the huge peculiarly shaped spire that he had seen when he was given the pile of concentrate. Again using the time of day and the position of the sun in relation to the spire, which, like all frontiersmen, he had learned to do for directions, he saw that the spire was now slightly southeastward from the place where he was now standing.

Before leaving him at The Strip, Cochise again asked him never to reveal to anyone the secret of how he got his rich gift. But when he arrived back at Fort McDowell later in the morning, he was so full of his adventure of the night before that he could not refrain from telling at least one person, his best friend, who from the best information the writer could obtain, was a First Lieutenant Fairchild. He swore Fairchild to absolute secrecy and gave him a piece of the concentrate both as a souvenir and as confirmation of what Thorne had told him.

Thorne then asked permission of his commanding officer to make a journey to visit his family at San Jose, a town near San Francisco, before going back to New Mexico.

He had a relaxing and enjoyable visit with his family, whom he had not seen since they went their separate ways in St. Louis, he to take up his medical studies and they to seek their fortunes on the Pacific Coast. He did not mention his gold to them, because he feared it would cause a great deal of excitement, speculation and inevitably, requests for loans and donations to this and that cause and all the other demands that descend on a person who is known to have come into a large sum. He knew, too, that the sum rises as the tale goes from mouth-to-ear-to-mouth until the total becomes so gigantic that it attracts the parasites, leeches, and con men from far and near—some of whom, according to the law of averages, are bound to become dangerous. Thorne avoided all this by quietly announcing after a few days with his relatives that he had to make a trip to San Francisco in order to deliver a trunk to the family of a good friend he had at Fort McDowell. The gold, of course, was in the trunk.

He had no difficulty in disposing of the concentrate once he had reached San Francisco. The gold not having been smelted out to its pure state, he had to sell the concentrate as it stood for a figure derived from an estimate after an assay had been made. He received an astonishingly large amount of money for it.

In the countless stories that have since gained currency about Dr. Thorne and his experiences with the Apaches, including their fabulous gift to him, there have been many guesstimates as to the amount of money he received from the mint, but he never, so far as is known, revealed the exact figure to anyone.

Before leaving San Jose, however, he did announce that he had had a windfall while at Fort McDowell, and he insisted on paying off a bank loan for his father that he had secured to expand the export-import business he was operating with two other sons. Thorne gave both brothers substantial gifts, too, that they might buy homes for themselves in San Jose.

At a local bank he had the balance of his money from the ore converted into the kind of draft that would be readily convertible in New Mexico.

Behind him at Fort McDowell he left a wealth of health and happiness, and even love, among the Apaches who lived on The Strip—people who had heretofore known little if any kindness, consideration, or even fairness at the hands of the white man. Still standing today on the site of the old Fort are the ruins of the sturdy little hospital he had built for treating seriously ill soldiers and Apaches. It was built mostly of wide, thick adobe slabs, by Mexican artisans and with the help of Apache braves—amazed at finding themselves doing women's work—and is the only original building at the Fort that survives.

Chapter 6

After the Civil War, when the sensation caused by the Peralta Massacre had almost been forgotten, especially since no more discoveries of the remains of gold-laden burros had occurred for more than a decade, the search for gold in Superstition was started up all over again at a much more feverish pace, by the appearance of Jacob von Walzer (later shortened by him to Jacob Walz). This interest has never slackened, but, if anything, is today even more intense.

Walz was born in the state of Württemberg, Germany, in 1808, and was educated at Heidelberg as a mining engineer. He worked around Prussian mines until he was about thirty years of age. Then he went to Australia in the wake of news of a big gold strike there. He returned to Germany after about ten years, broke and rather discouraged. But in the immemorial manner of gold prospectors he almost immediately set out for California when news reached him of the great gold strike there in 1848. He landed in New York as a German immigrant and worked his way west, prospecting around Sutter Creek, California, and later around Prescott, Arizona, for about fifteen years, interspersing his searching periodically with stints as an ordinary miner in order to raise grubstake money.

Old mining records show a claim filed by Walz in the Walker Mining District (near Prescott) in the early 1860s. For a time he lived there with Andy Starar on a tract of land next to one owned by Darrell Duppa, an Englishman of considerable education, who changed the name of the city of Swillings (named for Jack Swillings who is credited with choosing the site) to Phoenix, after the legendary bird that rose from its own ashes, after Swillings was almost entirely burned down, and then rebuilt bigger and better than ever.

In 1863 Walz turned up working as an ordinary miner in the Vulture Gold Mine near what is now Wickenburg, Arizona—named after Henry Wickenburg, the discoverer of this mine. Many millions of dollars were taken from the Vulture, legitimately by the owners, and by high-grading on the part of hired hands. In miner's lingo, "high-grading" is when a miner conceals and removes high-grade ore or nuggets of pure gold from a mine employing him.

Nowadays extraordinary precautions are taken by gold mine owners to prevent this; in some cases the miners are required to leave their clothes in locker rooms after arriving for their work shift, then must proceed nude to another room and don working clothes there. This process is reversed when they have completed their day's work.

The Vulture Mine was about the easiest to high-grade of any of which there is record, because strewn on the surface at first was a vast fortune in nuggets and chunks of exceedingly rich ore, from which the gold could be broken loose with an ordinary hammer, or even by hitting two chunks together. When this surface bonanza was exhausted and the digging began, the same rich ore and nuggets continued on down for various depths in several directions.

In the excitement and in view of the quantity of gold that was being honestly taken out daily, not much attention was paid to the bulging pockets and remarkably heavy dinner pails of some of the miners, when at the end of their shifts they wended their way to the shacks and tents where they lived. As a consequence some of them became rich, at the start anyway, right along with the owners.

Walz and some others who were suspected of this at the time were finally arrested and their belongings and quarters searched—a search that turned up something like $175,000 in obvious high-grade. But none was found that could be traced to Walz. All those caught with illicit high-grade were charged with theft. Those who were merely suspected, including Walz, were fired and warned not to be seen in the vicinity of the mine again, though rumors have persisted ever since that some of them were secretly hanged.

Some of the losers who were caught with ore were rather bitter about Walz, and for a very human reason: they resented, so the story goes, his alleged cleverness in getting his high-grade spirited out of camp each day by a beautiful seventeen-year-old Apache Indian girl, named Ken-tee, which means Sunshine in Apache, with whom he was on intimate terms. Some of his fellow workers were jealous about the girl, too. She was the prettiest girl the people of that frontier area had ever seen.

Walz himself was an extraordinary figure of a man in 1866, more than six feet tall, with massive shoulders, a trim waist, and heavily muscled arms from his decades of mining. He stood tall and proud like the Prussian-trained soldier he had been, and his thick head of hair and neatly trimmed Vandyke beard made him a distinctive figure in sparsely populated Phoenix and vicinity.

There was, then, as we already know, much intolerance for, and discrimination against, Indians in the Southwest. It was popular in those parts to regard Indians as something less than human, and a man who "took up" with an Indian girl was regarded as being several notches below his warm-hued consort. In the case of Ken-tee, her youthful attractiveness only added fuel to the resentment with which she was regarded by the largely weatherbeaten and work-worn pioneer women of the Territory. There was no denying the lissomeness of her body or the beauty of her luminous dark eyes and hair with the sheen and color of a crow's wing.

Ken-tee and Walz began living at Mesa, Arizona, in an Indian-type hogan about thirteen miles from Superstition Mountain, but they soon disappeared. When they returned after several weeks, they had two heavily laden burros in tether. The secret of what the burros carried was soon out when Walz appeared at the local Wells Fargo office to ship a quantity of nearly pure gold concentrate to the U.S. mint in San Francisco. In due course he received about nine thousand dollars for the shipment.

Soon after this a terrible tragedy overtook Ken-tee. The Apaches raided the Indian community where Walz and Ken-tee had their hogan, apparently for the sole purpose of carrying her off for having told Walz about the location of the Peralta mine, which, it afterwards developed, they *knew* she had done. They did succeed in seizing her temporarily, but her neighbors quickly rallied and, mounted on fresh horses, pursued the raiding party so fiercely, killing several of the Apache braves and some of their horses, that the remainder, to make good their escape, freed Ken-tee. But first they cut out her tongue. She died in Walz's arms within the hour from shock and loss of blood.

Walz was utterly devastated by Ken-tee's death. According to the old-timers around Phoenix, she loved him with a rare passion and single-mindedness. He was particularly bitter about how she had been treated socially at the hands of the frontier women, and was at some pains to point out during the years that followed, that in looks or as a wife, she didn't have her equal among those who professed to scorn her.

The first few years after her death he became largely a loner and took to drinking—apparently maintaining no close association with anyone. During those years, as near as can be determined, he never went near his gold find either. He used some of the money he got for the gold he and Ken-tee brought back from their expedition to buy a home on the outskirts of Phoenix, and he invested some more of it in a forty-acre plot of land near Sixteenth and Henshaw. Today, that forty acres alone is worth more than all the gold he is known to have mined.

He was increasingly less seen in public except in a saloon or on his way to and from one. Pictures of him at that time show his hair long and uncombed; the points of his mustache drooping below his chin and his clothes unkempt. He also developed a reputation as a brawler. Nevertheless, on the strength of that one expedition he made with Ken-tee, his fame grew until there was hardly a spot in the world where the stories about the Old Dutchman, as he had come to be known, hadn't appeared. People came from all over to see the man who discovered a fabulous gold mine and was ignoring it because of a personal tragedy. They vied with each other to buy him drinks and meals, and sought continually to entice him off to themselves in the hope that if they could get him sufficiently in his cups, he would at least drop a hint that might lead them to his mine. But they never had any success in trapping him, because Walz appeared only in places where there were bound to be several people at all time. He went armed with the standard .44 belt gun, and usually had a Sharps rifle in the crook of his arm when he went back and forth to his house where he lived. He allowed no one to walk with him on these occasions, and he never permitted anyone to enter his fortress of a house. He once said of his extraordinary precautions that neither he nor any man could tell when the power of gold might tempt someone into a desperate undertaking, such as kidnapping him and torturing him to reveal the location of his mine. It was why he had his house built like a veritable fortress, with adobe walls nearly four feet thick and shutters of heavy overlapping ironwood planking. The only outer door was the front one, and it also was constructed of layers of planking and swung on oiled hinges, specially forged to carry its weight.

Perhaps to discourage would-be marauders, he used to compete in the many shooting matches that were a favorite entertainment of the people of the Southwest, where proficiency with firearms often meant survival. He had been a crack shot with a rifle in the Prussian Army and became an extraordinary one during his years around Phoenix. He was very straight with his .44, too, but never mastered to any extent the art of the fast draw.

Sometime during the year 1869 another German immigrant by the name of Jacob Weiser appeared in company with Walz. He was as outgoing in his contacts with other people as Walz was an introvert, though he spoke only a little English. It was thought that Walz had sent for him and paid his passage from Germany. He had been a carpenter in Germany and began earning his living in Phoenix by building sluice boxes for miners and prospectors. On one occasion Weiser mentioned to a fellow German immigrant who ran a grocery store that Walz had promised that one day he would take him to his mine. Then came a period when it was noticed that neither of them was to be seen at his usual haunts.

In a matter of a month or so they were back in Phoenix and Walz again took some sacks of gold concentrate to the Phoenix Wells Fargo office from which, as usual, it was shipped to the U.S. mint. Almost immediately the two Jacobs started back to the Superstitions on another trip. Several days later a shoeless, shirtless Walz, exhausted and his feet torn, arrived at a ranch southwest of Superstition. Later he told the county sheriff that he and Weiser had been attacked by Apaches while they were sleeping and Weiser had been badly wounded and perhaps captured. Walz said he had escaped them by going over the top of Superstition, dressed only in his shirt, trousers, and stockings. He had torn his shirt into strips and wrapped them around his feet in lieu of shoes. He led a posse of mounted searchers back to the place where he and Weiser had been attacked, only to confirm that Weiser had disappeared!

At the campsite was irrefutable evidence that the attack was purely the work of vengeance on the part of the Apaches, to avenge—as they always did, or tried to do—any defilement of their Thunder God's abode: they had ignored at the camp a small fortune in incredibly rich gold concentrate!

Within a few days Walz learned that Weiser had managed to stagger along, though fearfully wounded by an Apache arrow that went through his left arm and on into his chest, until he encountered a hunting party of some friendly Pimas who brought him on one of their horses to the home of Dr. John D. Walker, on the nearby Pima reservation.

Walker's home was probably the best refuge the wounded Weiser could have been brought to, though Walker was a man who was bitter toward most of his former friends and asso-

ciates, and with good reason. Although he had helped save the
Territory of Arizona from annihilation at the hands of the
Apaches by his raising of a large force from among the Pimas
and other Indian tribes and training them into a highly efficient military force, peerless, as events proved, for the task of
out-thinking and out-fighting the Apaches, at a time when, according to its then Governor Goodwin, Arizona lay almost
wholly at their mercy, the settlers had nevertheless turned on
him and treated him shamefully, once they were safe, merely
because he had married Chur-ga.

Walker and Walz had a thing in common: the treatment
Chur-ga and Ken-tee had received at the hands of the white
women. These women had, even during the worst period of
the war, been mean-mouthing Walker because of his preference for Chur-ga, his captivating sweetheart, because she was a
Pima Indian. The women no doubt feared that the example of
his devotion to Chur-ga might catch on with other frontier
swains who admired the natural beauty of a few Indian girls
and responded to the appeal of their frank sensuality. This
fear and jealousy on the women's part helped put over the
miscegenation law that was passed by the Arizona territorial
legislature in 1865, directed to some extent at Walker, who
was engaged at the time with his volunteer force of Pimas in
defending the barely hatched Territory, and was too busy to
know or care about the law that was to have such a drastic
effect on him and his family in later years.

Walker's brilliant political appeal and rapidly increasing
prominence in Territorial affairs stemming from his conduct
of the campaign against the Apaches had also aroused much
jealousy among the usual type of frontier politicians, and they
were determined to destroy as much of his public standing as
they could.

After he married Chur-ga in the solemn Pima ceremony
despite the miscegenation law, his enemies saw their opportunity to down him. Walker forestalled them by withdrawing almost entirely into the life of his wife's people and never gave
them the chance. He no longer concerned himself with the
role of lion in Arizona's social, business, or political life he
had so briefly experienced, but which he had never liked anyway, as it was mostly contrary to his nature.

Walker, as a medical doctor, naturally did all he could for
Weiser, but nothing could have saved him by this time, so fa-

tally advanced had the infection in the wound become. During moments of lucidity he managed to relate the circumstances of the attack.

"We were coming from a gold mine; it must be the richest one in the world," he told Walker. "But it wouldn't be fair to my partner, Walz—he's my friend—to tell you where the mine is without talking to him about it. If I get well I'll ask him to give you a share in it—I promise you that."

The next day he died and the Pimas fashioned a coffin for him and carried it on their shoulders to his final resting place in a cemetery a mile or so down the river where they had for many years been burying the bodies of the white men they found dead of thirst or at the hands of Apaches.

The Pimas had a feeling that death is dangerous to the living, for the dead person is lonely and tries to take others with him if he can. Therefore, they buried their dead as quickly as possible and, even if they loved them, tried not to think of them again.

Walz had himself driven in a buggy to the funeral—his feet were still in bad shape. Afterwards he lingered as a guest while the doctor treated his feet. The strong bond between the two men was not entirely because Walz, too, had loved an Indian girl. They were both rugged individualists, and saw eye-to-eye in many other ways.

The crusty Prussian developed a great fondness for Churga, as almost everyone did who came in contact with her, and while she went happily about her household chores in the fine home that Walker had built on the Pima Indian Reservation, his eyes would follow her with a sad it-might-have-been-this-way-with-Ken-tee-and-myself look.

Walker said afterwards that he never mentioned to Walz the lost mine of the Peraltas, probably because he knew that it was quite certain it wouldn't produce any useful information if he did. He sensed, and no doubt correctly, that the fact that only Walz in the white community knew where the mine was, invested him with an importance that brought him attention—a thing that was vital to a lonely man. Although Walz said the attention only annoyed him, his actions indicated he valued it greatly. Besides, Walker was convinced that if the Peraltas had been working a rich gold mine—and he knew they had—he would eventually find it with the help of his Pimas.

One thing—a matter of individual preference—he and Walker did differ on, however, was Walz's recently acquired quirk of playing the old prospector to the hilt. Whenever he dropped by, he would be dusty and dirty and his clothes literally stiff with dirt and cooking grease, and his body unbathed, until Walker told him, "You smell worse—much worse—than your burros, and you'll simply have to take a thorough bath each time you're going to eat with us."

Chur-ga had some softly tanned and attractively embroidered buckskin duds made up for him by some of the Pima women who specialized in tanning hides for wearing apparel, and they were kept there for him for post-bath use. As soon as he appeared she would have the warm water prepared and put in a tub that had been made by sawing a wooden-staved hogshead cask in two. After the first occasion on which Walz had supposedly scrubbed himself in this commodious accommodation, Chur-ga suspected he hadn't done a very thorough job, and the next time he came by, she not only had the bath ready for him, but she had two giggling young girls standing by to help him with the scrubbing. It took a little while to get him used to this procedure, as well as to the top-less maidens, but once he did he went for the whole package with great enthusiasm. Chur-ga suspected that it also made his visits more frequent than otherwise might have been the case.

Walker once invited him to come and live near him in the village, but Walz refused, saying, "Indians never had a real doctor before the white men came, and the things you can cure or alleviate gives you a godlike standing with them that makes all the difference—it makes a wonderful life for you, really. But I feel that Indians don't ordinarily think overly much of a plain white man who comes to live with them; they sort of take their attitude from the way the whites regard them. I wouldn't like that."

Nevertheless, Walz was very much interested and warmed by the teeming life of the Pimas in their villages, and Walker, who had been making a close and deep study of their ways and arts, would talk to him for long hours about it.

But Walz, who was fast becoming a legendary figure during his own lifetime, was much more interesting to Walker than Walker was to Walz. "The whole business about Walz and his mine and the kind of man he was had an utter fascination for me," Walker said in after years.

The electrifying news that in Arizona a man, usually referred to as the "Old Dutchman," had discovered a gold mine so rich in high-grade ore that he could go to it and pick up a sack of almost pure concentrate any time he wished, excited the imagination of millions.

The stories about Walz multiplied and spread until there was hardly a place in the world where there weren't people who would ask American visitors, "Have they found it yet?" and most would know they meant Walz's mine.

The imagination-provoking stories that were contemporary about his bonanza were written during an era of a little more than two decades when stupendous gold and silver mines were being discovered in many parts of the western United States, which made any story about a mine, no matter how fantastic, easy to believe. The story of Walz became even more bizarre when it developed that he did not seem interested in exploiting his discovery in the usual way by working the mine with men and machinery, but was content with merely helping himself to more or less modest amounts of gold from time to time.

Researching his life and times one finds hundreds of newspaper stories, dozens of magazine articles, and several books that have been written about him. Practically anything written on the subject enthralled the periodical readers of every continent. In recent years, for instance, *this* writer wrote two magazine articles about him that were published, one in *True Magazine,* and the other for *Point West.*

To no one did he reveal the location of the mine, and the lure of it grew as the years went on and the number who searched for it swelled from hundreds to the thousands. The mystery became studded with countless legends and made it a steady source of eagerly read stories for magazines, especially the great mass-circulation magazines of the United States.

These stories have persisted through the years right up to the present. Besides this writer's magazine articles, the *Saturday Evening Post, Colliers,* the *American Magazine,* and many others in the past few decades, ran versions about the well-hidden mine on Superstition Mountain, the "Lorelei" mountain that lures so many to destruction. There have been at least three books about it in the past five years.

But there was no one in Walz's own time, or after, who could reveal satisfactorily what the man was really like or what motivated him, because no one knew him that well, even though literally hundreds of people in Phoenix and vicinity over a period of nearly thirty years became familiar with his face and figure. He had no intimates or even close friends in the ordinary sense of the term, not even Dr. Walker, who said, "Jake is an enigma wrapped in a mystery."

His nearest neighbor said: "He is not at all like you and me."

The pattern of the life he lived in Phoenix after the death of Ken-tee and Weiser, however, produces a picture that gives some insight into how he preferred to go about things during the years after he developed as a character, and makes for a certain amount of predictability regarding what would have been his probable course of action in given circumstances.

First, the murder of Ken-tee was a numbing shock from which, by all accounts, Walz's spirits and his once enormous zest for life were slow to recover, and in fact, never did recover to any extent. Second, he told Walker that after losing Ken-tee he felt drained of any feeling for courting another woman on any serious basis and had looked to the partnership with Weiser as the next best thing to stand off the loneliness and emptiness of old age, which he could see was in the offing for him. Then Weiser, too, was killed.

The accumulation of more wealth must have seemed a hollow and futile thing to the lonely man who was already fairly wealthy from the gold he had taken from his mine by the time of the Weiser tragedy.

Besides the probable lack of monetary incentive for returning to the mine, there was the deadly danger involved in the determination of the Apaches to drive out or kill everyone who tried to exploit the Mountain in what they considered a sacrilegious manner. For more gold he would be risking the remaining years of his life if the Apaches managed to trap him, and a cruel death besides.

Then there were the adventurers who were lying in wait for him at every turn, most of whom were willing to kill anyone for a profit. Also, beginning to appear in the United States with increasing frequency were the psychotic killers who killed for the thrill of watching their victims' death agonies.

The whole situation in and around Superstition Mountain was almost made to order for such sadistic practices.

The fact that the Apaches left the rich gold concentrate at the scene of the attack on him and Weiser did not encourage Walz. Wise in the ways of the Apaches, he knew that they had come to know the value of it. They had demonstrated this to Dr. Thorne. But when it came to the attack on Weiser and himself they obviously did not want to give the impression that robbery was their motive. They wanted it unmistakable that they were merely trying to serve their Thunder God.

To casual observers it might have appeared strange that in view of the ever increasing number of adventurers searching all over the Mountain, the Apaches didn't kill all of them out of hand. The explanation is simple: as long as intruders didn't stumble on the spot the Apaches considered their Thunder God's sacred area, it was not desecrated, according to the way Geronimo afterward described their attitude to Captain Walker.

The Apaches must have realized, too, that if they made it a practice to kill everybody who climbed the Mountain with a burro and some mining tools, they would set up a backlash that would bring soldiers to run every last Apache off Superstition Mountain forever, regardless of the time, expense, and trouble involved.

As it was, the Apaches were blamed for a sizable portion of the bushwhackings (no matter who was guilty) that began to occur up there in those days and are still continuing as this is written.

Quite a tent colony of adventurers and gold-seekers sprang up in the neighborhood of Walz's house in Phoenix, crowding in as near as the boundaries of the land on his river bank lot would permit. They had various planned procedures, but all their plans had one thing in common: they were determined to find his mine.

Some hoped to track him to it; others tried to make friends with him and gain his confidence. Some banded together and approached him with the proposition that for a cut of the gold they would give him "protection" on any journeys he might undertake to the lode. But the Old Dutchman kept to his "loner" ways after Weiser's death and did not attempt another trip to the Mountain for nearly ten years.

Among the forces that protected him, besides his reputation

of being a deadly man to tackle, was the realization that if he was killed during an attempt to kidnap and torture him for information, no one might ever find the mine. Then, too, it would have been practically impossible to spirit him off in full view of the numbers of people who watched him day and night. Some out-of-town people even formed syndicates and pooled their funds to hire watchers to keep a round-the-clock eye on him.

Among the personal relationships he'd once had, he kept up only his friendship with Captain Walker, though he also patronized quite a few of the saloons and gambling places that then abounded on Washington Street in Phoenix. A moderate drinker, the chief lure to him of the booze joints was the companionable atmosphere he found there, as well as the safety in numbers.

As the 1860s passed and the 1870s began and he made no more attempts to reach the mine, the number of people who watched and trailed him dwindled considerably and kept changing constantly. By their very natures most of them, aside from the syndicates, had little or no money to finance a long siege and they would get discouraged and leave. But a hard nucleus, its members often changing, was there as long as he lived.

Among those who came and went were journalists, novelists, and writers of all sorts—many of them distinguished— who tried to interview him. As far as can be learned none of them ever accomplished this. Among the famous ones who came to Phoenix and stayed for various lengths of time while trying to wangle at least a conversation with him were Mark Twain, Harriet Beecher Stowe, Thomas Hardy, Herman Melville, Walt Whitman, and Bret Harte. Numerous wealthy men tried to contact him through their agents, and in a few cases they came in person. They were willing to pay vast sums for a partnership with him. Many syndicates were expressly formed for that purpose also. He would stonily ignore those who approached him on such errands at a bar, which was the only place they could safely contact him personally—it was rightly considered very dangerous for anyone to try to force themselves on him while he was out on the street, or entering or leaving his house.

Along about 1875 or '76 he did a thing considered most uncharacteristic by those who thought they knew him: he made a personal project of buying shoes for the poor Negro,

Mexican, and Indian children of Phoenix, which he asked the Sisters of Charity to distribute. Once in a while he would include white children if he was convinced that their need was caused by the fact that the father drank and the mother was a slattern, "and if she wasn't," he once said, "she soon would be from living with a drunk. Anyway, I think the greatest need of a poor person is to have good shoes." He proved it by buying and having them distributed to children by the hundreds. He told Walker that he learned what shoes mean to a person when he was forced to flee in his stocking feet after the Apaches raided their camp and killed Weiser.

Strangely enough, he also would give away on occasions some of his gold, though only in a peculiarly personal way. He never lent people money, no matter how much, or how expertly they begged for it, but on impulse he would sometimes capriciously reach into one of his pockets and hand someone who had caught his sympathy a pinch of gold dust. Once or twice he did this with fairly sizable nuggets. He seemed to take a whimsical delight in this, as if to confound those who said, "He's probably getting his money from some other source; I doubt that he has a gold mine at all."

R. J. Holmes of Phoenix had a pair of cufflinks made from the nuggets the Dutchman gave him, using the whole nuggets on the outside of the cuff as an ornament, and wore them the rest of his life. They were a great conversation piece, and in after years became very valuable because of their source. His son Brownie, now a very old man, still owns the fabled cufflinks.

Along about 1878 the Old Dutchman, still comparatively physically vigorous, began returning to his mine for more gold, actuated by what motives no one knew. Perhaps he was bored or his pride was stung by remarks that he had lost his nerve. He may have been short of cash because of his charity of buying shoes for poor children, or handing out pinches of gold to suspected skeptics and friends had depleted his reserve or, as the Mexicans say, *"Quien sabe?"*

Also, he was getting rather old and he might have irresistibly felt the call of the old adventuresome spirit that had moved him to spectacular risks in the past, or he might merely have wanted to show people there was a lot left in the old boy. In any event, he decided to risk being able to give the slip to his trailers and avoid the Apaches once he reached the vicinity of the Mountain.

According to many eyewitnesses whose stories were collected by Barney Barnard, and personally related by him to this writer, the procession trailing after him on that first occasion, and on later expeditions continuing sporadically to about 1888, looked like a parade; some of the hundreds of people were on foot with backpacks, others rode horses or mules, or drove in buggies or buckboards, accommodating themselves to the slow pace of the Dutchman's burros, and his heavily laden mule, alongside of which he usually walked. "I welcome the walking," he told Walker. "It keeps me healthy and vigorous."

Barnard, a prominent Arizona rancher and businessman who became fascinated by the story of the Dutchman, devoted more than fifty years to collecting memorabilia of Walz and his mine that eventually became known as the *Lost* Dutchman Mine.

Probably nowhere else on earth is there such a wilderness of deep canyons, washes, and defiles—all thickly covered with nearly impenetrable cacti—as there is sloping down and fanning out for miles from the southwest end of Superstition Mountain. All Walz had to do was to lead his two burros after dark into one of the deep washes, and wait for it to become pitch dark, for he picked times when the moon suited this purpose. People soon learned to keep their distance from the place at which he halted. He was a crack shot and was credited with killing at least some of the dozen or more men who had been shot while trying to creep too close to keep contact no matter how dark it became later.

To prove that he shot any one of his pursuers was practically impossible, and the Old Dutchman knew this full well, because so many of these adventurer-desperados were always shooting each other, usually for no better reason, aside from those who were sadists and psychotics, than that they wanted the other fellow's outfit, any map he might have, his pocketbook, grub, arms and ammunition, or any other object of value, let alone a thing as valuable as the Old Dutchman's mine was reputed to be. And it was hopeless to try to say honestly what gun a bullet came from before ballistics tests were invented. Too, there were always the Apaches to blame.

In the West of those times, the man who shot first and

stayed alive was the man most admired, and Phoenix and vicinity was always as wild and woolly in this respect as they came. Of course, only a small fraction of persons were murdered around there in those days compared percentage-wise to the murders committed in Phoenix and vicinity in these enlightened times. But it *was* as tough an era in regard to *man-to-man killings* as the world has ever known. Tombstone, with its almost daily shoot-outs during the 1880s and '90s, only a couple of hundred miles south of Superstition, led the world in producing a horrifying example of this sort of thing. Many of the men who dogged the Old Dutchman are known to have come from there or went there afterward.

His trackers related they were almost certain that he put muffling pads and muzzles on his burros, before slipping away quietly in the dark. He would then shuttle in the maze until he deemed it was safe to make directly for the mine. Favoring his tactics was the fact that many of the deep slashes in that tortured area of volcanic rubble laced with cacti were interconnected. Most of the area was a perfect labyrinth—and still is. The crowd following him would not see him again till he was out of the mountains and suddenly appeared on some portion of the road back to Phoenix with the gold he came for.

On some of these trips he never even went near the mine, but on the first night out gave his trackers the slip, then turned right around, as a sardonic joke on those who sought to trap him, and came directly back to his house in Phoenix.

As the riches he derived from his mine piled up, and his age reached the seventy mark, his trips to the rich lode got farther and farther apart, and apparently much of the fun and satisfaction to his ego from the trips to the mine went out of it through repetition. Also, the necessity for being ever on the alert, once he put the pack saddles on the burros he kept, with his riding mule, in the tightly fenced-in tract of land back of his house must have put an almost unbearable strain on his nerves. He could feel the vigilant eyes of the many people who watched him day and night, month in and month out (year in and year out, for that matter).

Barnard told the writer that he had made more than half a dozen trips, some of them to San Francisco, and one to Germany, to search out the facts about Walz's early history and his activities after he came to this country. In New York he found Walz's immigration record, and in Philadelphia old mint records showing vouchers amounting to $254,000 that were made payable to Walz between 1879 and '85, some of them being only a few months apart, to pay for gold he shipped via Wells Fargo Express.

Although people no longer can follow the Old Dutchman in person, there are still those who seek the vicinity of where his house once stood before it was washed away in the great flood of 1891, thinking no doubt that he might have buried some of his gold under it or near it. Phoenix police have more than once been alerted because some householder in that area heard the thud of digging in his own, or a neighboring, backyard in the still watches of the night. The police always found it was being caused by someone digging for the Dutchman's gold—someone who had been fooling around with old city maps, or had one sold to them by a crook or prankster. Knowing that the owner of the property would hardly let them dig there without a big split, or even demanding the whole lot for himself, they thought that the best thing to do was to sneak in under cover of darkness.

Insofar as the writer knows, the only person still alive who knew the Old Dutchman and talked to him on occasion is Mrs. Gertrude Barkley, who as a child remembered him coming to her father's ranch near Superstition Mountain to water his mule and two burros while going out and back on expeditions to the Mountain, or roundabout to visit Walker. "We always knew the moment he appeared if he was merely visiting: he would be riding his mule. Otherwise he would have it loaded with equipment," Mrs. Barkley said. "He used to let us kids ride his wonderfully trained burros once in a while. 'I like those little rascals better than most humans I've met,' he told my father once. One he called Fortuna, and the other, Senator."

Gertrude married Tex Barkley, a young rancher, and they worked side-by-side for more than sixty years to build one of the largest cattle empires in Arizona, the western limits of which lay in the evening shadows of the southeast end of Superstition. They had three children, a boy, Bill, and two girls, all of whom had families, but are long dead. Alone now, Gertie is still interested in the management of the ranch, though totally blind. She lives in a beautiful and spacious modern house she built on top of a hill that is part of the original ranch. She was recently offered a small fortune for just a part of the spread. Her house has a breathtaking view, facing toward Superstition, over many parts of which she rode while punching cattle for her husband. As a matter of fact, she owns some of the Mountain and a good chunk of the area around it, too. Her still keen and alert mind coupled with her great age give her a commanding and fascinating viewpoint back down through the years, and bring many historians and writers to her hilltop home to ask her questions and to get her opinions and remembrances of the things of her youth. A recent caller was the late Erle Stanley Gardner, creator of Perry Mason, who was at the time writing a book called *Hunting Lost Mines by Helicopter,* in which he featured her. "I just grew to love that old lady," he said.

"I remember Walz very well," Mrs. Barkley, whose age is now approaching the century mark, said recently. "He dressed roughly and was kinda cross looking, but invariably courteous, though suspicious of most people—and with good reason. He had to live a life like the poor mockingbird fledgelings when there are cats around."

Chapter 7

The life with Chur-ga and the other Pimas on their reservation gradually took on more of an air of reality for Captain Walker than all the years of his life that had gone before. The time mounted almost imperceptibly and drifted ever more pleasantly by. The Pimas' customs charmed him more and more as he lingered among them. Increasingly he fell under the spell of the comparatively undemanding life and learned to banish or ignore most of the silly concerns and worries of the white man's world. He simply immersed himself in the languorous life of the village, spending long afternoons lolling in a little glade under the refreshing shade of some great cottonwood trees that whispered by the Gila River, or swimming in the cool embrace of a wide deep pool there, partially shaded by the massive trees. Fish teemed in the sparkling water—water as undefiled as the air he breathed—an air that was purified

by the rays of a sun almost hot enough to sterilize surgical in-
struments as it eddied and swirled over a desert that extended
for hundreds of miles in every direction.

Almost everyone in the village swam at one time or another
during the day, and they were as much at home in the water
as otters. They had no particular stroke to propel them; they
seemed to move as fish do: effortlessly and with the grace and
playfulness of porpoises. They mostly swam under the surface, only coming up for air, and had the lung capacity of
Japanese women pearl divers for staying under. Sometimes,
watching them disporting in the depths, their nude, golden-
tinted bodies rolling, darting, and jostling each other, their sleek
forms looking for all the world like playful dolphins, Walker
would reflect on what a shame it was that any other segment
of the human race had ever advanced beyond the point the
Pimas then occupied.

In that warm climate the Pimas did not need much clothing
at any time, though they had known for well over fifteen
hundred years, and probably much longer than that, how to
raise, spin, and weave cotton into cloth. The men usually
wore only cotton breechclouts. The women wore a sort of
wrap-around skirt made of doeskin or woven cotton cloth that
reached about halfway to the knees, something like mini-
skirts. They wore them mostly for the comfort they gave them
while sitting, though it was the Pima custom to spread a blanket whenever they wished to sit or lie down. They went bare-
breasted the year around and their breasts remained shapely
until well into old age and often as long as they lived. They
had never been taught or made to feel shame regarding any
portion of their body or of its functions; therefore, clothes
beyond the breechclout or the brief skirt were to them only a
convenience at certain periods. For cold weather, extra
clothes usually took the form of a blanket thrown over the
shoulders. During the fine weather of southern Arizona, men
wore their breechclouts principally for the support they gave,
especially when riding horses.

Children never wore anything at all before the age of puberty unless on some ceremonial occasion, when in order to
show them off their mother might wrap them in a piece of
beautifully embroidered buckskin, or in a wraparound of cotton material that was equally decorated with many colorful
designs from the excellent dyes the Pimas knew how to make.

The women were also adept at using dyes to paint beauty-spot designs on their skin, such as birds, shucks of corn and, often, butterflies. Their invariable custom of carrying burdens on their heads in gaily decorated baskets gave them a regal carriage, which Walker found a delight to the eye as they moved with the sleek grace of panthers to and fro from the fields, or while helping the men bring back game from hunting expeditions.

He found their sex habits, manner of marriage, and how they raised their children particularly fascinating.

As a girl approached the age of puberty, Chur-ga explained to him, she began wearing skirts only on more or less formal occasions, but wore them continuously after the second year of her puberty, at which time she was formally presented to the young men of the tribe as being fully nubile. The accompanying ceremony, invariably taking the form of a dance, almost exactly paralleled the rites attending the presentation of a girl to society with a debutante ball in modern U.S. social centers. The parents of the girl warmly invited everyone in the tribe, but some they invited more warmly than others, with special attention given to urging all eligible men of the tribe (read, having plenty of wampum) to take part.

Puberty dances were the gayest occasions in Pima social life. For four days before this event the girl lived at the "separate house" while some of the older women of her family instructed her in the facts of married life and taught her the exciting movements of the coming puberty dance and its meanings. At the dance the girls were supposed to wiggle and gyrate their hips in a meaningful manner. Centered in the pelvic and genital area, these elemental gestures were designed to be plainly suggestive of the amount of ability the girl potentially had to please a man after marriage.

At the "presentation ball" the boys stood in one line and the girls in another, facing each other. As the girls danced they moved provocatively toward the boys until their pelvises were nearly touching, then teasingly danced back. This often went on all night and, under the stimulus of the sexual feeling aroused, sometimes for many nights, provided the girl's family was able to come up with enough food and drink for a sumptuous meal each midnight.

The parents took entire charge of the marriage of their sons and daughters. Their reason for it was that two families in full accord toward uniting their offspring in marriage would be thus obligated to take special care of each other's welfare—a vital consideration throughout their history. The girl's parents had probably been looking for an industrious young man for her since she quit toddling. They usually chose him from another Pima village, since people in their own village were often related. If they had a daughter already married they would sometimes give a younger sister to the same husband, if he had proven himself a good husband, for they had no law against marrying more than one wife. They felt that if a man were industrious, i.e., a good provider, a girl would be better off with him and her sister than with some new man.

To propose the marriage, the parents went to the boy's relatives, or to the man himself if he had already married one of their daughters. Often they did not tell the girl anything about it until the last moment, either because she was too young (thirteen or fourteen) to choose wisely for herself, or she was known to be interested in some other young man.

When the time for the wedding arrived, the selected man came to the girl's house and laid with her for four nights under her mother's supervision. Then a marriage ceremony was performed by one of the leading Pima medicine men, followed by a big feast attended by all the relatives and most of the people of the village, after which the bridegroom took his bride back to live with his parents, for newlyweds were considered to be still like children. The boy remained under his father's direction and the girl took her place with his sisters working under her mother-in-law. When they had several children of their own and were at last considered grown up, they built a house near the husband's parents. The boy still worked in his father's fields and the girl and her sisters-in-law took turns at the family cooking.

If at any time in the future the couple did not want to stay together, they could be divorced merely by either or both deciding to separate. The woman went back to her father's house. If she had small children, she took them with her. Older ones, especially boys, might stay with the father. Her relatives soon found her another husband. Since she was required to do at least half the work of supporting her husband and children, she never lacked offers to mate.

But if her husband died, she expected one of his younger brothers to marry her and take care of her, because the husband's family and the wife's family did not want to separate, and no matter if he already had a wife, or even several wives. If the husband had no brothers it was customary for one of his cousins to marry the widow. In the same way, if a woman died, her husband would look to her family to give him one of her younger sisters or cousins as a wife.

When a child was to be born the mother went to the separate house for women, because it was thought dangerous to have a birth take place in the family house. She stayed there after the delivery until the moon had gone around "to where it was before," while her women relatives looked after her. Then she took her baby to the medicine man for a kind of baptism, for which he charged a pretty penny, as he did for all his services, and usually one of his wives was on hand to do the collecting.

The baby spent the first year of his daytime life tied to the cradleboard. In this way his active young mother could take him with her while she went to fetch wood and water. She placed the cradleboard against a tree while she was working and, when she was ready to go home, her back piled high with the stuff she had been gathering, she balanced the cradleboard on her head as she walked. Almost as soon as he could toddle, he began to follow his father or mother about and was always encouraged to try to do everything that they did. By the age of eight or nine years, if the child was a boy, he was out with bow and arrow learning to bring home small game for the family meal. If it was a girl, she was stirring a cookpot while her mother went after water and her grandmother taught her housekeeping.

The grandparents did most of the child-training while the young parents were busy working for the family. In the evening, as the family lay on their pallets around the fire, if it was cool, or under the stars back of the wickiup in the summer, the grandfather would talk, telling stories that helped teach the children how they must behave. It was thought that an even better time for this teaching was in the early morning while it was still dark. Then grandpa would take his grandchildren and perhaps a neighbor's tot, or two, out into the desert and tell them each day afresh how they must always work, because it was only by work that people kept alive, stayed happy, and grew strong to fight the enemy. The boys, he said, must practice running in the morning. Running was very important with the Pimas, for they needed it in hunting and the wide, empty desert was almost a natural course. This training made them phenomenal runners.

The boys ran until they were exhausted; then as they lay resting on the ground they might have a vision in which some animal would come to them. Animals, the grandfather said, had magic power, as witness how much better than man they understood how to get their food and how to escape from enemies.

Girls, the old man said, must also work hard, because no man would want a lazy woman for a wife. In particular they must be sure their man had cool water to drink and enough to eat so he would be able to work steadily and effectively raising crops.

The feet of both the men and the women were incredibly tough from going barefoot, with callouses built up through the years often thicker than the soles of modern dress shoes. But when making very long journeys they wore sandals of mountain sheepskin with extra layers for the soles because once they had left the comparative smoothness of the terrain along their rivers and got into nearby mountains, there were many sharp volcanic shards on the ground that could cut almost anything like a very sharp knife.

Most of the Pima men never cut their hair, but let it grow and kept it wrapped around their heads in massive braids, which when unraveled usually reached below their knees. The front hair was pulled forward and kept cut in the form of bangs. The women were limited by custom to hair around nine or ten inches in length.

When they built a shelter it was a wickiup. Very little material could be found in the desert for building, but fortunately they did not need much shelter except from the midsummer sun and occasional rains, and for storing their possessions. A wickiup had a roof in the form of a dome, made by bending rods across rafters that were supported by four uprights driven into the ground. The rafters were joined at a center point to form a support for the dome. Then they tied bundle after bundle of brush over the rafters until they had a surface all the way around that was sufficiently strong to support a thick covering of adobe mud. They plastered the mud over the brush until there was a smooth surface much like some of the old brick kilns one sees here and there left over from prerevolutionary days. The sun baked the mud until it was impervious to both the withering desert heat that sometimes reached 120 degrees and the occasional rains that came to the area.

There were no windows, just a small aperture at the center of the dome. Because of the usually salubrious climate, the cooking was mostly done out back of the wickiups in a little cleared circle where they had a fence of woven brush in a semicircle on the windward side to keep out blowing dust. The women of the family each brought their food, but cooked it together.

To keep enemies out and to make it easy to close the doors in bad weather, they were only large enough for one person at a time to crawl through. Generally the wickiups were built in small clusters known as "family groups" by the Pimas. The original shelter was for the parents and any later ones were for the married sons who brought their wives to live at home. Daughters went to live in the family group of their husbands.

Nearby was a small storehouse where each family group kept seed beans and corn. In the summer they had an arbor with a roof of woven fronds, in which they did their working, playing, lovemaking and eating except in very bad weather—a thing that was rare in that part of the Southwest.

Another small house some distance away from the family group had a door that designedly faced away from the group. This was where the women went once a month to be by themselves. The Pimas believed that at a certain time of the month women should not be around men and they were sequestered in this little house. Their food was brought to them by other women until the period of enforced solitude had passed.

Walker was to discover that long before the white people arrived in America the Pimas had learned about corn, beans, and squash, and how to raise them in abundance on fertile land bordering rivers. Their corn was of different colors, mostly white, blue, red, and black. Sometimes a strain of corn would be a mixture of all these colors and the Indians found this diverting and called the mixture "Laughing Corn." A particularly vivid combination was called "Crazy Corn." Archaeologists have been able to determine that corn was raised in the land of the Pima more than twelve hundred years ago. They also mastered the intricacies of irrigation at least that long ago.

The Pimas had been growing wheat seed and seeds of such vegetables as chick peas, onions, watermelons, and casaba melons, he learned, ever since the first Spanish missionary, Father Francisco Eusebio Kino, established a headquarters in 1687 in Alta Valley in Mexico and began making journeys north to get acquainted with the unknown Indians living along the Salt and Gila Rivers, and he brought these seeds with him. He presented these seeds to the Indians and taught how the Spanish cultivated them. He also introduced them to horses, cattle, and sheep, the first they had ever seen. They were quick to grasp the usefulness of these animals and they have had horses and cattle ever since.

The desert country of the Southwest is so big and parched to the eye of the uninitiated, that at first sight it had the look of death itself to Walker, and he was astonished to hear that the Pimas could live entirely off its products if they had to—and often they did—and always lived partially off them— products that have grown wild in this desert for centuries numbering beyond man's ability to determine.

They taught Walker that the buds of the cholla (pronounced choya) are very nourishing if they are baked properly in a bed of coals, how the prickly pear can be eaten raw after the thorns have been scraped off, and that even the giant saguaro cactus gives a fruitlike fig out of which can be made a drink and a sweet, colorful, delicious red jam. They also taught him that this fruit can be ground up into a flour and made into tasty cakes.

The women did all the work of gathering this sort of food and carried it home balanced on their heads, swinging along with the proud walk the balancing art gave them, and as if the burdens were light as baskets of feathers.

They made cellars by digging pits in the desert for surplus food against the day when winter would be upon them and the desert plants were sleeping like badgers until spring. Then from these cellars they could draw enough to keep them well nourished until spring and the plants and the badgers emerged together.

After a while Walker discovered that he had been made a member of a family clan. The clans were the most important divisions in the seven Pima villages, each headed by its oldest male member and all his descendants through his sons. Women belonged to the clan of their father, but when they married their children went with their husband's people. Walker's position being somewhat anomalous in this respect, he was therefore "assigned" to a clan—Chur-ga's clan.

Her father, Thunder at Dawn, explained to him how the clans were set up and operated. Most of the people in the villages, he said, were relatives, generally on their father's side. One man usually emerged who acted for *all* the clans as a sort of unofficial judge and watchdog over them. He had no power of enforcement, merely their respect as a persuader. He would suggest, for instance, how a particular quarrel should be settled, but had no means of settling it whether or no, nor was he expected to. He told them the best time to have ceremonies, and usually lived in the house where such meetings were held, but sometimes preferred to live in a smaller house beside it. At night he built a fire in the house, and standing on the roof called the men to come and discuss village affairs. Usually he was quite an old man and did not have a strong voice any longer, and he would appoint a man who was called his "legs," and also known as his "voice" because he called out the leader's announcements. This leader when Walker came to the villages, was from the Azul family, or clan.

Any kind of working democracy, said Thunder at Dawn, was abhorrent to the Pimas and they would resist majority rule to the death. "We do use persuasion on each other," he said, "but that's as far as we ever try to dominate any man's thinking or his freedom of choice."

Individuals desiring to take this or that action naturally clotted together from the attraction of the project that activated them and, equally as naturally, they tried to influence as many others as possible to go along, but there was no such thing as passing laws or rules with the end in view of *everyone* having to obey them. Those who favored whatever it was, pursued it; those who didn't were perfectly free to abstain and usually did.

According to Thunder at Dawn it was only when all of the men of the village met together that "persuasive" suggestions could be made. When they gathered in the council house the leader brought up any matters on the agenda and asked the advice of everyone, except the young men were not encouraged to speak during the meetings until they were past thirty. Their role, dictated by the old men, was to sit at the back of the house listening.

Thunder at Dawn was very curious about the time Walker had spent as an officer-physician with the California Column, and he was insatiable in his desire to know more about how the white men fought their wars. He was always amazed by what Walker had to tell him about the rules of so-called "civilized" warfare, and was flabbergasted when he heard what they did with their prisoners; how they were protected, fed, clothed, and returned to their families at the end of hostilities. The fate of being captured under such conditions impressed him as being far preferable to not being captured.

There was no mistaking the fact that the Pimas hated war and all its works, and by their very nature they could be happy forever just cultivating their fields, swimming, playing their running games, and having feasts, making love, resting, talking, and raising their families, and generally enjoying life in the villages, which was a very good life indeed. But they also had the reputation, which so impressed Governor Goodwin, of being the most devastating fighters of all Indians when they were forced into war. "There was always some ambitious chief in another tribe starting a war," Thunder at Dawn pointed out, "particularly among the Apaches. They always would rather risk being killed any day," he said bitterly, "than work for a living. It was this penchant on their part that forced us into our policy of *always* making them pay at least double for every one of us they killed or carried off. That largely cured them of it. You see, they wouldn't hunt—it was their nature to prefer to plunder for their food; consequently they were never as good marksmen with their arrows, nor can they make as good a bow as we can. We depend on our bows and arrows for all our meat, and getting within effective range of game with bow and arrow is much more difficult than getting close to human enemies in war. We are also very expert at tracking; they are not—we work at becoming expert at it, they won't. It is one of the reasons we start our children at running in the desert every morning almost from the time they can walk. They become fast and long-winded, and can even run down deer when it comes to endurance."

Most villages had a man to be a leader in war, he explained, whom they called the "hard man" or "bitter man," who was roughly equivalent to the white man's general. He was chosen because he was brave and presumably would not give in to the enemy. He had no actual authority, however, and the people took his orders only because of their confidence in him, and then only when they felt like it.

Walker became greatly interested, even fascinated, during his early days with them by the extreme skill of some of the outstanding bow and arrow shots among the Pimas, and curious as to how they obtained their arrow points. He made a trip with them to the mountains while they searched for a particular type of flint for this purpose, and he also learned how to recognize the stalks of the soapweed which at a particular time of year were green and ideal to cut and dry for arrow shafts.

Turkeys furnished the best feathers for arrows, but for war purposes the Pimas believed that arrows flew more often to the heart of the enemy if eagle feathers were used, because turkeys are notoriously not brave birds. When the Pimas were ready to make a new supply of arrows they took turns helping each other, assembling in a group, something like what the white man calls a "bee," and inviting an old man to be present who was known for his talent in chanting the special ballads used during arrow-making. Working all day they could make about a hundred arrows and it was up to their host, for whom each day's output of arrows was intended, to feed them while working.

They made bows out of boxthorn or mulberry. The wood was cut when it was full of sap; then shaped with a knife so that it was thick in the middle and slender at both ends. While it was still green and full of sap it was laid in hot ashes and bent into the proper shape with stone jigs. When it was thoroughly dried in this way it held its shape permanently. The sinews from a deer's back were ideal for bow strings, and a wise hunter always kept an extra one ready in case he pulled too strong a bow and broke it in the excitement of seeing a prime target, or in case the string simply frayed and broke.

The Pimas knew something about the value of herbs as medicine. First the medicine man sang over any stricken one, in the manner which among white people is praying. Then the ailments were treated by the women of the family with certain plants or roots that were known to have curative powers and, if the patient recovered, the medicine man claimed the credit and a fat fee. The women used leaves of the creosote bush, which grows so plentifully in the desert, for colds and to make a hot vapor bath for rheumatism, and broomwood for a medicinal tea. They washed sore eyes with a brew of a seed-like flax.

A man wishing power understood that he would do well to have the medicine man pray for him. A medicine man got his ability, it had been revealed long ago, by visions that began when he was very young and kept having until long after he was a grown man. He never told exactly what he had learned, for that would destroy his power. When he had thought over his visions a long time, he would announce that he was ready to practice.

Sometimes he would go with the others to the far western Big Water for salt, and other medicine men who lived *under* the Big Water might take him into their houses beneath the waves and give him the temporary power to breathe like a fish and there telling him the secrets of all diseases.

Most Pima medicine men did not attempt any curing. *Their* business, they said, was *only* to tell what bad magic had caused the disease. The medicine man sat down cross-legged by the patient with a gourd rattle in one hand and two long eagle feathers in the other. He shook the rattle and prayed softly in strange tongues that no one could understand—prayers to entice the wisdom he needed. Sometimes he carried a little bag of ore samples which he called his shining stones. He said that they gave light to see so that he knew where the sickness was. He watched them; then he prayed, waving his plumes until morning. At last he might say, "It is this or that kind of sickness."

Then the family gave him some hefty wampum. Medicine men were always paid better than anyone else. Their tough, merciless, even rapacious demands and utterly ruthless methods of collecting made them 'way ahead of their time.

After the medicine man had his fee, he went away and it was the business of the family to find someone who could cure the sickness. This might be any man in the village who had dreams. This fellow would be sent for, or if several had the same dreams they would all be invited.

The medicine man claimed to have power to bring rain by waving his eagle feathers. And if it didn't rain he would say it was because someone in the circle was a Jonah, then collect his fee, nevertheless, and leave.

Hunters used to take a medicine man to the mountains with

them because, it was said, he could "see" where the deer were hidden.

During war these medicine men professed to know where the warriors might best meet the enemy. Before the big games between the villages, rival medicine men would swallow sticks like swords and eat coals and the one who could out-perform the others with his feats was believed to be able to help his village win. They were the cheerleaders of their day.

But their hocus-pocus profession had its hazards too. The people believed that if a medicine man became mentally unstable he might work witchcraft to kill people instead of help them, and if a great many patients he prayed over died, the villagers would be sure he *was* working evil magic instead of good. Then, with the consent of the council, they would go out with their clubs and drive him out.

The uninhibited customs and the almost soporific pace of the life in his village increasingly charmed Walker, and the Pima philosophy deeply interested him as he lingered on among them, falling more and more under the spell of the kaleidoscopic charms of Chur-ga, who by this time fairly worshipped him.

To repay them for their unstinted, undemanding hospitality and friendliness, he gave his professional services free to all in the villages, and he made a point to be tactful enough to develop a sort of partnership with the medicine men, for whom he made the face-saving gesture of pretending to act as their consultant, while scientifically supplementing their magic treatments for exorcising simple ailments.

He advised the Pimas shrewdly and his ability to lead and teach in connection with many matters relating to their daily lives, particularly sanitation, and preserving meats and vegetables, and using herbs to season food caused them to be deeply grateful to him. No person could have done more or been more unselfishly devoted to their welfare or advanced it more.

The medicine men soon came to see the value of this for all. In particular they saw how they could profit from it by learning from him and using the information for their own benefit. "If you can't lick 'em—join 'em," became their pragmatic philosophy.

In this blend of the ancient and the modern, Walker progressively accommodated himself to the everyday life of the Pimas. In the winter they rested, played games, held races, and engaged in slow-paced talks around the fire, while the hovering women took care of them.

Sometimes they hunted deer in the mountains during the winter. It was no problem getting as many deer as one wanted in the summer—quite the contrary, as a matter of fact. They came down then to the banks of the Gila, attracted by the succulent crops. The Pimas never believed in killing anything except for food, and therefore they posted what were known as "deer watchers" to keep a continuing around-the-clock watch and shoo the deer away. Otherwise there would have been little or no crops to harvest. And not only the deer loved these succulent green shoots that were coming up out of the ground —they attracted hordes of rabbits, both jacks and cottontails, and ground squirrels by the hundreds.

The Pimas cooked meat in those days much as hunters do now—by holding it on the end of a stick or rod over a fire. The women also made delicious stews of rabbit meat, roots, and vegetables in a clay pot.

Sometimes during those "slow-paced talks around the fire," the elders and priests would re-tell their story of the beginning of the world, adding a bit to it here and there, and burnishing old bits. Each had his own way of telling it, and he told it with whatever histrionic ability he possessed, simulating the voices of the characters and illustrating the action of the tale by arm and body movements. In essence they were novelists.

Their story of how the world began was told only in the winter time. In summer when the men were needed in the fields to raise crops and the time was needed for sleeping away fatigue, the telling was discouraged.

In the beginning, the story went, Earthmaker, whom the Pimas later called Elder Brother, fashioned the whole world out of a little ball of dirt. He then danced on it until it spread and touched the edges of the sky. The Pimas implicitly believed He originated all the things they knew, or knew about. He had told their forebears long, long ago that He had found them under the ground and led them forth. He told them where to settle, and He showed them the fields they must cultivate, and He brought the rain to keep them well fed, and then gave them the delightful means and the overpowering urge to make love so they could perpetuate their race, and forever live in happiness.

The Pimas had other needs besides love and food. Every

man wanted to feel within himself a great primitive power to work and fight and endure hardships. Elder Brother said that all nature is full of these powers; the birds, the animals, and even the plants can do strange things which man cannot do. If the Pimas were virtuous and hard-working, an animal would one day speak to them and give them some of this magic. When he was out on the desert alone every boy watched for the eagle or the cunning mountain lion that might suddenly appear beside him, and from whom he might learn these great qualities.

In the spring the men cleaned the ditches, turned the water into them, and prepared for a full summer of planting and tending the crops that richly supplemented the things they ate such as game, or the plants that grew naturally in the desert.

Long before the white people had any idea of smoking to-bacco and chewing gum, the Pimas were raising both and used them liberally, Walker found. Smoking, however, was not merely a pleasurable act among them; on occasion it had an element of religious significance, too. For pipes they used a hollow reed that had a small opening at one end and a larger opening at the other end. They placed the end with the small opening in their mouth, put tobacco in the other end and lit it. No decisions of any consequence were made until those who had the responsibility had smoked on it. At council meetings, when a decision was needed, only one pipe was lit and it was passed from hand to hand, each man taking four puffs and passing it on to the man on his right.

They made a chewing gum from the juice of the milkweed vine, which hardens if it is heated and allowed to cool. There was also a sweet gum, though much inferior to the milkweed product, that could be found in the mesquite tree.

After a while Walker saw that in order for the Pimas to have many of the things that he felt they needed, such as schools, a hospital, and proper barns in which to store their crops, as well as metal plows, cultivators, fertilizer, and other simple tools with which to facilitate their farming, now thriving under his tutelage, they would need to sell some of their produce to get money for these things. So he began establishing trading posts at some of the stage depots along the river and sold the passengers food, drink, and lodging, and the hostler and wagon-train masters shelter for themselves, and hay and grain for their horses from the Pima farms. The trade in vividly dyed cotton blankets and beaded moccasins became so prosperous that he had several other Indian tribes busy helping the Pimas meet the demand. Soon all Arizona was buying his products.

A great boost in this direction was the fame of Captain Walker because of his successful generalship of the Indians that saved Arizona from the Apaches during the Civil War. Also, legends grew concerning his romantic marriage, and his choice of living among the Pimas, or as it was sometimes referred to by eastern newspapers, and some in the West, too, "among the savages under appallingly uncivilized conditions," spread nationwide and to Europe also. But it was his obvious and enormous uniqueness that intrigued them the most.

He became an object of much curiosity. Journalists and magazine writers from literally all over sought him out in the Indian village on the banks of the Gila. "Why," they invariably asked, "do you find this existence preferable to one among your own people?"

He had a practiced, but sincere answer for one and all such questions. "I find these honest, hospitable, affectionate, courageous, hard-working Pimas immeasurably, delightfully, and refreshingly separated from the white man's so-called culture, especially in regard to snobbery, pretense, hypocrisy, meanness toward guests, treachery toward friends and relatives—especially relatives—greed for money, and shame and embarrassment toward the natural appearance and functions of their bodies, such as my wife, Chur-ga, encountered among white people at Fort McDowell, and at the territorial capital in Prescott. Among the Pimas is a charming, satisfying atmosphere in which to live, and particularly for a surgeon and a doctor of medicine."

The stories they wrote about it all brought many fine people as well as curiosity-seekers to see for themselves. Soon touring Pimeria became the "thing to do."

Walker reveled in taking visitors on a tour of his particular village, as well as some of the other villages up and down the banks of the river and showing them the great progress the Pimas were making. He showed how they had many centuries ago learned to construct irrigation systems skillfully and to bring water to thousands of acres of arid land, which then became fertile almost beyond belief, as they could see for themselves in regard to the land bordering the Gila. He would also point out to them that contrary to the practices of other Indian peoples, it was the Pima *men* who planted the fields and looked after the crops.

"The Pimas," Walker would say, "have always been friendly to the white men, and I have yet to find an instance in which they even tried to harm an innocent person."

He also made a point of their not being nomads, having lived in this same area for thousands and thousands of years, subsisting by farming and hunting, and that their only warring activities had been confined solely to punishing other tribes for raiding them.

An air of superiority on *anyone's* part always had the capacity to annoy Walker, and sometimes well-nigh infuriate him. Many of the people coming from California, or going there from the East during the latter 1860s and the '70s in the numerous wagon trains and in the stages of the successors to the Butterfield Stage Line which then had a depot in his village, had heard of the famous hero turned "squaw man" and they were eager to meet him and see "what he is like," and to view the conditions under which he lived with the now legendary Chur-ga.

The first thing they were made aware of was that Walker was doing good business with these travelers. Few of the travelers lived so well or were so generally prosperous as Walker. The Pimas were likewise living in far better fashion than any other Indian tribes, and even better than over 90 percent of the European peasants.

The women from the wagon trains and stages were often positively affronted by the grace, erudition, and delicate beauty of the lissome Chur-ga, who might have been described to them as, after all, "just a savage" and many of them were no doubt prepared to patronize and lord it over her. Later, their comments among themselves would have been interesting to hear, especially if they'd had dinner at his gracious home.

Both the men and the women were at first astonished and then somewhat envious over the fine home Walker had built on a perfect vantage point by the river where, over coffee and cigars in his book-lined, spacious library, he would sometimes play host to the men after a fine dinner presided over by Chur-ga, and prepared and served by the Pima maidens she had trained who, dressed in their soft, exquisitely tanned and embroidered buckskin dresses, were a delight to the travel-weary stage riders, or at least to the men among them.

The precise setting of his dinner table by these maidens at such times, and the air with which they served it never failed to delight Walker and to amuse him when he observed the astonished faces of his guests. The girls took turns cooking—two of them at a time—and four of them had become excellent cooks.

They were all the pupils, as had been Chur-ga, of an elderly and proper Bostonian lady, Mrs. Priscilla James, whose husband had been killed fighting for the North, and who had come to Phoenix with her brother and his wife in the hope of finding work as a teacher or governess. Walker had hired her in 1867 to come and organize his new home, and give English lessons to Chur-ga and five other girls and five boys selected by Chur-ga for their general intelligence. "We will have to do something about their manners, too," Priscilla told him with some asperity. *"Esta en su casa,"* replied Walker with a wave of his hand.

Priscilla found it rather tough sledding at first, but she came from a long line of ancestors who buckled down in earnest about the time other people were considering quitting, and Chur-ga was a great help to her when it came to deportment lessons, which she herself had taken to like the proverbial duck to water. In less than three years the class had not only become fluent in English, but grammatical as all get-out; they could even dance a creditable minuet to an accompaniment by Walker on his violin. Priscilla, in turn, had learned the Pima language.

At first Priscilla had objected strenuously to these slender, firm-bodied, and rather well-developed thirteen-to-fourteen-year-old girls coming bare-breasted to class, and learning how to cook and wait on table in this innocent and, certainly in their case, very charming way of dress, but Walker told her that there was no way of *specifically* explaining to them, or their parents, or the Pimas as a whole for that matter, what objections might be found to this age-old custom without disgusting them. "It would all sound too nasty to minds conditioned since time immemorial to regard such things as perfectly normal," he explained. "As you can see," he said, "they don't wear *any* clothes until they are ten or eleven, and all over the villages you can see hundreds of women nursing their babies in front of their homes, or wherever, without a thought as to concealment of their breasts and, in any event, the Pimas certainly could never be made to understand, at least at this stage of their development what the *point* of such an objection would be, and I certainly wouldn't undertake any such explanations, and on the other hand would do all in my power to keep anyone else from attempting it around here."

As soon as the specially trained maidens married, and they were considered great catches by the young braves of the village, Priscilla trained new ones to take their place. They became known as Priscilla's Maidens.

Walker was not above having a little fun with some of the oldsters who came to his house of an evening and had an opportunity to observe Priscilla's girls at close range. "If you think an older man can't neigh and prance around a girl while he's sitting down, then you should have seen some of these fellows," he once said. As he described it, their eyes would light up like a locomotive headlight, and soon they would be making all sorts of hints to the effect that they would like to know one of these warm-hued nymphs a little better. Walker always pretended to take their hints seriously.

"Well, I don't know," he would say to any of them who were bald, or had foreheads that reached to the back of their crown, "there's Henrietta who might not mind walking down by the river with you, if only you had a little more hair. I'm afraid her boyfriend wouldn't be interested in the amount you have."

"You mean . . . ?" his guest would stammer.

"Exactly," his straight-faced host would reply.

In those days the mighty chieftain of the Apaches and implacable foe of the white man, Geronimo, was much in the talk of the people all over the United States, and travelers who used the stage lines that patronized Walker's stage stops were bound to bring up the subject of Geronimo sometime during the evening, though he was still some years away from starting his second war of extermination against Arizonians in 1881 to '86.

Anson Safford, who by this time had succeeded John N. Goodwin as governor of the Territory, and was a good friend of Walker and often visited him at his home among the Pimas, liked to tell how Walker relished teasing visitors who brought preconceived notions to Walker's attention.

"Too bad, seein' as how you're interested in Geronimo, you weren't here last night, when he stopped by for a visit," Walker would say casually, according to Safford, "and he might come by again this evening; he often does."

"Whaaat!" the tenderfoot present would exclaim, while the seasoned westerners who happened to be among them would grin and wink among themselves. "You mean you had that murderous savage right here in your house, *last* night?"

"Are you trying to say that a man who fights in wars for what he believes to be right is a murderer?" Walker would demand of them in pretended outrage, while transfixing them with a fierce look bolstered by his bristling eyebrows and hawklike eyes.

"Why-y, no, not exactly, but, but . . ."

"Now, you look here," Walker would say with finality, "I don't hold with anyone criticizing my neighbors, especially ones I am good friends with, and Old Geronny *lives* just over there," waving his arm toward the distant mountains rising palely in the moonlight against the eastern sky, "and *he* is as good a neighbor as whites could hope to have, that is, the whites who don't try to take from him what is his'n, and certainly isn't theirs."

True enough, according to Safford, Geronimo was very friendly with Walker, as were many other Indian chieftains, as well as braves of Arizona, and each and every one of them remained his friend and he theirs as long as they lived after the Civil War was over, despite the terrible wars they fought against the rest of the whites of Arizona, until the might of a considerable segment of the U.S. Army was brought in against them, and finally crushed all the Indians' aspirations to live on their own land free from interference and molestation.

Whenever he had an obnoxious guest from California aboard who might try to take Walker down a peg and disparage Indians as a whole by mentioning some of the rather primitive conditions they had noted in some Indian villages they had seen, Walker would offer to read them a passage from John C. Cremony's book, *Life Among the Apaches,* which was published in 1868 and was a best seller, not only in the U.S. but throughout much of the rest of the world besides. The book told of Cremony's many years of intimate experiences as a U.S. Army officer assigned more or less as a liaison officer to the Indian tribes of the Southwest. "I happen to have come here after quite a while in California," Walker would tell them, "and I would like you to hear what Cremony has to say about the effect the 'white civilization' has had on the Indians there."

"The deplorable condition of the California Indians," went the passage from Cremony's book, "after years of Jesuit teachings, and a foundation of numerous missions, surrounded with large and pacific Indian population, only offers proof . . . that instead of being better civilized and Christianized, they have adopted all the worst features of the white race and retained most of their own bad characteristics, while native dignity, courage, and primitive virtues have been completely annihilated. In all the attributes of manhood, in everything which dignifies human nature, the untamed tribes are infinitely their superiors.

"Superstition, cowardice, filth, sloth, drunkenness, moral depravity, and the most revolting licentiousness have replaced the sterner and more simple qualities of the so-called wild Indians. In the desire to do them good, they have been done great harm. In the hope of exorcising their savage defects, they have been inoculated instead with the most debilitating vices. This is a sad picture, but it cannot be denied."

Chapter 8

When the Civil War ended it became increasingly apparent to Dr. Thorne that the peacetime army was not for him. He had had understanding and respect for most of the formalities and restrictions he had endured as a part of military life during wartime, but chafed under them when they persisted into peacetime, leaving the last two years at Fort McDowell a period of diminishing interest for him, except for his work among the Indians on The Strip.

Therefore, when he reached his new assignment at Taos, New Mexico, after his transfer from Fort McDowell and spending his leave with his family in San Jose, California, Thorne mailed in his resignation from the army. As soon as his resignation had been accepted and processed, and the usual formalities completed, he left for Lemitar, New Mexico, where he had decided to make his permanent home.

With the cash he had in hand from the gold the Indians had led him to, and the anticipated returns from the practice of medicine in Lemitar, he figured he would be able to make a living for himself—one that would permit him to engage in the various forms of research he had in mind, as well as indulge a couple of personal hobbies.

Once he settled down in Lemitar he did not flaunt his modest affluence, contenting himself with buying a toy ranch just outside the town to insure the privacy he craved after years of school, college, and army life. On this spread he built a rather small home of adobe and then scouted around for a man of Mexican descent who had a green thumb for raising vegetables and fruit trees. He found Porfirio Armendairez, whom he hired to plant a large orchard of the various kinds of fruits that thrived in that altitude and place, and to prepare a plot of ground in back of his house for raising vegetables. Soon he had a fruitful orchard and vegetable garden, the produce from which he mostly gave to his neighbors.

Though he had fully intended to build only a rather modest medical practice, which would leave plenty of time for personal hobbies, the fame of his work among the Apaches had followed him, and he found many people eagerly seeking to have him take care of their health. Especially was this true of the Indians and Mexicans in the area; they literally stormed his home, and the women who came with their younger children would sit patiently waiting for him to come and talk to them about the pains or aches they or their youngsters had.

His popularity as a doctor was not lessened, one may be sure, by his ever-growing reputation for charging only nominal fees, and then only to those who could well afford it, and little or nothing to those whom he felt could not, and these latter encompassed most of the Mexicans and Indians.

But despite the care he had taken in regard to secrecy about the gold the Apaches had given him, somehow or other the tale, or at least distorted versions of it, spread around, and not only penetrated back to army headquarters at Taos, and then to Lemitar, but reached all the way to San Jose where his father and brothers were now operating a very prosperous export-import business.

As the years multiplied, the stories about the ledge of quartz heavy with gold somewhere on Superstition Mountain, Arizona, continued to spread, and the gift to Dr. Thorne from the Apache chiefs became one of the favorites. The adventuresome of the world were already excited by tales of the Old Dutchman's find and when the Thorne story reached them, they nodded sagely and lived more in their dreams than ever. The story made it seem that the Apaches had shown Thorne the location of the ledge itself and speculation grew until many considered it a certainty.

Thorne refused to discuss the matter and commonly turned off any inquiries with the statement, "It is a thing that I do not care to talk about with anyone under any circumstances." But this did little to lessen the constant pilgrimages to his house and the importuning of various societies as well as individuals. If he didn't want the gold for himself, said most of them, would he not let them have some of it to use for various worthy causes?

Finally, in 1872 his brother came all the way from San Jose to talk to him about the matter. "There is no use, Abe," said his brother, "of your trying to tell me that the 'windfall' you told us about years ago in San Jose was not part of a very large amount of gold that you received from the Apaches near Fort McDowell when you were there, because we are certain it was. We know also that they showed you a mine that contains hundreds of millions of dollars in gold ore so rich that it hardly has to be smelted."

Well, at this Thorne could only laugh helplessly and admit to his brother that, yes, he had received some gold concentrate from the Apaches as a gift in gratitude for some medical services he had rendered them, but there was no such mine as his brother imagined insofar as he knew. Then he told him the whole story. "I used some of the Apache windfall," Thorne told him, "for the gifts to you, our brother and father, which you know about, and to buy the land, build my house and furnish it, and so on. But most of the rest is gone because I have been using it to help out Mexicans and Indians, and even a white person now and then, who have fallen upon bad times, especially where the man of the house has been injured or has become too sick to work and needs food and clothes."

His brother immediately visualized this last statement as a perfect lever to pry from the good-hearted Doctor information as to where the "mine" was located. "Well," he said, pressing his point home, "if that's the case and there is so much need for money among your patients as well as the community at large, just think what you could do if you had enough money to be able to furnish almost unlimited help to those in need around here, as you have already been doing in a small way."

At first Thorne was not persuaded by this line of reasoning, because he still felt forever bound by his word of honor that he had given to the Apache chieftains never to reveal the circumstances under which he had received the concentrate and especially anything he knew about the location where he had received it. When he reminded his brother of this, the latter replied, "Yes, that is true, and I would be the last one to ask you to break your word of honor, but as you know, Cochise has completely withdrawn to his stronghold in the Chiricahuas, and most of the chiefs and braves of your time out there have been killed in the various Indian wars. Except for Geronimo, any of them that are left must be very old now and penned on the miserably barren reservations they were forced onto by federal troops. Think of what you could do for these Apaches, those friends of yours, if you had a vast amount of money; how you could make life easier for them on the reservations, and perhaps help their children to get an education and things like that."

He clinched his arguments by offering to finance an expedition to search for the scene where the Apaches had taken Thorne on that morning so very long ago to present him with the heap of rich concentrate.

The best that Thorne would promise his brother was that he "would go and talk with my friends among the Apaches, if I can find any." He arranged for another doctor to take care of the most pressing of his medical practice, left final instructions with Porfirio for the care of the orchard and the vegetable garden, and set out for Arizona. He specified to his brother that he would not accept any help with expenses until he knew whether he would ever be able to do anything in return for the financial assistance. Certainly, he said, he couldn't if the Apaches wouldn't go along with him.

When Thorne reached Arizona and discovered the condition of the Apaches there, it almost broke his heart. "I found them," he wrote, "suffering grievously from the two scourges

of the Indians after the white man began invading their terri-
tories, (1) the fatal desirability of the fertile land on which
they had lived and, (2) the machinations of the agents provoc-
ateurs, those persons whose ugly business it has been since
the dawn of history to go among those who can be easily
robbed if they can be made to seem disreputable to the rest of
the world, and then persuade or trick them by devious means
into committing some act, or acts, that will allow their enemies to point and say, 'See! They must be exterminated. They
are godless, cruel, untrustworthy, and there is no place for
them among men and women of good will. They must be captured or killed and placed in confinement where they can do
no more harm.' "

"My experiences with the Indians of Arizona," Thorne stated in a letter he once wrote to President Ulysses Grant, "reveal that the Indians, especially the Apache Indians, have
cruel elements in their midst who are capable of terrible
deeds, but this is never publicized on a percentage basis in
comparison to the white men. Rarely can those who, like me,
find the majority of the Indians of Arizona a much abused,
much maligned group of people, get the authorities back East
to investigate properly or give them the benefit of the doubt.
What is badly needed, in the interest of fairness, I think, is to
have the responsible newspapers and magazines call attention
once in a while to the percentage of white people throughout
the United States who are committing murders, robberies,
rape, and crimes of every sort imaginable—many of a type the
Indians never dream of committing. In their own way most of
the Indians of Arizona I know are an upright sort of people
according to their own lights, especially as to personal honor,
as is true of all other ethnic groups, as well as colors.

"Only the angels know the true facts of what is happening
to the Indian tribes as a whole in Arizona, and it must often
make them weep."

Thorne had probed around trying to find Apaches who
knew something about the trip he had made with Cochise for
the concentrate, but could not find any of his Indian friends
who would have anything to do with his project, and because
of his solemn promise he shrank from asking Cochise personally, even if he had made the long journey to his hidden
stronghold.

He was told that it was useless for him to try to contact

Geronimo personally because he was now being forced to live with his followers on a reservation, and was almost insanely bitter against any white man, good, bad, or indifferent. The U.S. Army was relentlessly rounding up almost every Indian band in Arizona, and even individual Indians, and forcing them onto mostly barren reservations in charge of politically appointed "Indian Agents."

Nevertheless, Thorne decided to try to get a message through. He was told that Geronimo still trusted him personally, but would not see him because he felt it might be bad for Thorne to have it known that Geronimo was a friend of his. He would accept a message, however, if it were sent to the San Carlos Reservation. So Thorne sent Geronimo a message by one of the braves who had had a good standing with him in the old days on The Strip. After about two weeks, while Thorne impatiently cooled his heels, the brave returned and reported that he made personal contact with Geronimo, who had said to him, "Tell Thorne me remember him well; me still good friend of him; me trust him in all things, but no know of mine; gold we gave him from mules."

Thorne couldn't make much sense out of his message, but he didn't want to proceed without the cooperation of the Apache high command, so he gave up the whole idea and returned to Lemitar.

Thorne wrote his brother of his experiences and his decision after he arrived back in New Mexico. Naturally the brother was deeply disappointed and persisted in trying to persuade Thorne to resume the quest. After a year or so Thorne made him a partial promise to attempt another expedition, this time letting the brother underwrite the expenses. "I know a man by the name of Bob Groom," he said in a letter to his brother, "who I believe knows more about mining and gold generally than almost anyone I have heard of out there. I will go back to Arizona and contact Groom and if he is willing to help, I will try to find the source of the ore."

Groom lived in Prescott, Arizona, and was famous for having discovered and operated the rich Groom Creek placer gold mine. Actually, Thorne wasn't too optimistic about enlisting the cooperation of Groom in the search for the source of the gold, but when he reached Prescott he found to his surprise that Groom seemed very interested, and listened closely. Groom asked many questions concerning every last detail of

Thorne's experiences with the Apaches generally, and particularly regarding his now-famous expedition into the Mountain after the gold. He told Thorne he would accompany him on the search, but would have to pick his own crew, because it was a dangerous situation. Some of the Apaches who were holed up in the Mountain were desperate, mean, and vengeful.

"In any event," said Groom, "if we discover the mine, the greed of men being what it is, it would create a situation to which I wouldn't care to expose myself unless the men around me were men I could trust with my life—because that's about what it would amount to," he said soberly, "if we found any considerable quantity of gold."

The men Groom selected were Joe Sugate, afterwards proprietor of a stage station on the Black Canyon Road from Phoenix to the Bradshaw Mountains; John Hewett, cattleman and owner of the Hewett Stage Station on the road from Florence to the Silver King Mine; and John B. Montgomery, rancher in the Salt River Valley, who later became sheriff at Phoenix.

They were all inclined to believe that, true to Geronimo's more or less cryptic message, the concentrate given Thorne had indeed come from the packsaddles of the mules and burros that were gathered up by the Apaches long after the Peralta Massacre. They also had a pessimistic feeling that if the concentrate had later been gathered from many of the packsaddles and dumped into a pile on the ground near where the animals were slaughtered and eaten at leisure, it was probably quite a distance from the small pile that was given to Thorne.

Under Groom's expert supervision an expedition was quickly mounted, provisioned, and on its way. They soon determined that the canyon which Dr. Thorne believed to be the one he had traveled up that morning blindfolded was Boulder Canyon and that the sharp peak he had seen limned against the sky was Weaver's Needle. They even identified the place where Boulder Canyon issued into the Salt River (now covered by the waters of Canyon Lake). It proved to be about twelve miles from The Strip, and about six or seven miles up Boulder Canyon and its west branch from the Salt to where the concentrate was probably piled. But though they traversed the entire length of the canyon and two of its branches, West Boulder Canyon and East Boulder Canyon, they could not find the *exact* place of steep walls where the actual transfer of

gold ore had taken place. Finally, they realized that somewhere along this tortuous canyon the Apaches had turned off
into a side canyon or gash in the mountains that surrounded
it. After coming to this conclusion they retraced their steps
and quickly found such a side slash off West Boulder Canyon
at a spot not far from the Massacre Ground, and Thorne was
even able to recognize the very spot where he had stood that
long-ago morning in a canyon of Superstition Mountain.

They searched the area thoroughly, but without success,
and became more and more convinced the gifting spot was
some distance from where the Apaches had the main cache.

"It is more than likely, I would say from my knowledge of
the way the Apaches' minds work," said Groom, "that they
had some other braves meet them there with the gold that
morning. Before taking the blindfold from Thorne's eyes they
had probably dumped the ore on the ground from the very
buckskin bags which they then proceeded to refill and hang
on his saddle. If this wasn't the case, why did they remove the
blindfold from Thorne's eyes unless they *wanted* him to see
Weaver's Needle, the most prominent landmark in the Superstitions, and deliberately wanted him to be misled?"

On thinking this over Thorne was practically convinced
that this was indeed what had happened. He realized that the
Apaches had been more devious in their dealings regarding
this gift than he had credited them with, and he couldn't honestly say in his heart of hearts that he blamed them one bit. It
was obvious that they were utterly sincere in wanting to make
him a rich gift to show their gratitude and good feeling for
him, but he could understand that their feelings did not extend to any other white men, at least not enough to duplicate
what they were doing for Thorne.

So he said to Groom, "Look, Bob, I am sorry, but I am
sure now that my Apache friends made certain that their
cache of concentrate, provided there is any left, is in a place
that we can never track down."

They disbanded the expedition, and Groom returned to his
mining at Prescott, and the other men of the party returned to
their own business interests.

Before going back to Lemitar, Dr. Thorne stopped for
awhile with Hewett at his home near Florence Junction,
Arizona, and discussed the whole thing with him in minute
detail. Hewett, who had lived in the vicinity of Superstition

Mountain almost all his life and was familiar with the details of the Peralta Massacre, agreed with Thorne that undoubtedly the gold had come not from an Apache mine, but exactly as Geronimo had told him: from the mules they had captured after the Massacre. "Of course," Hewett pointed out, "there were doubtless a few mules and burros overlooked by the Apaches and the scavengers that followed them, particularly Hurley and O'Connor. Massacre Ground, after all, is only a short distance from West Boulder Canyon and those skeletons may still have their loads of gold scattered among their bones. But if you'd been over Massacre Ground as many times as I have, you'd realize that searching there for the skeleton of a burro or mule after the years that have passed would make the search for the needle in the haystack seem like an easy undertaking."

Thorne went back more or less contentedly to Lemitar. After all, he had never wanted any great amount of gold for himself and while he had been tempted by his brother's arguments about the good he could do with his share of a rich gold mine, he also knew deep down inside that it would destroy his well-ordered life in Lemitar—a life he enjoyed extremely because it gave him more satisfaction to do good with his own modest monetary means and personal skills as a doctor, than a vast operation financed by much gold ever could.

As far as is known he never again gave any serious thought to Apache gold or discussed it further with anyone, including his father and brothers.

In the latter part of his life he was much in demand as a consultant and lecturer on Apache customs and such actions as sprang from their innate nature during the decade that surrounded the Civil War period. He was glad to act as a consultant for free, provided those seeking information on what it was like to live intimately with the Apaches came to visit him in Lemitar. When asked to lecture away from home, he required that his travel expenses be paid and he also charged a nominal fee which he contributed to a fund for teaching English to poor Mexican and Indian children.

"I know of a few cases besides mine," he stressed during his lectures, "where an Apache formed a friendship for a white man—known as 'White-eyes' to the southwestern Indians—and would do almost anything in his power for him, but this came purely from their hearts and was directly contrary to their training as to what is proper behavior. From infancy they were taught that the brave who could outwit more people than any other is the greatest and would receive the most favors from maidens, and other delectable rewards besides.

"Almost from the day they were born they were drilled into being different from anyone else," he told his audiences.

"Their extraordinary endurance, on which neither hunger, cold, thirst, nor lack of sleep had any appreciable effect, constantly amazed me," he said. "Certainly they weren't affected by these things in comparison to the effect they had on even the strongest white men. To complain about anything was, for an Apache, to disgrace himself. Even as babies, for instance, they were never allowed to cry; whenever they attempted it their mother or the midwife would simply hold a finger lightly to their Adam's apple, which didn't hurt them unless they tried to cry and then it became very uncomfortable indeed. By trying the same thing on myself I quickly got the idea as to why the Apache babies soon learned *never* to cry. Their children weren't allowed to scream at play because sometimes it was necessary for the whole tribe to remain in concealment, and it took advance training to fit the children for adapting themselves to this existence when it arose. No child ever disobeyed a parent, or showed disrespect for an elder, at least that I knew of, because they were taught that an instant whipping with a limber but tough switch would follow as certain as day follows night.

"Polygamy among them was not only permitted, it was encouraged because of the high incidence of fatalities the braves suffered, stemming from their warring on literally every other tribe within reach, and on white men, too, after they appeared. This naturally worked toward a great surplus of women, and the brave who didn't try to feed and house as many of these as he could obtain subsistence for, and do as much as he could toward producing a good crop of papooses was considered the Apache equivalent of a bad citizen. If he did do well in this regard he received the greatest honor and respect.

"An obvious weakness of the Apache women—and Lord knows they didn't permit themselves many—was their passion for the loudest dyes for their clothes they could distill, and as many trinkets to wear with them as they could obtain. A man who could afford many wives was considered the best catch, and any of the young girls would have much preferred to be one of seven wives of a well-off brave, than to be the sole wife of an impecunious one. The more wives, the less work each one had to do, and if a brave could afford a harem, then by the same token he could afford to deck them out in enough finery to make them the envy of his community. The girls, therefore, much preferred polygamy—no question about it—as a way of life, and they felt sorry for the woman who was the only wife of a brave and had to do *everything*—and frequently—for him.

"But the fact remained that courage or lack of it, or kindness or lack of it, had no bearing as far as I could tell on the attitude of the unmarried Apache girls when it came to picking out a hero for themselves. They would admire the gallantry of a mighty warrior in times of danger, and would like to be seen with him on any terms while danger hovered, but if he didn't also use this as an opportunity to enrich himself while he could, they regarded him as little better than the equivalent of one whom the Germans consider a *dumpkoph*.

"The moment dreaded periods of peace broke out—and despite the Apaches' constant efforts they would once in a while —braves hanging around the tepee, and generally underfoot, were scorned and largely ignored by the squaws.

"The chastity of Apache women was of awesome proportions where outsiders were concerned, stemming from centuries of training by their men that this was the best thing for them, or at least much preferred by the men. Young Apache girls were generally the most beautiful of all Indian girls before marriage, but the effect of all this work and lack of conjugal kindness and consideration of even the most elemental sort sadly changed them to veritable crones after only three or four years of marriage. The kind of life they led as wives quickly withered them, and soon they were wrinkled and muscular. After becoming widows, some of these hickory hard old-young women turned into the most feared of raiders. They learned to ride like centaurs and could shoot with the best of the marksmen. Though the braves used their women, once they were married to them, as little better than beasts of burden, they were very ardent during the courtship period and in turn were much affected by female praise or censure.

"I could never satisfy myself as to whether congenital bone laziness on the part of the Apache caused them to evolve a

For the filter.
For the taste.
For all the right reasons.

Mild, smooth taste.
Micronite filter.
Regular or Menthol.

What a good time for all the good things of a Kent.

KENT

Warning: The Surgeon General Has Determined That Cigarette Smoking Is Dangerous to Your Health

Coffee 'n Kent!

system that called for wives to do all the work, or whether it came from yielding to the natural industry born into these women, but the constant in the situation was plain: there was nothing an Apache man was *expected* by the squaws to do in the way of ordinary work. Anything not connected with war or plunder was considered unsuitable for his place as a male Apache. He would, and often did, suffer the pangs of hunger indefinitely rather than plant, much less tend a crop, and he even refused to hunt if the product thereof could possibly be stolen or robbed. But he would cheerfully undergo extreme hardships and privations when he hoped thereby to get into a position where he could steal something from another tribe, and as has already been mentioned, was raised to believe everyone was his enemy.

"The seemingly unreasonable determination of the Apache to exterminate the white man wherever he appeared was puzzling until you lived in their territory for a while. During the first two years I was there, I was to become only too sadly aware of the fact that terrible as the Apaches were, they were more than matched by the evil scum riding the crest of the overwhelming wave of white immigration that almost engulfed the decent immigrants. Beginning in about 1850, Arizona and New Mexico were scourged by hundreds of the worst kinds of criminals, all of them vomited out of the by-no-means intolerant communities farther to the East. Among these were many sadistic and perverted killers of the most loathsome description: those who murdered innocent men and women solely for the pleasure of watching their death throes—murdered them from ambush in the tractless desert, or in the mountain passes and defiles, where most of their bodies were found, but in the very nature of such things there can be no doubt that many were never found.

"Just in the cemetery of the Presidio of Tucson alone [Spanish fortress town] there were buried by 1860 the bodies of more than two hundred men who had been murdered for sport, or call it what you will."

Chapter 9

During the years he had spent in Arizona, Captain Walker had heard much talk of the Peralta Massacre and of the fabulous gold mine they were unquestionably working before they were annihilated. There was even much talk in California about this mine. All accounts agreed that it was somewhere on Superstition Mountain and that there was no one left alive who knew of its precise location but the Apaches, and that of the principal leaders of the attack which resulted in the massacre of Peralta and his men down to the last man, only Cochise survived; Mangas Coloradas had been treacherously murdered in 1863. But after the episode occurred involving the murder of Ken-tee, the name of Jacob Walz was generally added to the list of those who knew where the mine was.

Thoughts about the vast wealth of this mine and the power of such wealth haunted the dreams of most who heard about it, and among those was Walker. But probably unique among them, he was not thinking so much of what the gold could do for him personally as of what it could do for all the Pimas of Pimeria. He visualized a veritable nation of their own coming into existence in southern Arizona in the area watered by the Salt and Gila Rivers, financed by the many millions of dollars the gold from this mine would produce. But he never lost sight even while dreaming about this Golconda upon Superstition Mountain, of that aforementioned practical fact that one must catch the rabbit before rabbit stew can be prepared.

Now that his trading posts were flourishing, and his life in 1871 was organized and settled in the Pima villages, Walker decided to tackle in earnest the problem of finding the Peralta Mine. Although he was almost certain that some of the Pima chieftains probably knew where the mine was, he was even more sure that they would never reveal it. It was the one thing they more than likely wouldn't do for him. They had tragically good reasons for this. The Pimas, in conformity with *all* Indians of the Southwest, were in tacit agreement never to show a white man where gold could be mined unless *all* the tribal chieftains were consenting parties to the revelation. Experience had taught them that once mining operations began, the Indians in the vicinity were apt to suffer grievously from the kind of people who were attracted and usually transformed by gold fever and almost invariably for the worse. Many of those who fluttered into the incandescent vicinity of gold strikes as moths to a flame in the early days of the West were honest enough, but right along with them came some of the ugliest types in the world, those who seemingly were born to prey upon and mistreat others.

Indians also had bitter memories of the old days when, if they showed a mine to the Spaniards, they sooner or later were tortured—often just on suspicion—to make them reveal *more* mines and, if they honestly didn't know of the location of any other mines, the thought of the extent of the tortures this subjected them to by the skeptical conquistadors and priests fairly boggles the mind. This had occurred so often that the Indians of California, Arizona, New Mexico, and Sonora had a horror of the very word, "mine."

Therefore, Walker decided that to force the Pimas into turning him down for this information, merely on the off chance that they *might* let him have it, could easily, and probably would, permanently and drastically impair his present good relations with them. So he put this course out of his plan.

Of course, there was always Walz to ask about his mine, but Walker knew full well in common sense that the fierce and cranky Dutchman would never tell even him where it was. Besides, during his increasing visits to the Blackwater home of Chur-ga and Walker, Walz often hinted that he himself might never again visit the mine. Walker never believed this but, in any event, he came more and more to the conclusion that Walz had become too much of a misanthrope because of Ken-tee's treatment by both whites *and* Indians to ever want to help anyone, regardless of race, creed, or ethnic persuasion for purely humanistic reasons. He also realized that if he ever asked Jake for the information and was turned down, he would never see the Old Dutchman at his house again, and he most certainly didn't want that, since he had become rather attached to this mysterious, unpredictable man who was unlike any other human being he had ever known.

"His individualism was a powerful and highly interesting thing to be around," Walker said of him, "and I looked forward mightily to his visits."

Late one night during the period when Walker was weighing the pros and cons of how to go about looking for the Peralta Mine, Geronimo slipped into his house—one moment he was reading alone in his library; the next moment Geronimo appeared before him without his having heard a sound or movement connected with his coming.

In telling about it afterwards, Walker reported that approximately the following conversation took place.

"No can stay," Geronimo announced. "Much soldier after me; I say hello to you, my friend, and I say good-bye. I jump from reservation five suns ago to show I can do, but want get back before they catch me."

"But just one question first," said Walker. "Can you tell me how to find Peralta Mine? If you do and I can get legal possession I will divide any money I get from it three ways—one-third to Apaches, one-third to Pimas, and I'll take a third for myself."

"No can do," said the old copper-colored, fierce-eyed, ugly little man who had been the terror and scourge of literally all the White-eyes in Arizona for a generation, and who had been only intermittently at peace with them ever since the end of the Civil War, but was now living with the remnants of his band on a reservation.

Cochise was peacefully holed up in the Chiricahuas, and Arizonans were beginning to breathe easily and sleep nights.

"Why?" asked Walker. "Don't you know where it is?"

"Perhaps yes, perhaps no," he answered evasively. "Cochise one you must ask. Besides there be much trouble for me soon; maybe you, too, if you friend of mine. I take braves, leave reservation soon; we starve there. Now go on warpath."

Then he didn't so much seem to leave by stepping backwards, as sort of shrink in size until he backed through the doorway onto the porch and was gone, and gone utterly without sound.

Dr. Walker had already heard much of the frightful mistreatment of Indians who agreed after the Civil War to live on reservations and accept the seemingly liberal offer of the recently organized Federal Indian Bureau. But corrupt agents of this distant bureaucracy became hand-in-glove with those who bribed them for crooked "privileges." These privileges, according to U.S. Army Captain John C. Bourke, General George Crook's adjutant for many years, enabled them to steal, or help others to steal government-furnished supplies from the Indians as well as reservation land. Some agents, said Captain Bourke, issued supplies by throwing them through the rungs on a horizontal ladder—the Indians getting what stayed on the ladder.

General Crook himself said in his memoirs, "I have never yet seen an Indian that was not an example in honor and nobility compared to the wretches who plunder him of the little our government appropriates for him."

Finally, there were the seamy whiskey wagoners and petty thieves who were not averse to provoking the Indians, for a profit of a few dollars, into doing something that would provide some usually flimsy excuse for running them off any rich land some white man coveted.

Nevertheless, and in the face of all this, Walker decided to try and have a powwow with Cochise and effect some sort of deal with *him* that would persuade him to reveal the location of the mine. It was obvious that Cochise and his co-chiefs had, before wiping out the Peralta expedition, watched the mining operations for many months, and no matter how much pains the Peralta miners had taken to conceal the workings, the Apaches who had participated in the Massacre were bound to know exactly where it was. But Cochise, a bitter misanthrope by this time, was not going to be an easy man to treat with, especially where the white man's god—gold—was concerned.

When Cochise finally was contacted by one of Walker's emissaries, he demanded through his scouts that Walker state in advance exactly what he wanted of him, and when he learned that it was about the Peralta Mine, he flatly refused even to discuss it.

But, probably because Cochise began to think over Walker's increasing standing with Indians of Arizona, his taking up permanent residence on the Pima reservation, and his reputation for being honest and a man of his word, he finally sent word, after Walker had about given up hope, that he would talk with him, but stipulated that he would have to come alone, except for a certain Tom Jeffords, whom Walker would have to somehow persuade to guide him.

Thomas Jefferson Jeffords had a long and adventurous career in Arizona and New Mexico as a trapper, explorer, scout, and trader with the Indians, and he was highly respected and trusted by all the tribes, and the whites as well.

After locating Jeffords at Tularosa in New Mexico, Walker selected August as the best time for traveling in those high mountains, and knowing that Jeffords might take some persuading, especially as he was then acting as head scout for the U.S. Army cavalry units stationed at Tularosa, he decided to go there and contact him in person.

Meeting Jeffords for the first time, Walker found him to be a tall, red-haired, slim, soft-spoken, and quiet man, still in his thirties, who impressed him as having a considerable amount of formal schooling underneath his frontier drawl. He concluded at that first meeting that they would hit it off fine together.

His first move after arriving at Tularosa was to pay a courtesy call on the commanding officer of the garrison. The latter, when he learned that the purpose of the trip was to contact Cochise, readily agreed to allow Walker to "borrow" Jeffords for a short expedition. Very likely he figured nothing but good, at least from his standpoint, could come of it, in that once the exact whereabouts of Cochise was known it would be relatively simple for his men to capture him.

Jeffords quickly disabused the pragmatic frontier soldier of this idea after he called him in, in Walker's presence, to ask him if he would guide Walker, and throwing out a hint at the same time that he would eventually like to know where they found Cochise's baffling stronghold to be.

"I simply don't hold with any kind of treacherous goings-on," Jeffords told him. "I'd kill an Indian in a flash if I found him trying to do in a white man without no call to do it, an' I'd do as much for any white man I found trying to harm an Indian the same way. Cochise is my friend, an' I'm a friend of his, but what I said goes for any Indian or white man, anywhere, anytime, including Cochise. If you are still willing for me to go under those conditions, and Walker agrees to 'em too, then I'll go; otherwise, forget it."

"If I take you," Jeffords said to Walker, "you will have to go alone, that is without any of your own people. I'll have someone to help us tote supplies; perhaps I can get Chie and Ponce to come along. Chie is one of the sons of Mangas Coloradas, who was murdered in 1863 by some treacherous soldiers who were assigned to guard him. Ponce's father is a lifetime friend of Cochise. Also, you must do exactly what Ponce and Chie—if I can get 'em—and myself say throughout the entire trip, even though sometimes you might feel I was leading you into a trap, and no doubt there'll be times when you *will* think that. Is this agreed?"

Walker assured him it was and they began making preparations.

Ponce knew Spanish and would act as interpreter in areas of New Mexico where they would encounter many Mexicans. "Ponce," said Jeffords, "is a favorite of the Old Man's [which was how Jeffords almost invariably referred to Cochise], and having him and Chie with us will make me doubly welcome to his stronghold."

The trail that Jeffords took leaving New Mexico led past what are now the cities of Alamogordo, Las Cruces, and Deming, and slightly south of Lordsburg, winding among sandy hills and through the wastes of southwestern New Mexico until the Peloncillo Mountains loomed ahead. Beyond, more than two hundred miles away in the Chiricahua Mountains of Arizona, Jeffords said the "Old Man" could be found. As they moved toward the range the trail divided into several dim paths, but they merely followed the lead of Chie, who kept well ahead of the party when it was on the move. When they camped Chie made sure it was in a spot which had a high vantage point from which either Ponce or himself could keep watch in every direction for possible enemies. After they reached one such summit Chie set fire to some resinous pinecones in four separate piles in a line about ten feet apart. The fires caught quickly, and when partially smothered with damp leaves put up four clouds of smoke. "That's peace smoke, and tells there are four of us," Chie explained. He then made a sound like a hoot owl and was answered by a hoot from another "owl" on the mountain. They had reached an outpost of the fabulous chief, though his lair was still a hundred miles distant! Soon a strange Apache joined them. He smoked a pipe with Chie and Ponce. He was a Cochise scout, Chie explained.

That next day's ride of forty miles, with the scout leading them, was a rigorous one. Though late summer is supposed to be delightfully cool in that area, there had been no rain for a long time and several springs which Chie depended on were dry, and men and animals alike suffered from thirst. However, Ponce and Chie said they knew of a dependable spring of clear sweet water which they could reach before nightfall, but when they arrived there, it too was dry. They perforce pushed on, and just as night fell they came to some steep, clefted cliffs and heard the welcome sound of falling water. It was somersaulting down the face of a cliff from a high-up spring into a deep emerald pool at its base.

They kept on the next day for forty more miles across a wide valley to the foothills of the Dragoon Mountains, and reached Camp Bowie the next afternoon, where they rested until morning. Then they went through Apache Pass, more than five thousand feet high, and Chie pointed out the spot where his father, Coloradas, was murdered by army assassins.

Year in and year out for over thirty years this pass was considered to be *the* most dangerous spot on the average in the United States. For a dozen miles or so while approaching it, Walker and his party had been riding past the bones of oxen, horses, and mules, and the wreckage of trail wagons was so thickly distributed along the sides of the road that they were never out of the sight. They found the same was true for an equal distance on the other side of the pass.

That night around the campfire Chie told the story Cochise had told Thorne and added a few details. Apache Pass was the place where in 1861 Lieutenant Bascom, a West Point graduate, tried to capture Cochise through treachery. At the time the Chiricahua people were friendly with the white men and a party had been employed to cut wood for the stage station at Apache Pass on the route that ran through the Chiricahua Mountains. Lieutenant Bascom had asked, said Chie, that a conference of Chiricahua chieftains come to his tent, above which he would fly a white truce flag, to discuss the woodcutting contract, as well as a rumor that Cochise had abducted a young white boy by the name of Mickey Free, though Cochise had already sent word that he knew nothing of the kidnapping. When Cochise accepted the offer of a pow-wow under a white flag, Bascom attempted to take them prisoners, but Cochise escaped, though with three bullet wounds. Six of the minor chiefs, three of them Cochise's relatives, were captured by Bascom and his men and were later hanged from trees. Cochise later killed some of Bascom's men in reprisal.

The high ground on both sides of the pass is among the roughest to be found anywhere, and furnished almost ideal cover for the myriads of robbers and murderers then on the run from various points in both east and west who lurked there waiting for some small party, or one- or two-wagon-train party to come through that would give them a risk-free chance of bushwhacking. Some of these were psychotics, such as mentioned earlier, who usually killed their victims merely from blood lust. All were men with no loyalties, and their mental makeup was scarcely, if at all, human. They were of all colors—black, red, brown, white, and yellow—almost every ethnic group on earth had spawned them. Between hauls they habitually lived and caroused in Mexican border hell holes.

The Butterfield Overland Mail Stage Line had established a station there in 1858, which was very necessary, as there was a long, hard, waterless pull for the horses coming up on both sides, and near the pass was one of the steadiest flowing springs of cool, sweet water in Arizona. But the outlaws proved too tough for the stage company, and they quit the run. One year after they quit, on July 28, 1862, the government belatedly established Fort Bowie a half mile east of the pass to protect traffic in the area.

The stage line that succeeded the Butterfield outfit, which at the time Walker and party passed there on the way to find Cochise, had been protecting their station and their stages with their own armed guards while going through the pass, was also preparing to suspend operations, not only in the vicinity of the pass, but throughout the whole of southern Arizona.

Further south, they passed through the late afternoon shadow of the eight-thousand-foot mountain, now called Cochise Head, located near the Chiricahua National Monument, and finally came to a place late that day where, Jeffords said, was the beginning of the corridor to Cochise's hidden valley.

Chie placed his blanket and saddle under a tree, and took off without saying a word, but Jeffords seemed content with his departure. Ponce busied himself setting five signal fires— fires that indicated to any watchers that there were now five in his party and all came in peace.

During this time there was no other sign to indicate the nearness of Cochise or any of his clan.

Early the following morning a boy of about thirteen and a girl of fifteen rode in bareback on Indian ponies, dismounted, and looked everyone over searchingly. Then, with a grave air much at odds with his years, the boy pointed back the way they had come and said something to Ponce in rapid Apache. Later Jeffords told Walker that the boy had said he and the girl had been sent to fetch his party. Jeffords recognized the boy as Natchez, youngest son of Cochise.

Winding upward around the foothills to the left they followed the boy and girl along a twisting stream that was flowing down from the heart of the range. Suddenly, after they climbed to the summit of what appeared to be a pass, they found themselves looking down upon a valley that formed a natural amphitheater. Its bottom was a level expanse of about fifty acres of grassland, watered by several mountain streams that splashed down the high walls that surrounded it, except for the entrance in which they stood surveying the scene before them in awe and admiration. About a score of Apache women and children were lounging near this entrance under some trees. They appeared reserved, but not particularly unfriendly. Chie was waiting with them.

He said they were to camp there that night and wait for a sign from the Old Man.

The next morning two braves rode in. One was short, heavy, and hideously painted with stripes of black and vermilion. He had a fierce look and carried a long lance in his hand. He rapidly approached Jeffords, for whom he showed great friendliness. He turned out to be Taza, another son of Cochise. The other was the famous chief, Victorio, next in command to Cochise at that time.

Then a great shout and clamor arose from all the Indians as a magnificent figure, astride a big, fierce-looking stallion came riding hell-for-leather across the valley, seemingly having come out of one of the sandstone cliffs on the far side. It was Cochise!

After riding up, dismounting, and embracing Jeffords and addressing him in affectionate Spanish terms, he turned his blazing eyes on Walker. Cochise's over-six-foot form was still well proportioned and immensely strong-looking, though his great mop of thick hair was streaked here and there with silver. Dashes of vermilion adorned his face. The countenance beneath was set in dignified lines.

He led Walker and Jeffords to the traditional seat on a blanket that had been placed on a nearby mound. Then he seated himself on another blanket facing Walker, with Chie and Ponce flanking him. All the others present seated themselves in a semicircle at the bottom of the mound. After a peace pipe had been passed around to the leaders, including Walker, Cochise asked Jeffords to tell him what he could of Walker's mission.

In the end, Cochise refused to give him the information he came for.

"We did not give the Great White Medicine Man, Thorne, gold which we took from a mine," he said, speaking in the Apache tongue in which he knew Walker, like Jeffords, was fluent. "As my brother, Geronimo, told him, it came from the backs of burros we captured from Peralta and his men. The big hole in the ground from which they brought up their cursed gold is well hidden—we watched them hide it—and it is best that it stay that way. Long ago I forbade all those who were left of the warriors who fought with us to wipe out the Mexican, Peralta, and his men who worked like women, to reveal this mine's location or I would have them put to death by torture.

"Mines long ago became the Indian's curse," he concluded sadly, "and I will never do anything to add to the weight of that curse."

The powwow ended on that pronouncement, and Walker, after taking the usual ceremonious leave that was due an Indian chief, left the beautiful valley that today is known as Cochise Stronghold Memorial Park, and is very close to what was to become the notorious mining town of Tombstone. They traveled northwestward to the fledgeling town of Benson, where he parted with Jeffords, and then made his own way to Tucson and Coolidge, and back to his Blackwater home on what is now the Sacaton Indian Reservation.

A great benefit, however, came to the rest of the people of Arizona because of his trip. Jeffords reported the gist of his trip with Walker (though not Cochise's location of course) to the army staff, and as an almost direct result an army officer, Major General O. O. Howard, who had established an enviable record for treating with many Indian tribes, was dispatched from Washington by President Ulysses S. Grant to go with Jeffords to Cochise and make a treaty of peace with him, now that they knew he would talk to someone Jeffords brought to him. Jeffords did arrange the meeting in the summer of 1872 for General Howard, to whom Cochise sent word that he would also have to come to the meeting under the same circumstances as did Walker.

Since the trip with Walker, Chie had taken on another wife—a girl of thirteen—and was more or less honeymooning with her at Alamosa. At Jeffords's suggestion, General Howard journeyed there to ask him to go along. When he agreed, they went next to find Ponce who, it turned out, was living in an Indian camp near Fort Bowie, and he also decided to come along. Then, accompanied by Ponce, Chie, and Jeffords, the same threesome that went with Walker, the general set out to find Cochise, which they soon did. As a result of that meeting a peace was arranged with Cochise—a peace that permitted him and his people to remain in his Shangri-la valley. Later it was made a part of a reservation called the Chiricahua Indian Reservation that General Howard arranged to have set aside for the Chiricahuas after Cochise's death in 1874, with the provision that they did not molest anyone, and in turn they would not be molested. Cochise was the only chief in the history of the Southwest and its troubles with Indians, who did not have to go to a barren reservation and remain there.

Today many streets, mountains, and other historical places in Arizona are named after him, including a county in the southeast corner of the state.

Chapter 10

Whenever Geronimo broke out of a reservation and took hundreds of his followers with him—which he did on several occasions—plenty of white people said: "See—that's what we get for being good to those savages. We should have hunted down and exterminated every last one of them as soon as the Civil War was over, instead of putting them on reservations, with no work to do and feeding them at our expense."

Quite a different opinion was voiced by Frank Lockwood, the noted author on Indian affairs, who was known to have the ear of President Ulysses S. Grant, and was one of the outstanding authorities on the troubles with the Apaches. He declared that for a long time the cruel treatment of the Apaches of Arizona had caused stirrings of conscience in the souls of a vast number of good and informed citizens throughout the nation. There was now a widespread belief that the Apaches were not getting a square deal, that it was becoming more and more apparent that many government Indian agents were allied with certain hideous individuals who were responsible for deeds that were a stench in the nostrils of the civilized world.

Lockwood, through his writings and speeches, was able to arouse enough feeling among people of humanitarian instincts in the East to cause the creation in Washington in 1871 of the Permanent Board of Peace Commissioners (with the strong approval of President Grant), the object of which was to put an end to the injustices and cruelties visited upon the Indians and to introduce a sane, uniform, benevolent plan for the improvement of the red man.

This board was able to influence the giving of the command of the military department of Arizona in that same summer of 1871 to General George Crook, who was the most famous of all U.S. Indian fighters of that period. He was also noted for his wisdom, kindness where deserved, and what was still more extraordinary, an honesty that brooked no exceptions. It had been said of him that he would no more break his word to the leader of a pack of ragged Apaches than he would break his word to President Grant.

Fortunately for the Arizona settlers, there was little or no esprit de corps left among Apaches in general. Aware of this, General Crook decided to enlist the aid of disaffiliated Apaches who might persuade Apaches on the warpath, as well as bands of other Indians on the warpath, of the hopelessness of their struggle. If they would come back to their various reservations, Crook would pledge his word to wangle a new deal for them, and he would add his personal guarantee, as well as that of the Great White Father in Washington, that it would be kept to the letter.

By the end of the summer of 1874, General Crook's

Apache scouts had, and with a minimum of bloodshed, coaxed and persuaded most of the disaffected Indians to come back to their reservations, where they were settled down and, apparently, peacefully inclined. They were at least outwardly happy to be no longer hungry and tired, trying to wage an impossibly one-sided struggle against odds that were insuperable.

So good was the job that these scouts did that they became famous, not only throughout the United States, but throughout the world.

So pleased with the result was Governor Anson Safford that he gave it as his opinion that it was "almost a certainty" there would never again be a general Indian war in Arizona.

The first phase of General Crook's mission was now ended, but the second phase proved to be not so easy. It involved insulating the newly bucolic Apaches from white thieves, land-grabbers, and troublemakers with an angle.

In addressing a gathering of Indian agents shortly after peace was restored, General Crook said to them: "During the twenty-seven years of my experience with the Indian question I have never known a band of Indians to make peace with our government and then break it, or capriciously leave their reservation without some grounds, or a more or less valid complaint. When they do have such reasons, they will constantly give annoyance and trouble until their complaints are examined and adjusted."

He then went on to warn these agents that their reputation by and large had become a noisome one, "and in my opinion," he said, "this comes mostly from the political spoils systems under which you directly receive your appointments."

In the summing-up report which he sent through channels to President Grant, he once more reiterated his already well-known conviction that the Apaches were far more sinned against than sinning. They were not, he said, the vicious animals they were represented to be by those who wanted to grab fertile land, nor were they pious martyrs. They were ignorant, illiterate people who had become the almost constant target for extermination, "an experience that had made them the most polished masters of ruthless guerrilla fighting in the history of the United States."

Geronimo, for instance, had trained his warriors until they could cover forty miles a day on foot, shambling along in their sloppy legging-like moccasins, or could make seventy-five miles a day on horses specially trained for such endurance.

They could live off the country, while a civilized pursuer was perishing of hunger, thirst, and sunstroke. They could travel as invisibly as a ghost, appear or disappear as silently as a shadow.

These dusty warriors were seldom seen, and if seen were seldom hit, and if hit, were seldom killed.

Captain Bourke, General Crook's adjutant, became extremely well acquainted with Apaches and added this opinion to the report: "No Indian," he wrote, "has more virtues and none, admittedly, has been more truly ferocious when aroused. . . . For centuries he has been preeminent over the more peaceful nations about him for courage, skill, and daring in war; cunning in deceiving and evading his enemies; ferocity in attack when skillfully planned ambuscades have led an unwary foe into his clutches; cruelty and brutality to captives; patient endurance and fortitude under the greatest privations. . . . But in peace he is deserving of respect for keen-sighted intelligence, good fellowship, warmth of feeling for his friends, and impatience with wrong. . . ."

The greatest cause of trouble with the Apaches in the period immediately following the Civil War again in 1871 had been the arbitrary and almost continual shifting of them from their various home reservations to new reservations where they did not want to go. This was done by the Federal Indian Bureau, sometimes for reasons of legitimate operating efficiency. But sometimes the move was a shenanigan engineered by an Indian agent, or a group of them, to throw the business of supplying the reservation to some go-getting community.

These injustices always brought furious protests from the Chiricahua Apaches in New Mexico and Arizona. Somehow or other they managed to remain mostly on their Chiricahua Reservation, though it was most coveted by land-grabbers and Indian despoilers.

After the great Cochise died in 1874 in his exquisitely beautiful valley which had by then become part of the Chiricahua Reservation, trouble wasn't long in coming again.

In recognition of Jefford's work with Cochise, General Howard had had him appointed as the Indian agent for the Chiricahua Reservation, with his headquarters in Sulphur

Springs, a stage stop. Unfortunately, this stage stop was also the location of a ranch and a store operated by two tinhorn white men by the name of Rogers and Spence, who sold the Indians as much rotgut whiskey as they could pay for, despite Jefford's attempts to stop it.

When the Indians couldn't pay, Spence and Rogers were not above offering the whiskey to them on the condition that they induce, or force, Indian girls to commit prostitution with such of the passengers and employees of the busy stage line who were of the kind to indulge in such proceedings during overnight stops.

The chiefs who succeeded Cochise as joint rulers of the tribe, headed by his oldest son, Taza, also tried to put an end to this inhuman business, and during one discussion about it at the Rogers-Spence deadfall, one of Taza's fellow chiefs was shot and killed by a panderer.

That night some of the shamed and desperate wives who considered the murdered man as having been their champion, mobbed the killer and bit, beat, and knifed him to death. When friends of the victim, headed by an Indian scoundrel named Skinya, tried to punish the wives, Taza came to their rescue and a deadly fight ensued. Two of Skinya's braves and a grandchild of Cochise were killed.

There are several versions of what happened next, but according to Jeffords, an Indian named Pionsenay got to brooding over the matter and went to Sulphur Springs and killed Rogers and Spence.

Taza then proceeded to drive the troublemakers, headed by Skinya, off the reservation. They holed up on an all but inaccessible peak in the Dragoon Mountains for a short period, following which they sallied down shooting their way into Taza's camp. In the ensuing battle, Skinya and six men were killed and two seriously wounded. Natchez, son of Cochise, was said to have fired the shot that killed Skinya.

In what has been referred to by many, including Jeffords, as a colossal folly, the Federal Indian Bureau decided, because of this internecine battle to move the Chiricahua Indians from the reservation they had occupied since their joint agreement with General Howard, to the San Carlos Reservation, already overcrowded with tribes that hated each other, and regarded by the Chiricahua Apaches as a miserable place to live anyway. The Chiricahuas also found unbearably bitter the fact that their own reservation had been taken away from them, not because of the disloyalty or fault of themselves as a people, but as a result of trouble caused by the greed of white men for the land the Chiricahuas occupied.

Their being herded into San Carlos decided Geronimo to try once more to break out of San Carlos, and he threw in with the Chiricahuas and all other Indians he could persuade to go along with them. Thus began the final war between the Indians and the White-eyes that lasted more than ten years and took the lives of hundreds on both sides, during which Geronimo's superb generalship against fantastic odds made him one of the West's top celebrities, and one of the immortals of U.S. history.

When in the midst of this ten-year war the federal government attempted to consolidate the various Apache tribal divisions on no more than two reservations, the war intensified under the general leadership of Geronimo, with Victorio as his chief lieutenant, the latter having once been a second-in-command to Mangas Coloradas. The various Apache factions, accompanied by some warriors of the Mogollons, Mimbres, and Coyotero in-laws, began pillaging up and down the border country.

After Victorio was killed by Mexican troops in 1880, an old warrior named Nana led a battalion of warriors on numerous campaigns, fighting and winning a battle a week against a full regiment of U.S. troops, Texas Rangers, civilians, and some loaned troops from northern Mexico. Badly crippled with rheumatism, and some seventy or eighty years old at the time, Nana was so burdened with aches and pains he had to sleep in an upright position.

In 1875 General Crook had been sent away to the Black Hills in the Dakotas to fight the Sioux Indians when most of the people in Arizona believed, as did their Governor Anson Safford, that there was never again going to be another Indian war in their state. But he had to be brought back in 1882 to try and corral Geronimo, whereupon he reinstated his former patient roundup of hostile Apaches.

But Crook's superiors lost patience with his insistence on decent behavior and forbearance, and replaced him with General Nelson A. Miles, a blood-and-guts showman who inaugurated a relentless campaign of no-holds-barred.

Geronimo and his almost completely decimated followers

surrendered in 1886 and were exiled to Florida and later to Oklahoma as prisoners. Crook's old Apache scouts were included as prisoners, and so were the hundreds of Chiricahuas who had remained quietly, as long as they were allowed to, on Cochise's old reservation.

Very few, if any of them, ever again saw the hills of home.

General Crook was still waging a campaign in the halls of Congress for a fairer deal for the Apaches when he died of a heart attack in 1890.

Chapter 11

In 1873 Chur-ga gave birth at home in Blackwater to a brown-eyed, raven-haired, warmly-tinted and beautiful little daughter. They named her Juana and called her by the affectionate Spanish diminutive of Juanita.

Little Juanita became the special charge of Priscilla James, and was soon not only an ever-increasing delight to Chur-ga and Walker, but to Priscilla's maidens, as well as the whole of Pimeria. In Juanita they saw an amalgamation of the two cultures, and perhaps the beginning of an augury that could someday be a truly wonderful thing for the future of the United States. She was a healthy, happy, lovable child, and Walker, watching her unfold as the years went on, became utterly convinced that she was the most wonderful child in the world.

"She has a talent for music, like her father," he told a friend one day.

"How can you know that?" asked the astonished friend. "She isn't six months old yet."

"She cries with perfect pitch," replied Walker.

Though he was now a family man in the most direct sense, and prospering with his trading stations, which served the seven villages of Pimeria on the Gila, and several villages of other tribes within easy reaching distance, Walker did not give up thinking about the Peralta Mine. He remained keenly interested in the attempts of other men to find it and in rumors that were always cropping up as to its location.

But he was coming more and more to believe that Ken-tee had indeed revealed the location of the Peralta Mine to Walz, and that it was from there that he had been getting his gold. As his prosperity increased and his family life deepened and his contentment grew with things as they were, he found that he didn't even want to think of engaging in a struggle—perhaps a deadly one—with his friend Walz over the mine. Nor did he want to play an even more dangerous game of hide and seek with the Apaches who guarded their sacred place, and at the same time dodge the desperadoes who were coming in ever greater numbers to the Mountain and its vicinity to try and find the "ledge of rose quartz that was heavy with gold."

Thereafter as the years marched on, he forced all thought of finding the mine to the back of his mind, and threw himself during his spare time into studying the ways of the Pimas, with whom he now felt completely and almost solely at home. His fluency with their language had increased to a point where even the nuances of the least thing they said were clear to him.

He continued studying their ancient arts and crafts, which were many, in the hope that he could use more of these products as merchandise in his various posts at his stage stops. They were superb at handcrafting, and more income was much needed to improve their economic lot, of which they had a base of almost zero when he first came there.

The baskets the women made from tightly twisted cord were of a better quality than could be found anywhere else north of Mexico, and sold quickly at his posts. He tried organizing the women for the production of these baskets, because he found he could easily sell three or four times as many as they were producing, but this wasn't easy, because they preferred to only weave baskets when they weren't busy bringing in food, water, grinding corn, and doing other household chores. They had all been so thoroughly indoctrinated in the belief that taking care of their home, men and children came first *always,* that it was as strong as a religion with them. But they were very proud of their basketwork and an intensive rivalry grew among the women to see which could make the most beautiful pattern, and soon the volume began steadily to increase.

The baskets were put together with something like a crochet stitch, and dyed in various interesting designs with colors that included blue from fire soot and red from a volcanic clay found in the nearby mountains.

The women also wove baskets out of willow strands. For strength, willow was the best material for basketry and plenty of it grew on the banks of the Gila. These baskets were useful for almost every conceivable purpose except cooking. They could even turn one type upside down to use as a drum.

They also were astonishingly adept at fashioning rope. They used a very simple type to tie together their beams and rafters, consisting of only two strands plaited together and made from the fibers of the yucca and bear grease. It was extremely strong and impervious to weather, and it securely held together the materials that supported the clay while it baked hard to form a weathertight cover on the house.

Their finer cords and strings were made from the fiber of the century plant, called the *maguey* by the Mexicans. They separated the fiber by pounding the leaves of the plant on a stone similar to the dishlike metates on which they ground their corn and other materials for food. Then a man twisted it into string by rolling it up and down on his bare leg with the palm of his hand. String-making was not man's work among most Indian tribes but the Pima men did practically all of it. They made many useful things from this string, including the woven bags, called "carrying nets," with which to carry cuts of meat back from hunting expeditions, as well as other burdens while traveling. In those days no Pima woman would be caught without her carrying net. When the load was extra heavy they commonly ran with them at a jog trot and declared that the load on their back pushed them on. These nets looked rough and somewhat on the fragile side, but they were incredibly strong and would last almost indefinitely.

They made cradleboards for their papooses from long strips of rawhide. Light sticks bound closely together by strips of thin but strong rawhide formed the doors of their houses. Rawhide was also used to fashion traps for small animals. For finer work, such as bow strings, they used deer sinew and kept a bundle of it stuck in the thatch of their roofs at all times.

Several of the women vied with each other to see who could produce the most beautiful cradleboard for Juanita. Chur-ga accepted them all and diplomatically used a different one each day.

The older women were clever at forming and glazing the

earthen pots that were used for holding water and cooking, but rarely used for carrying things when they moved about because they were breakable. These pots were instant sellers in Walker's posts, but according to Pima custom only a few of the women at a time had been taught the craft of making pots, and even though they were kept busy at it, could only make a few more at first than their own needs demanded. But as in the case of the baskets, their output grew apace.

When a big jar was needed for the storage of water—and the bigger the better—it was usually made out of coarse clay and not glazed, which let the water seep through. The resulting evaporation over the entire surface of the jar kept the water cool. In the summer the water from the Gila (which in those days was as pure as the driven snow) was slightly more than lukewarm.

The women potmakers also made large round glazed clay plates to be used as griddles that could be heated over fire coals until they were very hot. When cornmeal batter was dropped on them it formed griddle cakes very similar to the tortillas of the Mexicans.

Walker helped the Pimas make a good thing of trading cotton string and cloth to other Indian tribes. He succeeded in organizing the old men into spinners and weavers, according to the aptitude they showed. The spinners twisted the cotton into string with a spindle, a slender stick with a slab wheel on the end to make it whirl. They held it between their toes and twisted the fibers around the spindle stick as people used to do in ancient times.

The weavers then wove the string into strips of cloth long enough for a woman's skirt. Using the smooth rods which grow inside the saguaro cactus and called the "cactus skeleton," they made a simple loom by tying four of these together with string and placing them on short sticks driven into the ground so that it looked something like a bedframe on legs. The weave was perfectly plain except that sometimes they put a few threads at the border which were dyed red with the extract from the root of a plant known to the Pimas.

Women almost never wove cloth, although on occasion the old women helped with the spinning.

During food-hunting expeditions in the mountains the men also hunted for stone slabs of a suitable size and shape for being fashioned into metates. These metates are today much prized as souvenirs of the Indians of the old West and can be found now in the courtyards of many Arizona restaurants and souvenir places, usually not for sale but to attract the curious interest of passersby and customers. The older people among the Pimas still use these stones like mortar and pestle or board and rolling pin to grind the corn to the way they like it for cooking.

For a long time it had been an open secret that the Pima Indians had a very rich silver mine to which through the centuries they made expeditions, cloaked by fantastically secret precautions to obtain enough ore from which to refine silver for the many silver ornaments they loved to wear. But Captain Walker was always careful never to betray the slightest curiosity about it for fear it would make his interest in them suspect. Besides, as time went on and the decade of the 1870s drew to a close, he found that he cared less and less for wealth in view of his present situation. He really had everything he wanted: a lovely and loving and many-faceted wife, a daughter who was a constant delight, a fine house, a very profitable business, and his own fertile farm on which he employed many Pimas. They raised food in profusion and in abundant variety for the stage stations and for his own and their tables. He had a steady income from taking care of the emergency medical needs of some of the white settlers and their families; he would treat whites only in emergencies.

Then one day Antonio Azul, Walker's top sergeant during the campaign that broke the lordly power of the Apaches, told Walker that the council of Pima elders had decided to reveal to him the location of the mine where they had been getting the ore for their silver ornaments through the ages in order that he, Walker, might make arrangements for it to be worked with modern methods and machinery. The money would be devoted in part to improving the tribe's lot.

At first, Walker refused. He was older and wiser now and feared that general prosperity might destroy his Eden. But eventually he agreed. He stipulated, however, that the preliminaries must be undertaken under conditions of the utmost secrecy.

They started out one midnight in the hope of evading Peter Brady, a shrewd, persistent, and patient old prospector who for years had been trying to trace the source of the Pima's silver. But, it turned out, Brady had bribed a corrupt and drunken old Pima who, though not in the confidence of the elders, was in a position to watch every move Walker and Chief Azul made—and could also follow tracks and signs during night or day better than many motorists of today can find their way between cities over the broad highways. Tipped off to the midnight foray by his Pima spy, Brady arrived on the scene at the mine just as Walker was erecting the markers necessary to file a claim and demanded equal rights in the discovery. Chief Azul wanted to settle the matter then and there by the simple expedient of killing both Brady and his tracker, but Walker vetoed this and subsequently settled with Brady for the sum of sixty thousand dollars in cash for Brady's nebulous "right" to the location. Walker said afterwards he didn't think he would get a square deal in Arizona courts if Brady claimed the mine.

Located about thirty-four miles west-southwest of Casa Grande, Arizona, this claim was to become known the world over as the Vekol (which means "grandmother" in Pima language) Mine, one of the richest ever discovered. It is said that Walker recovered the sixty thousand dollars during the first ten days he worked the mine. The outcrop from which the Indians had secured their ore led to a great chimney of rich ore just under the surface.

In an era of Arizona history filled with violence and bloodshed, the Vekol silver mining camp and the town of the same name that sprang up around it, lived out a long, serene period of unmarred peace until the ore was exhausted in 1912. The Pimas benefited a great deal from the Vekol profits, with Walker keeping a much smaller share for himself. The official history of Arizona credits him with taking over two million dollars from the mine.

Farish, Arizona's official historian, wrote that, "Captain Walker spent most of his millions on the Pima Indians."

Walker was appointed probate judge of Pinal County, which encompassed his mine and the Pima villages, and discharged the duties of this office, according to Farish's official account, "with fidelity and intelligence. His word was as good as his bond," Farish wrote. "No one ever knew John D. Walker to go back on his word in any way." After this he was always referred to by whites as "Judge" Walker. While sitting as a judge he lived that part of the time in Florence, the seat of Pinal County.

The disciplined leadership of Judge Walker produced a sort of utopia for the nearly two hundred Indians and their folks who inhabited the town of Vekol at its peak of operations. He mostly allowed only Pimas and Maricopas to work in the mine, but did hire a few White-eyes who had satisfied him they didn't smoke or drink, and he permitted white storekeepers and other businessmen to operate freely. This writer interviewed a few old-timers who worked there, and they spoke reverently of Walker. He was undoubtedly a model of sobriety, justice, leadership, and simplicity.

Mrs. Mabel Ludwig, a resident of Casa Grande, Arizona, now past ninety, was one of those early dwellers in the camp the writer talked to. As a child she moved to Vekol with her family in the middle 1880s. Her father was Thomas Day, mine superintendent for Walker.

"Vekol could be described as neither a holy nor an unholy place—there wasn't a saloon or a church in the camp," she recalls. "Alcohol and churches were the judge's two prejudices; he would allow neither one at Vekol. In the days when Tombstone was at its infamous peak, we had no liquor trouble. Mostly this was due to Judge Walker's ban against whiskey."

The corners of her mouth twitched in a smile as she recalled a humorous incident.

"My mother had a very powerful voice for a woman, and one day she was singing and accompanying herself on the organ she'd just brought from the East.

"While she was thus occupied, Judge Walker approached my father and asked him if there hadn't been a breach of the liquor manifesto. 'None that I know of, Judge,' my father replied.

"'Well then, how do you account for that singing?' came the quick rejoinder. 'Unless your wife's had a whack at the bottle!'"

In his personal life, music was very important to Walker, who was an accomplished violinist. One day, while amusing himself by playing variations on a Beethoven sonata, he was amazed to hear Chur-ga humming along in tune with him and showing a very good feeling for following a melody. It struck him that she had, perhaps, a talent for learning to sing well, and that if he taught her technique she could accompany him for their personal pleasure, and maybe entertain gatherings of the tribe on occasion. She was instantly and enormously intrigued with the idea.

He started her on breath control and, next, rhythm and pitch; how to produce a singing tone, then scales. "There are as many technical aspects connected with singing," he warned her, "as there are in learning to play an instrument."

She practiced the scales faithfully and he was astonished when she soon produced a clear and resonant vowel sound, especially in view of the fact that the Pima language is dominated by gutturals.

Next came learning to keep a very relaxed throat and jaw, the latter with a feeling of a downward pull, as though someone had taken her chin in his hand and pressed down on it; and to work away from the beginner's fault: opening the mouth sideways from left to right rather than up and down which gives the tone a harsh, strident quality.

One day while she was practicing breath control, he described to her how, when he was training them for the campaign against the Apaches, he taught his Pima warriors to stand while undergoing inspection in ranks with shoulders raised up high, the chest pushed out and the stomach pulled in. Then he made her laugh by having her assume this same position and telling her to try to sing. Of course, she couldn't very well, because it was the exact opposite from the posture the body needs for singing, or for any other activity that requires considerable breath control. Her stomach, he said, should be pushed out when she sang, otherwise she was cramping off about half of her lung capacity, as her diaphragm separated the top half of her body from the bottom half, and breathing in and out pushed this diaphragm up and down. When it was up it restricted her lung capacity, but when down let her lungs extend as far as they could, increasing the air cavity and giving her a greater capacity for rich, resonant, full sound.

He cautioned her against overdoing the vibrato—for in his opinion few faults in singing sounded worse.

She made steady progress on the physical requirements while he continued drilling her on the scale over and over again. Striking a note on his violin, he would say, "All right, sing that note for me, then sing the full scale, do, re, me, fa, so, la, ti, do. Not bad; now do it again."

She learned about intervals, whole steps and half steps, key signatures, and how to count time to get the rhythm of the piece.

As millions had before her, and as millions have done since, she had to practice committing esoteric musical terms to *memory* until it became a part of her conscious and sub-conscious—that a note, for instance, is not a sound but the written symbol for a sound and indicates the pitch that sound should have, and is drawn on the music sheet in such a way that its shape, when blacked in, or left open, or has a flag on it, a dot next to it, and by many other symbols, tells how long the sound should be.

Over and over she had to repeat to herself that notes are placed on five lines with four spaces in between, each line and space representing a pitch, and that this is called the staff, and that a whole note is an egg-shaped thing left blank in the mid-dle; a half note is like the whole note but having a stem on it; the quarter note like the half note, except the oval is blacked in; the eighth note looks like the quarter note except it has a little flag down from the stem, and a sixteenth note has two flags.

She practiced and she memorized until she dreamed about it almost nightly, how music is divided into little boxes, each one having an equal number of beats in it—maybe four beats, maybe three, maybe six, maybe nine, just so each one of the measures in a piece of music has the same number of beats in it to keep the music rhythmical. A time signature is the two little numbers that are the beginning of a piece of music; then what lines and spaces are for, and how the first seven letters of the alphabet, A through G, each stand for a certain musical pitch, the first line on the staff being E, the space above that F, and the line above that, G, and when, while practicing she got to G, she was to start over again with A and go to B, C, D, E, F, G, and then once more over again, A-B-C-D-E-F-etc., to familiarize herself with tones or pitches rising in sound.

When they had progressed to the point where she could sing simple little pieces, accompanied by his violin, he would criticize her technical faults until she got it right.

Soon he could hand her some music and say, "Hum it back to me," and her voice would shape it almost perfectly. Within three years she was well on her way to becoming an accomplished singer. Fortunately, both had all the time they needed for teaching, practicing, and learning. Walker had embraced so much of the Pima psychology of living by this time that he did everything in a leisurely fashion—indeed many things had drifted out of his consciousness that he had considered important in the years when he had been a boy in Illinois and a man in California.

While Chur-ga loved to learn and delighted in pleasing her husband, music alone would have been incentive enough for her. It made her expand and blossom and gave her an increasing sense of fulfillment. As her technical knowledge of music steadily increased and her capacity to reproduce it with her voice kept pace, the world of music and singing began unfolding its beauties. She could transport herself simply by singing certain pieces that had especial power over her emotions. Her voice began to develop wings, and to soar and hover, rise and fall at call as if on an eagle's pinions, and she more and more could round off the notes and flow from one to the other with an ease that sounded as natural as the song of the mockingbird at dawn.

She was not immune, either, to the stimulation that the awe in the faces of the tribe gave her as they listened to the sensuous power of her voice as it poured forth with ever-increasing beauty. Untutored in music they certainly were, but their senses thirsted as have those of men and women through the ages for the sounds and sights that lift the heart, delight the mind and tighten the throat with tingling emotion, and experiencing these emotions when she sang they knew that a miracle had come to one of their people, and through her to them.

Sometimes in the afternoons she would stroll with Walker to a little glade in a small grove of cottonwood trees a half hour's walk down the bank of the river—a place that they liked to think was known only to them. Of course it wasn't; it simply was that the Pimas knew of their preference for this retreat and respected it to the extent that it was tacitly understood among them that it was to be left inviolate for Chur-ga and their blood brother, El Capitan, the Spanish term by which they always referred to him.

To this spot, which Chur-ga always called "our secret place," Walker would bring his violin and play the airs he loved while she sang softly along with his music.

They would talk by the hour there. "The mine is making

more money for us than you can even imagine," he told her once, "and one day soon I will take you to see the whole world. We will go to New York, Washington, London, Paris, Berlin, and Rome and many other places, and we will come home by way of Atlanta and New Orleans. You'll see and hear all of the great concert artists; we will spend years on the trip—forever if we want to, because I already have enough money from the mine so that we could hardly spend it if we started throwing it away. Besides, they are digging more out of the ground at Vekol every day."

"But how will the women treat me in those places?" Churga wondered. "Don't they hate Indian girls there, too?"

"It is exactly the opposite there," he said. "Beautiful Indian girls are all the rage. Besides, when they hear you sing they will be at your feet. Oh, it will be wonderful; you will become gay and you will be laughing the day long—and nights, too; you'll see.

"I will buy for you the most beautiful emerald necklace in the world—no matter who owns it; I will tempt them with money until they sell it to me. Emeralds were designed by the Creator for your warm skin. I'll buy you a tiara for your hair; I will have the world's greatest jeweler, whoever he is, fashion a diamond brooch for you with a heart-shaped ruby in the center that will be the envy of all. The dressmakers who do clothes for the wives of presidents and kings will enhance your beauty. You will see.

"Juanita is even now a famous heiress. Accomplished teachers will educate her at the best schools. When she is sixteen we'll move to Washington, D.C., and I will buy a great house there so that we can properly introduce her to society. She'll have beaus aplenty—you shall see."

One evening in 1875 a stage came from California on the way to Tucson and points east and, as was invariably the case, the passengers alighted to have dinner at the stage depot, some of them sitting around afterwards talking, while others went sightseeing in the village. (This combined stage station, restaurant, and general store, built of enduring adobe blocks, though now in ruins, can still be seen at Blackwater. Although it was built in the 1880s, the outer walls still stand straight and in plumb and the original plaster is to be seen on parts of the inside.) One of them, who happened to be a concert pianist, was gone about an hour or so, and then came back to the depot in great excitement and told the others that he had just heard an Indian girl, dressed exquisitely in embroidered doeskin, singing to some children in the village with such a beautifully clear tone that he could hardly believe it. "Actually she sounded to me as if she had had considerable voice training; I'd swear she was singing something from Brahms."

Walker, who was visiting with some of the travelers, was greatly amused. "She *has* had a little training," he said, "and probably the piece she was singing *was* something by Johannes Brahms—a little lullaby of his. She loves to sing it to the children. And thank you for noticing she is beautiful. She *is* beautiful—inside and out, with a beautiful heart and mind and nature, and I love her for all these things, and many more; also, thanks to a kind Providence, she is my wife."

Chur-ga loved singing so much she even loved her practicing and the happiness her great gift gave her found its most joyous expression in singing for her husband's pleasure. He was always her most treasured audience. Next to him came children, but each year, as her voice grew sweeter and more moving and soared more easily, she was ever more in demand, even in Tucson and Phoenix, and she was able to raise a great deal of money with her voice for the education of her people. A mezzo-soprano, she had developed an extraordinary range of three octaves, from C below middle C to high C. To understand how unusual this is, it is only necessary to consider that most opera arias require a range of no more than two octaves, and modern popular songs less than one. An octave can best be described to those who haven't studied music as eight notes, or the equivalent of eight keys on a standard-sized eighty-eight-key piano.

One evening when Walker came back from Vekol to his home in Blackwater, full of news about some more plans for their world trip now planned for that fall, it appeared to him that Chur-ga was slightly listless. Even her voice when she sang Juanita to sleep didn't sound as vibrant and sweet as usual. As the days went on a deepening shadow seemed to fall over her and around her, and it became only too evident to him that she was not feeling well. She acted disinterested in things that ordinarily she enjoyed; she rarely sang, and soon not at all. When he grew anxious about her, she laughed and ridiculed his fears. When this was no longer possible, she said that it was just a persistent headache, and that she'd had others and they had passed, and this one would too. But it didn't and soon she took to lying down for longer and longer periods with cool, dampened cloths on her forehead. This was so unlike her—she who had always been the very epitome of vitality, that Walker couldn't help becoming deeply worried.

He examined her on several occasions with all the professional skill he could summon, but couldn't find anything organically wrong; she tested out, as near as he could determine, as sound as could be, except for feeling weak and having constant headaches that were obviously growing in intensity.

Then came a day when she had to lean heavily on his arm in order to make it down to her beloved secret place and, once there, she didn't want to sing, or even talk, but lay in his arms pale and quiet and was plainly and dreadfully ill.

Almost beside himself with anxiety, he sent to St. Louis and to New Orleans for doctors whose reputations ranked them among the greatest, and accompanied his requests that they drop everything and come and treat his wife with the assurance that money, even if they demanded a king's ransom, was no object to him where her health was concerned. The doctors came and soon he knew that there was no hope—Chur-ga had leukemia.

In a matter of weeks she was gone. There had come a morning when he was sitting by her bed, holding her hand, and one moment she was breathing and the next moment she wasn't.

He sat alone by her side the rest of the day and refused to let anyone, even Juanita, come into the room. That night he wrapped her in the intricately patterned and beautiful blanket that her long-dead mother had woven for her as a wedding gift and carried her in his arms to their place in the glade under the cottonwood trees by the river and began digging her grave by moonlight between the roots of one of the great trees. They were to hold her while she slept. He had it finished by midnight and when he laid her in it and covered her over, he left not only her there, but a great part of himself.

According to all accounts, Judge Walker had been a born iconoclast, but after Chur-ga's death he became a king-sized one. It was an attitude which served to protect and insulate him against time-wasting, money-consuming social or religious yokes, a protection which he now desired more than ever. He also avoided as he would a plague any social foolishness or fashion, racket, superstition, demagoguery, and self-serving politicians, as well as literally hundreds of other traps he saw as originated or utilized by clever human wolves to make other people do, or conform to, so those "wolves" could reap the benefits. Yet, though taciturn to an unusual degree, and not one to listen to the uninformed politelyfi or to outright fools patiently, he had a never-satisfied thirst to listen to travelers from far places, or those who could discourse with unusual intelligence on any subject.

There was practically no consideration that could induce him to go along, or even be diplomatic or neutral about something he didn't believe in, much less objected to. He thought that the besetting sin of the vast majority of the human race was that they would not think or analyze to any sufficiently self-protecting extent the things they were told, or heard, or read, or about the means that were used to persuade them to do things that benefitted others.

"The ability," he said, "to keep from being one of the human sheep who, symbolically at least, are too often sheared, and finally butchered and eaten, and to be instead one of those who get to wear the wool for warmth and to eat the end product for pleasure and sustenance, lies in the extremely rare capacity to be always determined to inform oneself on who designedly benefits from the things one is being asked to do, such as vote for, give to, accept in a sacrificial spirit, suffer for, work for, or even die for, and—and the names of these things are legion—to submerge one's own identity for.

"The misleading import of the signs that direct people to keep on the road to slavery, and to stay there, are plentiful," he often said, "and the purpose of them plain to those who have the divine courage to question their wording. The most frequent of these signs, 'Don't rock the boat!', is the admonition of those who have all the fat and power."

The five greatest needs of human beings, he felt, were food, water, sleep, love, and to be noticed and listened to. "And not necessarily in that order," he would add with a twinkle.

But, despite the deadening effect of Chur-ga's loss, he still, in a measure, enjoyed the simple fact of living, for he had a vast curiosity and interest in just about everything. His indulgence in, and remarkable insistence on, freedom of body, mind, and soul from the banal and venally enslaving, was aided mightily by the fact that he had the rare ability to become accomplished at almost any skill he turned his hand to. He avoided intimate human contacts as much as possible, but filled his now lonely days with other interesting pursuits, expending on Juanita what warmth was left in him. But he no longer wanted to send her away to the "best schools" or buy the "great house" in Washington. He only wanted to be where he could make his daily pilgrimage to the secret place to visit Chur-ga.

Walker's iconoclastic beliefs, coupled with his celebrated physical and mental courage and extraordinary intelligence, left him free of the inhibitions, superstitions, and crippling mores that in practice condemn most people to be the hewers of wood and drawers of water all their lives without surcease, and enabled him to live about the only way he could have roused himself to live after Chur-ga died.

Almost his sole unalloyed enjoyment was watching Juanita grow up. He participated vicariously in all her youthfully oriented doings. As his only child she was a great prospective heiress, and her favor was much sought after by the coldly calculating, socially conscious mammas and papas—most of them of the very same families who had scorned and put down her mother, but who now, with their limp sons in mind, wanted to be in on the ground floor of her favor.

But he took to neglecting to eat properly and to brooding long hours by himself, spells which became harder and harder for him to shake off, and the periods he spent at the secret place became longer and longer. One night he didn't come home at all, and when they searched for him he was discovered there sleeping the sleep of exhaustion, covered with dew. This began happening with greater frequency and his health, though he was barely fifty, began to deteriorate alarmingly.

Yet, according to historian Farish, he did not flag in his consideration of others. Being a natural linguist and having mastered the Pima language, he increased his efforts to originate their first grammar, which he completed, and then he set himself to reducing it to a written language, and he finished this task also.

"I remember," wrote Major Doran, "that Judge Walker heard during this final period of his life that the Smithsonian

Institution claimed that the Gila Monster was not poisonous. Being something of a scientist, and realizing from personal experience besides, that if this belief gained wide currency in the West it could cause the loss of many lives, and untold misery in many other cases, he wrote a dissertation upon the subject, contending that it was poisonous, and sent a specimen to them for analysis. They reversed their decision, with thanks to him, and stated the Gila Monster was indeed poisonous."

In 1888, when Juanita was about fifteen, the shadows began to draw heavily about him, and so did the relatives who couldn't wait, at least with any grace, for the day when they might get some of his considerable estate. On December 24, 1889, Lucien E. Walker, a brother, applied for a guardianship over him (#109, page 120, Book 120; page 140, Book 128; Superior Court, Pinal County, Arizona) on the grounds that the judge had now become of unsound mind. Reading those old musty records is a rather horrible experience. They reek of all the ugly things that ordinarily feature such procedures where a lot of money is at stake. A lower court judge granted the petition, then it was thrown out by a higher judge, who remarked in effect as he handed down his ruling, "I can't understand how this man could ever have been adjudged of unsound mind; he is merely hard of hearing."

Then Judge Walker went to Napa, California, to seek medical treatment for a heart ailment and died suddenly there on September 2, 1891. His relatives had him buried there, disregarding his dying wish that he be laid beside Chur-ga.

In referring to him after his death, Farish said: "He was a good physician, and a man of extraordinary intelligence and something of a scientist . . . he had a wonderful fund of information on almost every subject, and he was very precise, a thoughtful man and somewhat of a philosopher. The least that can be said of him was that he was a man of fine attainments, generous to a fault; the best type of the western man, which embodies everything that is bold, chivalrous and honorable."

He died intestate, they said. No one could find a will, though he had told Juanita repeatedly that he had made a will and left the bulk of his estate to her.

At the time of his death he was still a resident of Pinal County. On September 18, 1891, A. J. Doran was appointed administrator of his estate by the probate court of Pinal County.

Rosetta Jones, Juanita's guardian because she was still under legal age, filed a petition in this probate court on the twelfth day of May 1893 in behalf of Juanita, asking that the estate be turned over to her as the sole heir of her father, John D. Walker.

In the petition, Rosetta stated that, "(1) Juanita was born at Blackwater, on the Sacaton Indian Reservation, (2) that her mother was a Pima Indian named Chur-ga, and (3) that Juanita was the child of Chur-ga and John D. Walker, and was conceived during lawful wedlock contracted on the reservation, and that Juanita ever since and until the death of her father was recognized and acknowledged by him to be his child."

Walker's three brothers and four sisters, all living outside Arizona, countered this through their lawyers by specifically citing the Arizona law (section 2, c 30, p. 317, "Marriages," Comp. Laws Ariz. 1877) which states in part: "All marriages of white persons with Negroes, Mulattos, Indians, or Mongolians are declared illegal and void." Therefore, they contended, John D. Walker and Chur-ga had never legally been married, and that in effect, Juanita was a legal bastard, and his only lawful heirs were his brothers and sisters. The plea totally ignored the rightful and age-old sovereignty of the Pima people.

The case was tried in Pinal County probate court, and on July 28, 1893, judgment was in favor of Juanita.

The brothers and sisters appealed the case to the Supreme Court of the Territory and it was tried at the Pinal County Courthouse at Florence, Arizona, commencing on the twenty-third day of March 1894.

There then ensued what was probably one of the most shameful miscarriages of justice involving the repudiation of the U.S. Constitution and Bill of Rights in the history of Arizona, or anywhere else for that matter. But stripping Indians, who by white man's laws had been made almost legally defenseless at all levels, had long been so profitable to white people in the Southwest that it was ridiculous to even hope that Juanita's interests would be adjudicated according to any moral considerations. It might set a bad precedent, you see.

Even so, a large number of the best and most respected

lawyers in Arizona, some as volunteers, represented her in the matter. They included Fitch and Campbell, J. B. Woodward, Abram S. Humphries, T. B. McCabe, Barclay Henley, C. W. Wright, and Street and Frazier.

Juanita contended through these lawyers that "the relationship between Walker and Chur-ga was a valid marriage, because it had been performed under Pima laws and customs, and existed between her parents on the Pima reservation according to these laws and customs of the Pimas, and that, therefore, the laws of Arizona could not be and should not be in the sight of God and man used to make invalid such a marriage; and that furthermore, *any* marriage performed according to the laws and customs of the Indians upon a reservation, perforce must be valid everywhere; i.e., such a reservation is the same as any separate jurisdiction operating under its own laws, and a marriage valid in any other country or jurisdiction was legally entitled to be recognized as valid in Arizona. It would be most horribly unjust," they stated, "to make a grossly discriminatory exception of the Pima marriage ceremony especially in this case, where great love had existed and endured until death ended it between the father and mother of the beautiful and cultured young girl here defending herself against the wholly unworthy and unfair designs of her father's relatives on the estate."

But a vast pressure, both tangible and intangible, was on the judges not to render a verdict that might encourage other Indian victims to seek redress—to try and reverse the results of the rapacity that had robbed them of their good bottom lands, timberlands, mines, and virtually everything else they had possessed through the centuries, and forced them onto unbelievably barren reservations in odd corners of the state.

The courtroom and the adjacent premises swarmed every day with those who had profited to some degree—and many of them hugely—from the way the Indians had been despoiled, first by the might of the U.S. Army, and then by the civilian authorities armed with clever, if hideously discriminatory laws. Most of them came for the express purpose of glaring day after day at the "dispensers of justice" to impress on them to whom they owed their jobs.

When what was, perhaps, the inevitable verdict against her was handed down by the court that simply ignored equity and conscience, if any, and took refuge in the letter of the 1865

...niscegenation law, it stripped her of even the least ...n her father's estate. She found herself virtually penni-...Worse, she had been held by the judges to be a "bastard" ...e word is taken from the legal transcript of the proceedings). The verdict was appealed, according to Farish, to the Supreme Court of the United States. She lost both appeals.

She found herself sneered at as that "half-breed" and many other worse names by those who had been fawning on her a short while before for the sake of her presumed great wealth, especially after the probate court had handed down its favorable decision. Closing in on her also were all those who derive a keen pleasure from using minorities meanly and sadistically, reveling in cruelty toward the helpless.

After the trial that violated the glorious and hard-won tenets the pioneers came to America to establish, she was brokenhearted and decided to give up the ways of the white people, as her father had done before her, and completely embrace the ways of her mother's people. She cancelled in her mind any aspirations she had toward becoming part of the fashionable world, and she devoted the rest of her life to helping her people advance in health and education.

She died in need in Tucson in 1923.

In 1962 the Arizona Legislature tardily struck down the infamous miscegenation law that had so long been a disgrace to Arizona and which caused Walker and Chur-ga so much anguish, impoverished Juanita, and broke her heart.

Chapter 12

It was from a copy of the *Phoenix Gazette,* of September 3, 1891, that Jacob Walz, the Old Dutchman of worldwide fame, learned that his closest friend, John D. Walker, had suddenly died the day before in Napa County, California, just north of San Francisco.

As Walz read the brief wire dispatch he must have thought that Napa County was a lonely distance from his village of Blackwater on the Gila River for Walker to die, with not even his beautiful young daughter, Juanita, by his side.

And not far from the thoughts of that dauntless Old Dutchman must have been his own death—indeed, it was to occur the following month—and his immediate situation was even more unlikely than the circumstances under which Judge Walker spent his last hours on earth. Walz was lying sick-unto-death on a makeshift pallet in the living room of a warmhearted black woman, Julia Thomas, who owned and ran a small store and restaurant at 35 East Washington Street, Phoenix, and who was neglecting her little business in order to see that he had food and shelter, and to nurse him back to health, a role that the women of her race have so often and nobly played in America.

Once, when asked what was the reason for her devotion to the desperately ill old man, she said: "Whenever he come to my place, he spoke nice to me, an' ain't many ever done that. Besides he always gave me all the eggs his chickens laid, an' there were plenty others he coulda done hi' self more good with if he gave 'em to them."

Phoenix had suffered the worst flood in its history in March when the Salt River overflowed its banks, and is always referred to in Arizona as the Great Flood. It rose so high in the vicinity of Walz's home on its north bank that at one stage he said he was forced to climb a tall cottonwood tree that fortunately stood just in front of his house. He lashed himself to the limbs with a rope, because at eighty-three he knew that otherwise either lack of sleep or fatigue would soon cause him to fall out.

As the flood waters began to abate and rescuers searched for survivors, Holmes (who made the cufflinks from Walz's nuggets) and Albert Schaffer decided to see if Walz was all right. The adobe, of which Walz's house was made, had by this time partially melted in the flood and they found the Old Dutchman inside its crumbling walls, wet, shivering, and obviously quite sick from exposure and fatigue. The flood waters, now receded, had soaked everything in the house, including the cot Walz was lying on. They carried him to the cottage of Julia Thomas, who they knew was friendly with Walz. As they were taking him there he begged them to be sure and look after his more or less pet chickens, whose shelter had been washed away while they took refuge in trees. They were now scratching happily in the flood-enriched mud, which was teeming with worms and grubs.

While Mrs. Gertrude Barkley, among the many who knew the Old Dutchman, is the only one still alive (as this book is being published), there was at least one other friend—a ninety-six-year-old man, who was alive, hale, and hearty at the time the writer first began working on this book. He was Frank T. Alkire, of Phoenix, Arizona, a member of a still flourishing Arizona pioneer family. He told the writer that on the occasion of the Great Flood, his father, Josiah, who was a friend of Walz's, became worried about the Old Dutchman because the water was known to be extremely high in the vicinity of his house. He asked Frank to go as soon as the water subsided somewhat to see how the old man was making out. Phoenix, an inland city, almost entirely lacked boats. (Frank had become friendly with Walz, a valued customer of the bank where Frank was a teller during school vacations.)

By the time Josiah asked Frank to check on Walz's situation, Schaffer and Holmes had already taken him to Julia's home, where Frank finally located him.

"Walz was lying in a bed in one corner of the front room of her small house, very shrunken and white and didn't seem to have all his senses. I could see he wasn't going to last long," Frank related.

"While I was there a rather curious thing happened which, it turned out, made more of an impression on my young mind than the situation of old Mr. Walz. Julia was throwing a magic powder into the fireplace which produced multi-colored flames, and was charging twenty-five cents for this show to a few people she let in at a time from the large crowd that had quickly gathered in the street outside when the word spread that Walz was in her house and dying. After I left I heard that she later raised the price to fifty cents, and finally, by various stages to two dollars and that, even so, her living room was continually crowded. Some of the customers would have paid any price, and Julia knew it, to get in and try to talk to Walz and ask him questions. But all they got for their money was to see the dancing colors in the fireplace. Holmes, Schaffer, and Julia took turns guarding Walz from anything that might further weaken him. Evidently they figured the heavy traffic in and out of the sightseers was a sort of tonic for him, but that night he could not hear them, or was past caring if he did.

"But Walz rallied somewhat following my visit, which was only the first of many on my part that summer. He hung on until October, when he died in the presence of Julia, Schaffer, and Holmes on the twenty-fourth. They made arrangements with a man named Ryder to build a coffin for him and two days later he was buried in Phoenix Cemetery, Lot Nineteen, grave four.

"A raft of stuff has been written about him since—much of it seemed fanciful to me—but one thing is certain about him: he could be a tough, rough man when necessary. I saw him around quite a bit during the ten years I knew him before he died—Phoenix was barely more than a good-sized village then—and he was its number one curiosity, though perhaps celebrity is a better word. The first time I ever remember seeing him was when I was about sixteen. I had gotten a job working during school vacations as a bank teller, and that very first summer he came to my window on at least three or four occasions. He used to send regular sums to various relatives in Germany, and a few who lived in this country, in St. Louis, as I recall.

"His long, striding walk and unusually erect carriage are the things I remember most clearly about him, because rarely does an old man walk that way, though you wouldn't forget his eyes, either. They were very piercing and when he looked straight at you he always seemed to be trying to probe you."

When Holmes and Schaffer brought Walz from his wrecked home after the flood, he had a canvas sack tied to his belt. In his last hours he stipulated that its contents be divided among the three who were with him at the end. It was found to contain about fifteen thousand dollars' worth of gold-rich concentrate, including a number of pure gold nuggets, some of them good-sized.

The Old Dutchman had scarcely been laid in his grave before a rumor started that during his last moments he had whispered to Julia some directions about the location of his mine. Apparently this story was true, because almost immediately she began an expedition to locate the mine in company with a seventeen-year-old boy, Reiney Petrasch, who had worked in her restaurant, and whose father, Gottfried, was a long-time acquaintance of Walz. She, too, had to slip out and resort to all sorts of evasive tactics as she neared the northwest end of the Mountain to elude the many people who were hoping to follow her to the mine.

After some months had elapsed and she had not found the mine, she appealed to Reiney's father, Gottfried, and his brother, Herman, in St. Louis, experienced prospectors and miners, to come and join her, and they agreed. They helped her search fruitlessly for another year or so, and then they all gave up for good.

Shortly before she died in abject poverty many years later —she had sold her business and beggared herself trying to locate the mine—Julia divulged the details of the information Walz had given her to Jim Bark, a prominent Arizona rancher, owner of the Bark Ranch near the southwest end of Superstition Mountain, who had also been an acquaintance of Walz in his latter years. Bark, who arrived in Arizona in 1879, held many important jobs in the state's history, including first president of the Arizona Cattle-Growers Association, and was one of those to whom Walz would talk casually on occasion. He was convinced that the Old Dutchman had given Julia the correct directions, and following her death he, too, searched for the mine for nearly fifteen years. Finally he formed a partnership with Sims Ely, engineer-manager of Arizona's Salt River Valley Water Users Association, and another believer in the existence of the mine, to help him search. They camped for various periods of almost every year in the Superstitions and searched until they concluded that, short of a foot-by-foot search of the area—an almost impossible task—it was hopeless.

Both Bark and Ely were highly regarded and respected in Arizona because of the reputation for integrity they earned through long lifetimes of holding high positions, and being generally successful in their undertakings. The high estate both had attained in their respective callings, and in the regard of all who knew them, shows that they were unusually astute and straight-thinking men, and makes one wonder what it was that the Old Dutchman said to Julia that made both her and them search for his mine so tenaciously and for so long.

Julia never revealed to anyone but Bark what the Old Dutchman had told her, but shortly before Ely died, after his fruitless years of searching for the mine, he told some of his close friends that Bark had confided to him long ago that Walz had told Julia that " . . . the mine can be found at the spot on which the shadow of the tip of Weaver's Needle rests at exactly four P.M."

The trouble where Julia, and later Bark, were concerned, and countless thousands of searchers since that time, was that this shadow apex follows a slightly curved line that ranges from a compass point of 91 degrees at its farthest southerly point in summer, to a compass point of 51 degrees at its winter solstice. These measurements, plus the fact that the sun's shadow is longer in winter than in summer, causes the shadow's tip to traverse a large fan-shaped area. When the places it rests on each day at 4 P.M. during the 365 days of the year are added up, it can easily be seen that it presented an almost impossible challenge to a lone searcher, or even a group of searchers.

Chapter 13

Just before the turn of the century, a story circulated in Phoenix that three amateur prospectors, J. R. Morse, C. R. Hakes, and Orrin Merrill, Mormons from the nearby colony in Mesa, Arizona, had filed mining claims on an area not far from the site of the Peralta Massacre. Close on this news came another story that caused a virtual stampede toward the old Massacre Ground; it quoted a neighbor of one of these three prospectors as saying that he and his two companions were acting on a tip that Jake Weiser had told his grocer friend shortly before his fatal trip to the mine, that the Old Dutchman didn't have a mine of his own behind Superstition Mountain, but was getting rich concentrate that had been stashed in the Peralta mine Ken-tee had led him to, only a little west of the slope where the Apache holocaust overtook Peralta and his men.

Shortly afterwards the word was out that the mining claims, which the three Mormons called the Mormon Stope, and described as more than a mile or so west of the Massacre Ground, were for sale.

A man named Charles Hall from Denver, then working in Prescott, Arizona, bought their claims for fifty thousand dollars, with twenty-five thousand dollars paid down. He organized a regular mining operation and called it the Mammoth Mine, though it was generally referred to by everyone else as the Goldfield Mine after "Goldfield," the name by which Massacre Ground was sometimes called. The town that immediately sprang up near the mine also became known as Goldfield, and it appears under this name on official U.S. maps today, while the old Massacre Ground is simply marked: "Massacre Ground."

In later years a story got around that all Hall bought for his twenty-five thousand dollars down was the story allegedly told by the grocer that the site of the Peralta mine was on the top of a hill a little way west of the Massacre Ground and was marked by a huge boulder that stood upright on it. It seems that the three Mormons had located the "huge boulder" and sure enough it was on the exact top of a hill overlooking the Massacre Ground, and they filed their claims merely on the strength of the fact that it was the only huge boulder standing upright for many miles around. But they became discouraged when they could find no signs of gold in the area and decided to try and sell their claims.

But after Hall had bought the claims, he revealed that his reasons for buying them were not that simple. "When I heard that the three men had filed out there, and the reason for it, I took a few days off, came to Mesa and rode to the hill on a horse to check around some. Perhaps I was a little more experienced prospector and mining man than the Mormons were, but, anyway, I found some distinct evidence on the surface of the top of the hill where the boulder stood that told me gold ore had been transported over it not too long ago. Therefore, I figured that the active diggings must have been on top of the hill, because why would anyone transport the concentrate *to* the top of the hill instead of down? Another thing, there were no other boulders like that one anywhere in that part of the country. This told me two things; one, it took a great number of men to bring it there and, two, there must have been an important reason for so doing. It became obvious that the purpose was to so plainly mark the location that *anyone* could find it forever afterwards if they had been told what to look for, and only Peralta ever had enough men in that vicinity to get that boulder there."

Hall brought in up-to-date machinery, including a small

stamp mill, hired some men, promoted the building of a few stores, boardinghouses, and saloons to give the budding town of Goldfield a proper nucleus, and began mining rich ore from his claim. It is a matter of record that in a few years he took millions of dollars worth of gold from the Goldfield mine he sunk at the exact top of the hill.

Meanwhile, the mining town of Goldfield, about a mile from the site of the mine, rose to a population of 1,500, and became a rip-roaring pleasure and gambling hell that attracted unsavory characters from all over the West, making it very hard for Hall's around-the-clock shifts of miners to hang onto their pay beyond a few hours after they got it.

From time to time during the course of the mining operation, Hall's miners found many Spanish relics, such as rusted mining tools and weapons, and bones, both animal and human.

Hall crushed and smelted his ore into gold on the spot, and many are the stories that have been told and printed about the precautions he had to take to get the gold bullion safely to Mesa and shipped from there. The West was more than usually plagued by outlaws during those years, and the Territory of Arizona always had its share of those haters of honest work that were a scourge on most parts of the West of that time. Stories about the shipments of gold and silver from fabulously rich mines abounding in the Territory during the 1880s and '90s was one of the main attractions for them, and Hall was almost constantly receiving reports that one or another of them was making plans to hijack his periodic gold shipments. But he always managed to outwit them with the aid of professional gunfighters for guards and new route procedures.

What the Apaches thought of all this can only be conjectured, but they were finally able to point out what they believed their Thunder God atop Superstition Mountain *did* about it. One day after the mine had been operating for a few years, black clouds began to build up and lightning flashed blindingly over the Mountain, followed by a deluge of rain the like of which was never seen before or since in that area. Many of the miners said that several separate torrents of water, miniature Niagaras, could be seen pouring off the crags and down the crevices of the northwest end of the Mountain —the very spot where the Apaches believe their Thunder God abides—to join into a single awesome torrent that swept down a huge, but usually dry wash. Another devastating torrent from mountains to the northwest roared right over Hall's mine and filled all his workings with sand, gravel, and boulders, and buried mine and machinery under thousands of tons of dirt, gravel, and rock.

A short time after the flood, Hall, who was quite old, died, and the mine remained buried. The miners, after waiting a few months, drifted away. Goldfield became practically a ghost town, with only a few merchants hanging on, hoping the mine would be reopened. Today it is set up largely as a tourist attraction.

The ruined mine was inherited by Hall's two daughters, who lived in Denver. Various interests tried to purchase it, and years passed before the estate was settled and the price agreed upon. Then the daughters sold it to George U. Young, an ex-mayor of Phoenix. Young installed new machinery and began probing for the vein, the flood having even changed the topography where Hall had been mining. He employed even more miners than Hall had, and once more the town of Goldfield began to roar night and day.

Not being able to locate the mother lode under the debris, Young sank a shaft straight down as a sort of probe. At about eleven hundred feet—very deep for those days—he hit an underground river that was under such enormous pressure it forced water up the shaft to within one hundred feet of the top of the hill upon which it stood. Although he installed huge steam-operated pumps, they couldn't lower the water an inch. Today one can climb to the top of this hill and look down the open top of the old shaft and still see the water level exactly where it was when the last pumping attempt was discontinued.

When World War I came along, one of the first acts of Congress was to order all gold mines shut down "for the duration." Before Young could get started again after the war to find some new way to combat the flooding, he, too, died.

The property remained in his estate, and his family received many inquiries, but always the negative reports of mining engineers regarding the flooding from the underground river discouraged prospective purchasers. Things dragged along like this for years, until finally the property was foreclosed by a bank, which ultimately sold it to L. Dow Shumway and his brother Ernest, of Phoenix.

Chapter 14

During the years Hall operated the Goldfield mine, and obviously was taking a great deal of gold from the claim, the feverish search for Walz's mine—and all the deadly happenings it bred—went right on over on the Mountain, only a mile or two away. The clanking machinery at his mine, and regularly patrolling armed guards, was too prosaic an operation to interest the type of adventurers who are attracted by stories and legends of a hidden or lost treasure. Some of them probably hated Hall's operation as an unwelcome intrusion, at least insofar as they were concerned, of civilization. What they obviously craved, even if unconsciously, was the atmosphere of deadly danger imparted by the steady stream of killings overtaking searchers for the lost gold mine they sought on Superstition's back-of-beyond.

Swelling the number of prospectors combing the Mountain and vicinity, as well as adding greaty to the carnage, was the effect from the snowstorm of fake maps that began showing up soon after the Peralta Massacre purporting to be true copies of one left by Peralta with his family in Mexico before he undertook the ill-fated expedition that resulted in the massacre of himself and his followers by the Apaches. Others were hawked around by the hundreds as true copies of one said to have been given by the Old Dutchman to Julia. The buyer was assured by the seller that these maps gave directions on how to find what had become known after Walz's death, and after Julia's fruitless attempts to find it, as the Lost Dutchman Gold Mine. These, and many other varieties of utterly false and worthless maps were, and still are, figuratively sold during the dark of the moon and under other contrived mysterious circumstances, often as elaborate as a stage play. The buyer is sworn to secrecy and is warned he might otherwise be killed by avaricious persons who covet the map. The price is commensurate with how much of a fool the con man thinks the buyer is.

He is also cautioned to go alone to the Mountain for the

gold. If the seller is asked why he doesn't go for the gold himself, he usually replies disarmingly that he is too much of a coward to take the risks he knows are involved. The subtle compliment that the map-buyer, of course, *is* a man of supreme courage, seems reasonable to the chump. The real reason the con man wants his victim to observe secrecy about the map is, of course, that he hopes to sell other maps around town.

As you are reading this there are many persons prospecting up back-of-beyond, and others hieing themselves into the Superstitions to scoop up the gold. Some spend large sums in the process and others, lamentably, don't or can't, though "Back of Superstition" is no place to go on a shoestring, or to go alone without eyes in the back of your head. The carnage that has been caused by these maps, and is still being caused by them, and by human greed in its normal course, and by those who seek the Mountain as a perfect place to commit murder for kicks, is incalculable.

"Some of the seemingly well-heeled ones who hire me to pack 'em in," says Tom Daly, "are so secretive about the map that lured them there that it's both ridiculous and pathetic. They will tell me to take them and their too-often skimpy camping outfits [which usually have a telltale shovel and pick bundle sticking out of them] to some point, like for instance the southeast end of the Mountain, and then, they say, they will tell me where to go from there. Periodically they will slip off by themselves behind a large bush, or around a turn of the trail for a few minutes—no doubt to study a map they have in their pocket—and by and by they will come back and tell me to go a little further in a certain direction. This sometimes goes on for days, but sooner or later they imagine they recognize the vicinity they are searching for. At this point most of them tell me they won't be needing me any more. With all that gold almost in their grasp, they are thinking that it would be hazardous to trust me any further. As I leave 'em up there I never fail to hope to God they won't need me again, at least in the way I fear."

An uncanny example of how a prospector can disappear behind Superstition was told the writer in a tape-recorded interview by the late John de Graffenreid, who was another famous guide in the Superstition area. "A few years ago," he said, "while I was packing in some dudes we came to a faintly smoldering campfire over which a skillet was suspended that had warm food still in it. There was complete and rather elaborate camping and mining equipment at the site, but no sign of the owner anywhere around, though he had obviously been cooking a meal a few moments before we arrived. We made a search of the vicinity at the time, and a thorough canvass of the area on the way back a few days later. Everything at the camp was still in precisely the same undisturbed condition as the first day we'd seen it. But whoever its owner was, he had disappeared, no doubt forever. Nor was there the least sign of any identifying marks of anything; it was as if the owner had deliberately made sure that no one could learn who he was by examining his equipment. That sort of precaution wasn't very rare because, probably, these types were figuring that if they didn't find the mine they didn't want relatives or friends, or anyone, to know they'd been searching for it. But I've often wondered what took this particular one off, and why so precipitately while he was in the midst of preparing a meal. Somewhere up there, there are only his bones left now—probably in a deep, narrow crevice, with the skull missing."

Aside from the many identifiable bodies found mercilessly done to death without rhyme or reason, there are countless old, old skeletons of men, and occasionally those of women, scattered all over the immense area that is suspended between the mountains back of Superstition. They turn up far too regularly.

One of these skeletons provides a tantalizing mystery. It was found during the early part of this century in a cave shielded by an overhang thousands of feet up on the side of a precipitous cliff near the top of the Mountain by a hardy prospector who saw the mouth of the cave through field glasses and decided to explore it by means of ropes and pitons. The bones were adjudged by the coroner of Pinal County to be those of a Caucasian girl about eighteen years old with perfect teeth. There were no indications to tell how or where she had died. She had been carefully laid out with her arms crossed on her chest, her legs carefully arranged and a smooth rock placed under her head bier fashion, obviously by someone who had a sentimental attachment for her. The deepest part of the mystery arose from the fact that this person, or persons, had either completely undressed her after bringing her there and carried off her clothes with them, or had brought her there entirely nude. Not a button or other sign of her clothes could be found. Even more mysterious was how she was taken up to that all-but-inaccessible spot if she was already dead; or how she was persuaded to undertake the enormous difficulty of going up there willingly and, if she was persuaded, what reason was given her?

When Barney Barnard died a couple of years ago, he left behind many thousands of words recorded on tape during interviews with the writer relating to events in and around the Mountain. During the over five decades he lived and ranched near the Mountain he or one of his cowboys had to go into the Superstitions countless times to find stray cattle, and never had they been in there through all those years without seeing plenty of signs that a good many people were at that moment prowling all over its vastness. Some were willing to be openly encountered, but others obviously were skulking either in fear of their life because of the precious map they carried or because they were looking for a chance to bushwhack someone.

Barney, a blood brother of the Apaches, held several positions of honor in their tribe. After serving in World War I with two Apache braves of the White Mountain tribe, Homer Red Lightning and Jesse Whitebear, who saved his life during the battle of Belleau Wood. Later in the same battle Barney saved Whitebear's life and was badly wounded in the process—wounds he suffered constant pain from the rest of his life. Yet he never tried to say that some of his Apache blood brothers were not doing some of the killing, especially where the heads were cut off and carried away. Actually, he was convinced that on occasion they *were* doing it. He flatly stated this to the writer. He knew their ways and was in their confidence and realized beyond doubt that there was no length to which fanatics among them wouldn't go to keep undefiled the sacred abode of their Thunder God.

He was often retained by one or another of the various law officers of Pinal and Maricopa Counties to go into the Mountain and search for lost treasure hunters. Besides usually finding the particular ones he was hunting for, he sometimes, during the course of these expeditions, brought out an "extra" murdered body, as well as others dead from various causes, which he stumbled on. He felt the known number of accidentally discovered dead proved many other skeletons must still lie moldering in this almost unbelievable wasteland.

One of Barney's favorite stories was about a tourist named Aloysious Baird, who came from Middleton, Ohio, to spend his vacations in the vicinity of the Mountain each year for about five years. He cautiously probed its outer edges and, in order to find his way out again, carefully studied and memorized the brutal terrain as he advanced further and further each year into its mysterious and deadly depths. On his last such trip he became quite bold and worked his way from the comparatively gentle topography of the southeast end of the Mountain to quite a distance up toward Bluff Springs Mountain, when suddenly he heard shots and what were plainly Indian war whoops coming from over the ridge on his right. "I'll tell you frankly," said Mr. Baird afterwards, "I was plenty scared." Nevertheless, driven by a curiosity too strong to resist, he crawled up the slope until he could peer over its crest, whereupon to his utter astonishment and disbelief he saw a band of Indians clad only in breechclouts and mounted bareback on ponies, pursuing a detachment of blue-uniformed U.S. cavalrymen. The Indians were loosing arrows at the fleeing soldiers, several of whom, as Baird watched in stupefaction, rolled from their horses and fell heavily to the ground. Horses too were falling and rolling end over end. The bluecoats were firing back at the Indians with muskets and scoring punishingly. The screams of the wounded, the neighing of the injured horses, and the sound of gunfire made a horrible cacophony and the carnage was obviously frightful. Then the word "Cut!" boomed out, the leader of the bluecoats held up his hand for his squad to halt and Baird recognized him. He was a famous Hollywood movie star.

Tom Daly also has a favorite story about back-of-beyond. It is about the hair-raising experience he had up there one time. He was moseying along on his horse at the head of a group of mounted tenderfeet over a wild, rough trail near Picacho Butte ("I like to give 'em all the tough horseback riding I can," says Tom), with mules and burros carrying the camping gear following along, when suddenly there burst on their ears what sounded like the most unearthly caterwauling. Quickly shepherding his party into the shelter of a barranca by the side of the trail, Tom tried to locate the eerie screaming. He had about concluded that it might be a lunatic mountain lion, when there appeared around a bend in the trail, a broad-shouldered, stocky figure marching on sturdy legs, dressed in the resplendent tartan kilt of the Scottish high-landers, and squeezing a bagpipe. It was Grady Haskin, Apache Junction's constable, indulging his love for the wearing of the ceremonial dress of his ancestors while he practiced his pipes! "I didn't want anyone to hear me practice," he said sheepishly. Then, peering over the edge of the barranca, he took in the situation at a glance. "This'll bring 'em up out of there," he promised and swung his pipes into a tingling rendition of the March of the Cameron Men. "I'll never forget their expressions," says Tom, "as they scrambled out and saw the colorfully dressed Grady, now playing the pipes tunefully and sweetly in the midst of one of the most desolate regions on earth."

An organization of a group of men active in the business and professional life of Phoenix, known as the Dons Club, undertook some years ago as a public service to cut down somewhat on the loss of life in the Superstitions by giving the tourists who come to Arizona a thrill or two, as well as a warning. They staged a nonprofit day-long outing at the base of a cliff on the southern facade of the Mountain for five dollars per person. A short trek along the canyon into its interior followed, supervised by expert guides among the Dons, who also gave a prepared talk as the short trip into the Mountain progressed. These treks have become nationally known and nowadays the Dons' limit of a thousand persons *always* come. Because of this yearly limit the Dons have set, the tickets are much prized. Most of the tourists go on the trek up into the Mountain over the well-marked trail to a vantage point from which they can get a clear, comprehensive view of Weaver's Needle and, at the same time, a shuddery look at what they would be facing if they ever decided to go in there alone. When these pilgrims return to the picnic grounds the Dons' wives, called "Donas," all dressed in beautiful formal Spanish gowns and mantillas, have a hearty, piping hot supper waiting for them, which is included in the five-dollar charge. After dark a stage show depicts the story of the Peraltas and the Old Dutchman. Some of the Dons play supporting roles, but the part of Jacob Walz was played for some years by a professional character actor, Bob Pollard. The climax of the show is a spectacular "Fire Fall" from a very high cliff, showering sparks down its face in the clear Arizona star-studded night.

The mounting toll of dead—if no more than only those discovered—climbed appallingly as the decades came and went following the Peralta Massacre. The legends attached to their lost mine, or Walz's lost mine, were thick as barnacles on the hull of an old square-rigged sailing ship. The ones who prepared themselves to go all alone into the Superstitions to find the "lost mine" with the aid of the vague and artistically aged map they'd bought were, on the record alone, taking a very grim chance on their lives.

From all over the globe, and especially from almost every part of the United States, there have been men (and sometimes women too) already dead in the Superstitions whom their relatives still thought were somewhere else on an ordinary errand. While unidentifiable skeletons regularly turn up back of Superstition, many of the bodies that *have* been identified were of persons not yet reported missing by relatives. They came, as we said before, from the ranks of those who had been exhorted to adopt this deliberate deception as to their actual motives in leaving their home and loved ones by the heartless scoundrels from whom they bought the inevitable map.

Not all, or even a majority, of those who died on the Mountain met death by foul play, of course. It is easy to get lost in that incredible wilderness and die quickly of dehydration in the desert heat that hovers between 100 and 120 degrees in the summer daytimes in the dozens of deep canyons. Conversely, you can freeze to death up there. The temperature can drop below zero in winter, and blizzards have raged among the peaks.

To add to the danger and misery facing those not wise to the ways of the desert, even the summer nights turn chilly on Superstition's over five-thousand-foot-high plateaus. The conditions surrounding the discovery of a great many of the bodies showed only too eloquently how woefully inadequate were the preparations the treasure hunters had made, and how recklessly they depended on their pitiable map, or whatever, to carry them straight to the treasure without the need for provisions for more than a day or two at most, even to the extent that they had not told their friends, or even their relatives, where they were going.

As an example of this dependence on maps, and lack of proper preparations thus engendered, the sheriff's deputies once identified the body of a man found in the Superstitions, who had not been reported missing, as William Harvey, Jr., from San Francisco, from papers in a wallet found at a meagerly equipped nearby campsite. He practically had no provisions with him at all in one of the wildest spots on earth. No doubt armed as he probably was with a map, he felt that he would be out of the Mountain before needing many provisions, and back home with the gold before more time had elapsed than would have been necessary for the short business trip he had said he was taking.

So many others found killed there had obviously thought the same thing.

Gold alone was merely the synonym—the excuse—used by these adventurers, who were in the majority honest, but plagued by the criminal types who regarded Superstition as their turf. The honest ones mostly *needed* to seek high, wild adventure—the *seeking* alone was the most important thing, though in many cases they may not have realized this themselves. They thirsted, those who came from the quiet places, the backwater regions, the safe jobs and professions, all the vocations that make those who work at them grit their teeth and symbolically gird their loins each morning in horrified anticipation of facing and getting through another day of sameness, to test their manhood, to see how they would stand up to life in the raw. They longed to pit their bodies and courage against the worst nature could throw at them.

Then there were those who perhaps did not think of themselves as killers, but who, when they needed a grubstake, or a burro or two, or they suspected a lonely prospector had some money in his packsaddle, did not hesitate overlong to kill him from ambush, or in any other way handy, to possess themselves of one or all of these "necessities."

As for the born killers at heart, Superstition Mountain was and is, on the record, probably one of the most perfect places to commit murder and get away with it that has ever existed.

Other types of killers also flocked there—those who, as has been redundantly proved by events, and ghastly as the thought is, were tired of killing gentle rabbits, deer, raffish, clownish mendicant bears, moose and sweet ducks and geese —animals and birds which have often demonstrated after being tamed that they probably always longed to be friendly with humans.

Mayhap a few of these "hunters" had been on big game hunting safaris and had been bored by the normal practice of hiring beaters to run animals past them while they waited in safe places with guns ineptly poised, and a crack-shot guide to shoot the trophy if they missed. Now they wanted to hunt back of Superstition Mountain for *human* game. The records show that many of them did so and were successful.

Chapter 15

Adolph Ruth was not thought of as a person easily duped. Rather he was a man noted for his cool analytical mind. But the lure of gold is such that, when combined with the prospect of adventure, it often causes even judicious persons to do strange, often foolish, and sometimes terrible things.

Ruth left his home in Washington, D.C., with a map in 1931, and, driven by the dizzying dreams that apparently beset him after he studied it, went to Superstition to search for the Old Dutchman's mine near the spot where the tip of the phallic shadow of Weaver's Needle touched at 4 P.M.

Various stories have been circulated concerning how Ruth obtained the map that finally led him to camp one night near Weaver's Needle, at a point where West Boulder Canyon, Needle Canyon, and East Boulder Canyon join and flow into the Salt River as Boulder Canyon. One such story is the map was given to him by his son, Dr. Erwin C. Ruth, who had obtained it while working for the U.S. Government in Mexico, inspecting cattle for hoof and mouth disease that were due to be sold to meat packing interests in the States. Dr. Ruth is said to have earned the gratitude of the Peralta family while on this mission, and to show their goodwill toward him they gave him the map that indicated where their family's ancient gold mine was located in the *Sierra de la Espuma*.

Whatever the source of the map that was Ruth's evil lodestar, it is extremely unlikely that it was a valid one. If it came from the Peralta family, and they thought it was a true one, it is hard to believe that they would have turned it over to *any-*

one, much less have kept it under wraps ever since the Massacre, a matter of over a hundred years, without doing something about finding the gold. After all, Sonora is only a few driving hours from the Mountain, and mining arrangements are easy for *anyone* to make with our government authorities. What is likely is that Miguel Peralta never made a map—he knew where the mine was. As for the others, the swiftness of the Apache preparations for the attack and the deadly efficiency with which it was pressed left them too little time to worry about who would work their mine in the melancholy event they were all gathered to their fathers during the coming battle.

It is about as certain as anything can be that depends on humans that the relatives of Don Peralta never knew the exact location of the mine, or during those hundred years they would have made strenuous efforts to profit from it. Miguel probably no more trusted his relatives *in toto* than would any other intelligent leader. No doubt his surviving relatives *did* make secret attempts to locate it from time to time, but fared no better than all the others from around the world who tried the same thing.

However, there is no question but that the elder Ruth trusted and believed in his map. Many facts point to the conclusion that the inner Ruth was a person of fire and courage who only needed an excuse to go adventuring and whose indomitable disposition would have left him willing, if the odds weren't too bad, to risk letting the Devil take the hindmost.

It is hard to estimate the number of people in this world who lead lives of quiet desperation, but they must be in the millions. Dreaming about hunting lost treasure is the mental refuge of a vast number of them, but if they don't break away early enough, age and the infirmities that come with it, especially the waning of the drives and enthusiasms of youth, cause them to wind up after retirement sitting in some city park, or whittling in front of the village general store. Too old for sexual love, they often substitute a love of the sound of their own voice, and more often than not couple this with the fatal conversational fault that many older people have of wanting only to talk of their children, their grandchildren and of themselves, and particularly of the great moments of their youth—things that are absorbing to themselves, but hardly are to anyone else. So they wind up being generally avoided and lonesome as the wind that wanders the prairie.

But Adolph was of different stuff. Some people who knew him well have pointed out that he felt he had lived too quietly all his life, especially during the decades when he worked in government service in Washington, D.C., which to most people is a stultifying existence at best. When he retired with a small but adequate retirement pension for one of his simple tastes, he was only too glad to put all remembrances of things past behind him and to strike out for a new life, one of *high* adventure where he could accumulate experiences that *would* be worth listening to, though he never expected to stop long enough to tell about them.

His first blooding occurred when his younger son, Erwin, and he went to search for a lost mine in the mountains northeast of San Diego, dubbed the "Mountains of the Moon" by those who know them because of their extreme barrenness. It was another supposedly "lost mine" that Erwin had got wind of while he was in Mexico. It was an ill-fated expedition from every standpoint. They spent quite a bit of money outfitting and supporting the expedition and found no treasure. Worst of all, Adolph fell over a cliff and broke one of his legs. The injury never healed well and he had to wear a silver plate permanently attached to the bone and was lame for the rest of his life.

While his accident dismayed his wife and his other son, Early, he himself learned neither caution nor humility from it. A man who knew him during this period says that he didn't mind his cane too much. He regarded it as the symbol of the set of circumstances that brought it about, as something like a badge of courage, and rather preened in front of acquaintances whose idea of daring was to plead with their spouses for one night out a week to attend a lodge meeting.

Meantime, to temporarily sustain the tiger that prowled within him, he had the map that would surely lead him to the Lost Dutchman Mine. How he must have hugged to himself the thought of the desperate rather than glorious adventures he would have as he followed its directions through the deadly maze up behind Superstition Mountain that he had read about—and which had cost the lives of so many, including experienced mountaineers and miners.

Far from fearing the fate that might overtake him if he

made a single misstep in its compounded confusion of draws and canyons and thickets of cactus, mesquite, and catclaw, Ruth was instead of the breed, frail though he was of body, that welcomed such dangers. Of course, his wife and two sons tried to talk him out of it, but can one still the ocean waves with persuasion or march storm clouds in formation? And when has one of his kind ever heeded the fears of their loved ones? Already their eyes are fixed to catch the first glimpse of the far place they are dreaming of reaching and their minds range scarcely a step behind, mostly oblivious to all else.

He had learned quite a few lessons while on that fruitless quest in the Mountains of the Moon, and he put them to good use when it came to outfitting himself for the trip to *the* Mountain. It was in the latter part of May 1931 that he felt his preparations were finished and that he was as ready in all ways as he ever could be. He had bought a used car which he figured on driving from Washington to the vicinity of Superstition, but at the last moment he learned of a man who was going to the State of Washington who would relieve him of the fatigue and boredom of driving his car in return for a ride as far as Phoenix. It took them less than a month to make the journey, even though they lingered here and there in order to savor some of the features of their great country as they drove along.

He had learned from a letter he wrote to a bank in Phoenix that he could probably obtain shelter, advice, and hospitality at the Jim Bark Ranch, which was located slightly southwest of the Mountain. "The ranch is now owned by Mr. and Mrs. W. A. (Tex) Barkley, and you couldn't do better than to let them advise you," the letter said. The ranch was so huge, the letter went on to say, that it encompassed about all the grazing and browsing land there was near the Mountain and in the valleys and canyons of the Mountain, and not only was Barkley, the owner, thoroughly familiar with every foot of the Mountain, but so were his wife, son, and two daughters, all of whom constantly helped the large force of cowboys work the herds.

Ruth had learned from an automobile travel map that Apache Junction was the closest town to the Mountain. When they reached the Junction, Ruth stood with his companion on the porch of a little general store there and looked eastward across a barren stretch of desert, and there was the Mountain, the gigantic and perpendicular cliffs of its west face towering up to five thousand feet and appearing so close in the dry, sparkling clean air, even though nearly three miles away, that they literally seemed to crowd in on him. He caught his breath at the sight and an exaltation flooded through him that brought with it a feeling of almost complete happiness.

Before him in overpowering grandeur was the mighty Mountain he had pictured countless times in his mind's eye—and pictured so inadequately, he now realized—during the dreary years of servitude among the hundreds of thousands of bureaucratic mediocrities in Washington. As he looked at it he didn't even think, any more than he ever had, of the dangers inherent in the scheme he had for despoiling it of its gold. He now suddenly realized that gold was a poor second to the motivation that had been growing in him for years: the determination to wring from the Mountain excitement such as few men have ever known; to challenge it to throw at him the worst it could—and he, armed only with a couple of blankets, a miner's pick and a small shovel, and a few staples, would master it.

The many Zane Grey stories he had read had given him a vivid conception of what living the challenge would be like. Sharp and clear in his mind as he stood there was the picture of him lying between his blankets in the cool winelike air thousands of feet above the sweltering desert, looking at the stars that appear so close in the rarefied air of a mountain top, while the healthy drowsiness induced by a day of prospecting drifted him toward a deep sleep only children and those who work, live and sleep in the open can know. His last thoughts before surrendering to sleep would be of the pot of coffee he would brew in the morning over a bright, hot, almost smokeless little fire he would make from the dry brittle bones of old cactus plants. As he thought about it there on the stoop of that ramshackle little store, he imagined he could already smell the crisp bacon in the pan and the flapjacks he would bake in the bacon-greased pan afterwards.

But his companion on the cross-country trip dreamed no such dreams; he thought of danger as something to be avoided. His ideal of a good life was a comfortable home, a wife who was patient about sex, and a willing, talented cook, with perhaps a meal in some excellent restaurant occasionally to spell her. Therefore, he shook hands with Ruth, wished him luck and Godspeed and cut out for the State of Washington aboard a Southern Pacific train after Ruth drove him to the Union Depot in Phoenix.

That same afternoon Ruth drove back to Apache Junction where he found a cowboy lounging at the general store whom he hired to guide him to the Bark Ranch.

"I recall quite well his arriving at the ranch that evening," Mrs. Gertrude Barkley told the writer during one of the several tape-recorded interviews he had with her about the Old Dutchman and the Mountain. "I happened to glance out the kitchen window where the girls and I were helping the cook get supper and there was an automobile pulling up by the corral near the gate in the fence that we'd put around a half acre, in the middle of which our house sat. I kept a vegetable garden out back and with occasional help from one or another of the cowboys I raised quite a bit of produce in it. The climate being warm most of the time, we always had some fresh green stuff for the table. The fence and the gate were needed to keep the livestock around the place from getting in and enjoying our garden produce before we had first dibs at it.

"I noticed that two men were getting out of the car and, as we didn't have many visitors in those days, I was rather curious about who it was. One I soon recognized as a rather no-account part-time cowboy who did occasional jobs to get money to spend boozing around Apache Junction or for a spree in Phoenix when he'd saved an extra big stake. The other was a little old man, frail, walking with quite a limp and leaning on a cane each step he took. I met them at the door and the elderly man asked if the proprietor of the ranch was about the premises.

" 'That would be my husband, Tex Barkley,' I told him, 'but Tex is not here now. He's up on one of the ranges working some cattle. If you care to come in and sit for a while I am sure he will be back for supper, which we usually have about a half hour from now.'

"I invited him to stay for a bite with us, and with a naturalness that quite won me, he said, 'I would sure like that, ma'am, and to stay a night or two also, if I may,' Naturally I told him we'd be delighted to have him, and the Lord knows I was telling him the truth, because such company coming to the ranch was about the only social diversion we had for long stretches at a time in those days.

"I told the cowboy to go down to the bunkhouse and have something to eat for himself when our cook fed the hands, and make himself at home until the next morning when one of our wagons would be going into Apache Junction and he could hitch a ride with them.

"While we waited for Tex (who incidentally I always called 'Gus' when we were alone together), the stranger told me something about himself. He said his name was Adolph Ruth and that he had driven all the way across country from Washington, D.C., where he had recently retired from government service and that he had come out to Arizona and to our ranch to find the Lost Dutchman Gold Mine.

"Now this didn't strike me as anything at all unusual, because in those days there were always people traipsing back and forth across our ranch to get in back of the Mountain via Willow Canyon, with the announced intention of finding the mine. But of all the people who had stopped at our place for water or food or to get somebody to guide them into the Mountain, Mr. Ruth seemed the most unlikely of them to have a go at it. He obviously was not strong physically, though he had a vigorous voice and fine snapping bright eyes that showed that there was an inner fire in him and a strong spirit. But my common sense told me that his body certainly wasn't up to what he said he was going to put it through. Of course, he didn't know what he was facing on the physical side; no one could who hadn't had thorough experience with this awful Mountain. He told me that he got a bad leg quite a few years ago while searching for another mine in some mountains east of San Diego.

"Adolph was very interested in the kind of work and business we did on the ranch and I told him how Jim Bark had sold us his ranch in 1911 and was now living in Phoenix, and that we ran cattle on all our holdings well into the thousands of head.

"The house we were living in then was, like most ranch houses of that period, rather on the plain side, really it was little better than a rambling shack, and I know he must have been curious about how my big talk fitted into the picture this gave.

"Of course, I couldn't mention it to Mr. Ruth, but Tex was always promising me that when we got rich and prosperous we would have a big, new house, but every time we had a good year with the cattle, the money went back into more cattle, more land and more facilities for the new herds of cattle we were expanding. But you could bet your last calf that making Tex happy was more important to me than making myself happy. He was one of the great citizens who helped build Arizona and, dear God, how I wish he were still here and I still was trying to make him happy and keep the love for me in his eyes that never left them.

"In those early days, from about 1890 to 1946 I punched cattle along with the rest and did a full stint in the saddle almost every day, winter or summer, right with the hardiest of the hired hands. I never took more than a week out of the saddle—usually less—after young Bill and the girls were born. I had a sling rigged to carry them right in front of me, just back of the pommel. Bill actually learned to ride a horse before he was able to walk, and it was about the same with the girls. When a steer would break out of the bunch I would wrap one arm around the baby of the time and ride hell-for-leather after him.

"The babies just loved this part of riding herd on the cattle; I never recall any one of them crying with fear, even when those highly trained horses, almost human in their intelligence and ability to think fast and act accordingly, would cut across the steer, and sometimes wheel on a dime and head him off when he reversed his direction, and most of those rebel steer critters were pretty smart about that. The babies, all three of them, would chortle delightedly through all these tag contests, especially when the steer had a head start and my horse, always one of the two or three finest from our large remuda, would put his belly almost on the ground as he ran flat out to head him. Sometimes I would have to wrap the reins around the pommel and let the horse do all the maneuvering, except for what guidance I could give him with my knees and voice, while I got my rope on a pesky calf.

"It was a rigorous life that called for long hours, hard work, and often brutal exposure to the weather. It can get very hot up in those Superstition Mountains in the summer and very cold in the winter, especially during the long nights and early mornings, but we thrived on it. One day not long ago a friend said to me, 'Do you miss your horse and riding the range, and eating off the back of the chuck wagon?' How can you answer that? How can you put in words how it feels to see the sun come up from the back of a quarter horse, range bred and knowing more in some ways about handling cattle than you yourself will ever know? How can you make people who haven't experienced it know how breakfast tastes after a couple of hours in the saddle? How can you describe what it's like to be accepted as one of the hands by men who are all lean in the waist and broad across the chest and who wouldn't be doing what they were unless they had courage to burn and the character to ride herd on it? I know there is no way to make city folks *feel* what it is like to sit around a campfire after a day of moving cattle from one range to another—not talking much, so tired that just sitting and watching the moon come up to hover over us all is a delicious feeling, but I think most of them can understand.

"These days I live in this fine big house that I had built a few years ago on the top of this hill. It is located on what we called the 'Old Ranch.' I picked the site out long, long ago. Notice how the picture window in front of us frames the finest view of the Mountain there is? But I can't enjoy it any more. I'm totally blind now, and very, very old, but a kind of happiness increases in me these days as I know it won't be long before I'll be with Tex again."

"The night that Ruth arrived, Tex and our son, Bill, brought some of our top hands with them to supper—he'd promised them, as a sort of bonus for some good riding they'd done rounding up outlaw steers, a smokin' hot meal prepared by me instead of having to go to the bunkhouse for their usual chow. He also had two prospectors with him who were on their way out of the Mountain after a disappointing search for the usual thing up there.

"That evening after supper Mr. Ruth talked at great length about his plans and dreams and his hope of finding the Dutchman's Mine, though admitting that he had read about thousands of others who had sought it in vain, and in support of his confidence he mentioned the map and documents he had with him, and which he hoped would guide him to the exact location of the mine.

"You can imagine with what feelings Tex and I listened to this aging tenderfoot tell how he planned to tackle one of the wildest and most primitive areas on earth, where he planned to camp out for weeks at a time with only the meager supplies he had brought with him in his automobile. 'Of course,' he said to Tex, 'I would like to make arrangements with you or one of your men to bring me some new supplies every so often, after someone, preferably yourself, guides me to a place near Weaver's Needle, which I will point out to you on my map.'

"Can you imagine his telling us that he would point out Weaver's Needle for us on his map! We not only saw it practically every working day of our lives, but once you were up back of the southern parapet it could be seen from almost every vantage point on the rest of that old razor blade country up there.

"In regard to practically all the maps people showed up with, Weaver's Needle was the principal reference point which the victim was supposed to find. Back in the very beginning or right after the Peralta Massacre, Weaver's Needle got into the first fake map that was ever peddled, mostly I guess, because Miguel told his family that he used it as a reference point. Then the old Dutchman used it in his instructions to Julia Thomas, and the various swindlers concentrated on this salient landmark, mainly because, no doubt, if the dupe did any checking before buying the map, he would quickly learn that there not only *was* a spectacular peak behind Superstition named Weaver's Needle, but that it was the most prominent landmark there. This tended to give him confidence that the rest of the map must be authentic, too. Invariably traced on the maps, also, were the main canyons of the area.

"Incidentally," she said, "I think that old Walz, like all people who, no matter how sick or hurt they are, are yet certain that they are not actually going to die then and there, gave poor Julia Thomas a cock-and-bull story about where his mine was, figuring, no doubt, that out of gratitude for this she would take good care of him during his convalescence. But whatever his motive, he certainly didn't tell her the truth, and it not only ruined the rest of her life, but raised hell with Jim Bark and Sims Ely too, and they were two of the finest men that ever lived. On the basis of what Walz allegedly told Julia, they devoted all of what should have been the sweet leisurely years of their lives searching for the spot where the shadow touched at four P.M. The Old Dutchman was fully capable of doing such a mean trick, because I've come to believe that to a certain extent he was insane with hatred toward people because of what some of them had done to Ken-tee.

"Naturally, Ruth's plans and map were depressingly old stuff to Tex and myself, and to the cowboys, too, because we had heard it so many times before. For that matter few of our cowboys hadn't had dreams of finding that mine themselves—some, I suspect, are still clinging to them. Many had, like the various tenderfeet, invested in maps from slickers they met in downtown Phoenix while they were taking time out to spree a bit. 'Psst, Podner, wanna buy a map to the Lost Dutchman Mine?' was heard about as frequently around Arizona by tourists in those days as marijuana pitches to college students are today, and the dreams both produce have a lot in common, too, according to what I read. The people who follow these dreams also wind up about the same.

"But most of the people who worked for us in those days soon gave up these notions and tucked their maps away after they had been on a few cattle roundups up in back of Superstition and had a chance to see for themselves one of the wildest and most confusing areas on this earth, and listened to some of the old-timers (anyone with more than a couple of years with our brand, the Quarter Circle D) telling about the number of map owners who streamed into the Mountain each year, a gruesomely large percentage of whom never came out under their own power, or were never even heard of again.

"Naturally Tex did everything he politely could that night to dissuade Mr. Ruth from camping alone in the Mountain, even to the point of flatly refusing to have anything to do with it himself, or to allow any of his men to have a part in it. 'I would feel I would be guilty of risking your life if I had any part in putting you up there where you want to go,' Tex told him.

" 'Well, now, all I want to do for the time being,' said Ruth placatingly, 'is to camp near Weaver's Needle and have a good look at the terrain and the situation, and compare my map and other papers and information I have in my possession with the actual terrain, once I'm on the ground there. Is there any water near that peak?'

"Tex reluctantly admitted that there *was* water about two miles from the peak—clear, sweet water in a spring-fed pool in West Boulder Canyon. Under further pressing from Ruth, Tex said that if one *had* to make his way up to the vicinity of

Weaver's Needle, the best route was up Willow Canyon which began only a mile or so from our ranch. There was a well-marked trail in this canyon, he explained, and on up to a summit near the Needle. From there the trail went down and northwestward into West Boulder, and to the water, which was only about a half mile down from this summit.

" 'I sure hate like heck,' Tex, that big softie of a husband of mine, finally said, 'to see you go ramming around up there by yourself, but if you are bound to go, I'll take you in, if, that is, you'll wait until I come back from Phoenix where I'm shipping some cattle in the next couple of days.'

"Ruth professed himself as being quite pleased and grateful for this offer, and on that note we all went to bed.

"But before sunup the next morning after Tex and the boys had started with the cattle for the shipping station near Phoenix, Ruth, either fearing that Tex would change his mind, or put some other obstacle in the path of his getting up in the Mountain, evidently approached the two prospectors—who had also stayed over night with us—with the proposition that he would pay them well to guide him up to the Needle without waiting for Tex to return. They struck a bargain with him and the first thing I knew about it he was up on one of their pack burros, and they had his gear from his Ford car diamond-hitched on two mules they themselves had ridden into and out of the Mountain. The last I ever saw of Adolph Ruth he was riding that burro toward Willow Canyon, while the two prospectors led their mules. It was the fourteenth day of June.

"The Needle, I might add, was within comparatively easy distance from the ranch. Heck! You could see it after a couple hours' walking. The whole way to it could be negotiated each direction in a day, and it was easier walking back than going up because coming back it was mostly downhill. Though, as a matter of fact, the walk to the Needle from the Bark ranch is not an easy one. It takes a man in pretty good shape to keep steadily walking and climbing until he reaches the Needle. Anyway, the two prospectors returned to the ranch late the next day with their mules and burro and said they had packed Ruth into the vicinity of the Needle and found him a good camping site on high ground not far from the water hole in West Boulder Canyon, and had helped him make camp before they left him. Then they rode off and we never saw them again.

"When Tex came back a few days later and learned about what had happened, he was about as furious as I had ever known him to be. 'That poor old fellow,' he said, 'couldn't find his way alone to our backhouse, let alone to a hidden mine up in that mess behind Superstition, one of the most God-awful places for anybody to try to find their way around in the whole world, I reckon. Look how we sometimes have to hunt a whole herd of cattle up there for days before we find 'em, so just imagine a tenderfoot trying to find a little itty-bitty mining shaft—if there ever was one—that goes into the side, or top, or bottom of one of the hundreds and hundreds of cliffs and clefts up there.'

"He brooded irritably around the ranch buildings most of the rest of the morning, which wasn't like him at all, because he rarely spent any time near the ranch house itself—he liked to be back out on the range the moment he returned from a trip. After a meal and a sleep he would be off again, usually at the crack of dawn. Finally about noontime he came in and told me, 'I've just got to go and find that old coot, Gertie, before the Apaches or some of those characters that are always prowling around up there, broke, hungry, desperate, or just plain mean, kill him, as they've killed so many others, for kicks if nothing else.' "

One can only wonder what thoughts must have been Adolph Ruth's after the prospectors had left him on a rise overlooking West Boulder Canyon and he had settled down for the night. The only sounds that one could hear in the evening then or today up around the place where Ruth camped are mostly quails calling to each other, and coyotes calling to the moon, the scream of mountain lions and wildcats near and far, and the night songs of mockingbirds.

Adolph had, of course, lived a great many years and doubtless regarded himself as a rather sophisticated man, but actually the type of life he had led, with only a few little breakouts now and then such as his search for the lost mine in the Mountains of the Moon area, gave him no idea of the steady percentage of evil characters that humanity produces, and has produced since time immemorial, even though their doings were chronicled day after day in his newspaper. It would have been impossible for him to imagine as he busied himself about his campfire that first night that not far away cruel eyes were watching him from bushy concealment and a plan had been hatched to murder him at the first good opportunity to get an easy shot at his back. At the moment everything must have looked to him as though things were coming his way! He had his pallet shaken down, with his blankets ready to slide between for a long sleep that night; he had had his evening meal over his crackling fire of desert cactus sticks, just as he had always envisioned it. Happy he must have been, and eagerly looking forward to the 'morrow when he would get his first opportunity to check the directions on his map and locate the magic spot marked with an X. Before he got between his blankets he made sure that he was faced where he could see the moon lighting up Weaver's Needle, looking more than ever like the Finger of God, as it did to Peralta's peons.

But the next day was to be his last day on earth. As he rose and had his breakfast he must have been almost beside himself with pleasure and contentment as he brewed his pot of coffee, fried bacon in his pan to just the crisp turn that he liked, and then made himself one enormous flapjack that covered the entire bottom of the pan and soaked it in enough mouth-watering bacon grease to lend it flavor, just like he always thought he would.

Before that breakfast was over, there came the dull crash of a couple of shots from a heavy pistol that echoed back and forth in the canyon, and Ruth was dead before his body crumpled to the ground.

"When Tex reached the area and found Ruth's camp," Gertie said, "he could easily see that the old man had not been there since that first breakfast. He was very adept at reading what the Indians call 'sign'; he had been tracking cattle and the varmints who prey off them, and rustle 'em practically all of his life; therefore, it was easy for him to reconstruct the breakfast, except for the two shots of course.

"He and the cowboy he had brought with him searched for Ruth until nearly dark, then they came back home. Since Superstition Mountain lies in two Arizona counties, Maricopa and Pinal, Tex telephoned both sheriffs. Deputies arrived the next day, and Tex went back up with them to show them the camp and they made another thorough search, but found nothing, and finally gave up for the time being.

"That summer Mrs. Adolph Ruth offered a reward, and her

son, Erwin, came to Phoenix to direct a family-financed search.

"Things continued about like this until December, with the mystery almost continuously occupying prominent space in newspapers and magazines, all around the world. Then the publisher of Phoenix's morning newspaper, the *Arizona Republic,* decided that he would finance a more thorough and more organized search than had been heretofore mounted. He put this expedition in charge of Mr. Harvey Mott, the news editor, and Mr. Odd S. Halseth, an ornithologist and park superintendent of Phoenix. Also included were a regular *Republic* photographer, some trained dogs, a cook, and Barney Barnard for his expert knowledge of the wilderness behind the western facade of the Mountain.

"It was one of the dogs who found a skull on the bushy ridge about one hundred feet above the floor of West Boulder Canyon. Though having no direct proof, the search party strongly suspected that this was Ruth's skull, so they shipped it to Washington to be examined by Ruth's dentist, who positively identified it as that of his former patient.

"Dr. Alex Hardlica, the staff anthropologist of the National Museum, a branch of the Smithsonian Institution, confirmed that the two holes in the skull were what everybody suspected they were—bullet holes that had been fired at an angle which showed the victim had been taken unaware by an assassin who was someone he knew and had reason to trust, or a bushwhacker who sneaked up behind him. Dr. Hardlica gave it as his opinion that the bullet was a forty-four caliber and had come from an ancient model army revolver.

"But where was the body? 'If they can find a thing as small as a skull,' said my husband Tex, 'then they should have kept on until they found the body; it can't be far off from where the skull was.' Finally this curiosity and his pique at the searchers who had found the dismembered head and then abandoned the search, drove him to enlist the services of Jeff Adams, a deputy sheriff in whose tracking skill in wild country he had great confidence. Tex and Jeff went up to the bushy ridge where the head had been found and began making a minute search of the area, traveling in widening circles like the experienced trackers both of them were.

"They soon discovered that Tex had been wrong when he thought that the body must be somewhere close to where the head was found, but they persisted all of that January of 1932 until they *did* find it, in a deep narrow crevice a considerable distance from where the *Republic* expedition had found the head. There was no need this time to send the bones to Washington for identification, for there among the scattered parts of the skeleton was the silver surgical plate from his leg that Ruth had mentioned that night while describing his lameness and a little about how he acquired the injury. Also among the bones were various objects such as a man will have in his pockets—all of which were positively identified by members of the Ruth family when they were shown them.

"But there was no map, a circumstance that to my mind told of the motive for the murder."

The sheriff's deputies did find a little book of Ruth's in which there had been carefully written in his handwriting what were obviously instructions supplementary to the map. It apparently did not occur to the assassin to look in the book once he had located the map in his victim's pockets.

"It lies within an imaginary circle," the words in the little book read, "whose diameter is not more than five miles and whose center is marked by Weaver's Needle among a confusion of smaller peaks and mountains formed by volcanic rock. The first gorge on the south side from the west end of the range—they found a blazed trail which led them northward over a high ridge and then downward into a long canyon running north, and finally to a tributary canyon very deep, rocky and densely covered with a continuous thicket of scrub oak ... about two hundred feet across from a cave."

Then, well down on the page on which this was written were these famous words: "Veni, vidi, vici" [I came, I saw, I conquered], words that hark back to the time of Julius Caesar, who uttered them when he returned from a triumphant campaign.

They were words that produced a worldwide sensation because they comprised the last thing written by a man who was on a quest for treasure, and who had been murdered near the spot where the stolen map said it would be. Did the words mean he had found the fabulous mine after no more than a day and a half on the scene to which his map led him?

The words of Caesar that were borrowed by Ruth were the high point of the murder story and did more than any other feature of the shuddery affair to cause it to continue to be dealt with as a newspaper and magazine sensation, and heightened the speculation, of course, as to who had committed the awful crime.

"Along with the rest of the world," said Gertie, "Tex and I talked it over a great deal. We knew more than anyone else about the last hours of this fine and decent man, and we arrived at the conclusion almost immediately that he was not killed for any personal motives. Even if there were persons who harbored feelings of hatred or revenge against him [which all the evidence showed was extremely unlikely], they hardly could have been Johnny-on-the-spot up there in the Mountain where the murderer was who fired the shots. Nor was it the Apaches. Gus could tell by certain things that it wasn't them. That head being cut off and being carried back to near Ruth's camp, where searchers would be sure to find it, didn't fool him for a minute. In our minds we eliminated all but one motive—what money he had with him and the map—a map that was utterly worthless but deadly, because it got him killed. And we knew that there were only a few people who knew he was in the Mountain with a map, and fewer still who knew *exactly* where he was in the Superstitions during the pitifully brief hours he was there alive.

"Being human, we came to a fairly strong tentative conclusion as to who bore the guilt, but we realized we didn't have anything but circumstantial conjectures to go on, so we had to let it rest at that."

Chapter 16

The deaths on Superstition Mountain have not decreased, but rather increased during recent years. Nor have the bizarre circumstances that attend most of them lessened. The revolting compulsion, for instance, that causes a murderer to cut off the head of his victim is cloaked from understanding by the same mystery that masks the motivation underlying all psychotic acts. The strain of people with this macabre decapitation addiction have strongly featured civilization's every step, and the history of Superstition Mountain is replete with them.

James Cravey, who came from Kansas City, was among those who learned this the hard way as he searched near Weaver's Needle for the ledge of "almost pure gold." Like Ruth, they found his body there with the head missing.

There were many others, such as Dr. John Burns. His extensive medical education could not deter him from leaving his practice in Oregon to respond to the lure of a map he bought that the seller proclaimed would lead him straight to the Lost Dutchman Mine. What he found on Superstition Mountain was a bullet hole through his body that his medical knowledge could not heal. He had been long dead when they found him.

The Mountain serves as a grave marker for Joseph H. Kelly of Dayton, Ohio. They found him there, a victim of the Thunder God's vengeance, and in his pack was a map that he had evidently banked on to head him straight to the Old Dutchman's ledge of rose quartz heavily laced with wire gold. Keeping him company there forever are the skeletons of two California youths, Ross Bley and Charles Harshbarger, whom the searchers for Kelly buried nearby in a common grave.

Charles Massey of Tucson, who had been reared only slightly more than a hundred miles from the Mountain, listening to all the tales—most of them wild ones—that have been told since the Peralta Massacre, nevertheless absorbed enough of what he believed to be the true version and kept a rendezvous with death "up behind the Mountain."

A man with the extraordinary name of Guy "Hematite" Frank, who was wise in the ways of the Mountain and a close friend of Barnard, used to regularly raise grubstakes by working at various jobs and then prospect along the line made by the shadow of Weaver's Needle at four o'clock in the afternoon. He saw the shadow of the "Finger of God" begin its travel one morning, but when it neared the fateful afternoon hour he never noticed it pass over him, though he was lying in its path. Thunder God's vengeance had claimed him.

It is a remarkable fact that despite all the killings that stem from the Peralta gold discovery over a hundred years ago, it wasn't until 1959 that anyone was ever punished for one of them. Benjamin Ferreira, twenty-one, who with his buddy Stanley Fernandez, twenty-two, came from Honolulu to

Apache Junction armed with the inevitable map to the Lost Dutchman Gold Mine, earned this distinction for himself.

Stopping only to procure about enough equipment for a two-day picnic, they hired John de Graffenreid to take them to the foot of a canyon shown on the map they brought with them, where they dismissed him and plunged in. It was their back luck to discover almost immediately a vein of fool's gold many feet thick that glittered in the wall by the side of the trail they followed. The Spaniards, reportedly, were the first to be conned by this vein in the long, long ago. Many others had seen it since and joked about what a fool it made of them. It has a fatal quality of looking more like the real thing than the richest gold ore that has ever been unearthed.

The two young men danced a wild rigadoon in their elation and then broke off a chunk of the ore to have it assayed. That night, April 15, 1959, Benjamin, obsessed by God knows what greedy thoughts that brought on homicidal ones, shot Stanley through the head while he was in his sleeping bag, with the rifle they had bought to protect themselves from robbers should they discover gold. He made his way to Tucson by hitchhiking and then to the nearest assay office, where with no more than a pitying glance the assayer in charge gave him the answer that told him his buddy lay dead in Superstition Mountain for nothing—nothing, and that all he really had for having killed his buddy was the mark of Cain on his brow forever and ever.

He fled to Honolulu, but when Stanley's body was finally discovered he was brought back to stand trial and was allowed to plead guilty to manslaughter.

"There's something out in that Mountain that drives men mad," was his bewildered explanation.

The year 1959 was unusually bad for killings on Superstition Mountain. Ferreira's gunning down of Fernandez was merely the first.

Among the many thousands of persons who heard about the Old Dutchman and Weaver's Needle and the ledge of gold reputedly near it, and have come to search for it, was Celeste Marie Jones. She proved to be one of the strangest of them all as to belief and procedure. A Negress of magnificent physical proportions, Celeste entered the Superstitions a few years ago at the head of a company of workmen and armed guards, and announced that in response to a vision she'd had of its having a solid gold core, she was going to drill a hole clear through the Needle until she reached the "core of gold."

Though her theory was generally scoffed at, she was reported to have recruited several hundred followers whom she had convinced of the soundness of her plan to the extent that they were financing it with small but regular donations. Despite the ridicule and having one of her guards, Robert St. Marie, killed by prospector Edward Piper, she persisted. At last reports she still hadn't given up the idea, though she was in a rest home.

St. Marie, twenty-one, who, before going to work for Miss Jones, had said, "I'm going to find gold up there, or die in the attempt," proved a true prophet. He was shot to death on Armistice Day, November 11, 1959, on one of the highest accessible points on Weaver's Needle, by Piper, who said St. Marie was trying to jump his claim. A coroner's jury called Piper's act "self-defense." A few months later Piper himself found his own death on that claim. An autopsy gave the cause of death as a "perforated ulcer," but the Apaches chalked it up to their Thunder God.

Scarcely two weeks after Piper gunned down Celeste's guard, another name was added to the macabre list. Laverne Rowlee, thirty-two, on a prospecting trip with Ralph Thomas, twenty-six, and Ralph's wife, Donna, twenty-four, was shot through the stomach by Ralph after an argument on the slope of Tortilla Mountain. Rowlee was grateful for the pain-dulling numbness that crept over his body as the eternal shadow closed around him. "It isn't so hard to die," he said comfortingly to the sobbing Donna who was trying to staunch his mortal wound.

A few months later occurred another of those puzzling beheadings that have added so much to the grisly tales of this infamous locality, when a group of amateur prospectors came upon a headless body lying in one of the tortuous defiles that abound behind Superstition by the thousands. Four days later a skull with two bullet holes in it was found a few hundred yards away. It belonged to Franz Harrer, a student all the way from Austria. He had, according to the FBI, mysteriously deserted his studies and added to the American tradition of "dying with his boots on," his head still filled with the dreams that thoughts of gold bring.

Walter J. Mowry was a most unlikely person to be found

shot to death in Superstition's Needle Canyon. He was a fifty-seven-year-old Denver, Colorado, machinist, known to be a very common sense sort of fellow. But they found his bullet-riddled body there on March 21, 1961, after reports had gone around that he and a companion on an earlier trip had discovered traces of gold in the canyon.

The extent of the sadism behind some of the vicious acts that have occurred in the vicinity of Weaver's Needle is hard to believe, even for those who have seen examples of it. Almost on the stroke of midnight on January 19, 1962, a dynamiter blew up the Weaver's Needle water hole—the only water for eight miles in that deadly wilderness. Five prospectors, who were asleep at the time in a dry depression about fifty yards from the spring, narrowly escaped death from hurtling rocks. "I had the spooky feeling that someone was watching me all day," said Bill Gay, a Kingsville, Texas, ranch hand who was one of the prospectors. "I told him he was crazy," said a companion, Fred Hammell, " 'the only ghosts you have to fear are the live ones.' It turned out we were both right." Fred and Bill said they did not know the names of the three others who had camped with them there that night, not an unusual thing among the people who hunt gold behind the Mountain. "I've been going up there for twenty-five years," said Hammell, "and sore feet are all I've got out of it so far, but I'm going to keep on trying."

The only man to have the unenviable distinction of being killed directly *by* Weaver's Needle was Vance Bacon, thirty, a Phoenix mining engineer, who was hired by Celeste in 1963 to plan procedure for further work on the mining operation involving her tunnel through the Needle. On March 25, Bacon, with a companion, Ray Gatewood, after climbing to the top of the Needle, slipped and fell five hundred feet to his death down the sheer east face of the extinct old volcanic plug, which is what Weaver's Needle really is.

A good year for the Thunder God vengeance was 1964.

Jay Clapp has the year 1964 engraved on his tombstone. He was a determined man with courage to burn, as the saying goes, and had a lifetime dream of some day finding the Lost Dutchman Mine. He had bought the equipment for the long search in the Superstitions that a study of the subject told him might be necessary, and he had saved enough money to last him over at least a five-year stretch of prospecting, no matter how tough. The feeling of the bulge the money belt around his waist under his shirt gave him was good, and his study of the needs and difficulties involved had not only made him expert from a logistical standpoint, but had left him with absolutely no illusions as to the dangers involved.

He entered the Mountain over what's known as the Dons' Trail riding a mule and leading a pack mule and a pack burro. On March 22, 1964, David Hermosillo, thirty-two, from Indio, California, was also looking for the Dutchman's mine about five miles northeast of Weaver's Needle, stumbled across a skeleton wearing a backpack and minus the skull, which even a minute search of the area later failed to turn up. Papers in the knapsack revealed to Sheriff Coy deArman of bordering Pinal County, whom Hermosillo guided to the scene, that the headless skeleton was that of Jay Clapp. They never found his head.

Next to die on Superstition's fearful ramparts were two young men who dared to invade the area made sacred to the Apaches by their religious beliefs. Of those who have died there, Richard Kremis, twenty-one, a boy more handsome than most movie stars, and his brother, Robert, seventeen, had much to lose, for they were talented, physically attractive, and barely on the threshold of lives that promised them much because of the lavish endowments of nature with which they were so blessed.

They parked their car near the foot of the Mountain on November 15, and began their climb at daybreak. "We're going hunting," Richard said to his bride, Barbara. The next time she saw him was five days later when Robert and he were carried from the Mountain by sheriff's deputies, after having been found dead at the foot of one of its cliffs. J. D. Breedlove, Pinal County undersheriff, told her as gently as that rugged man, a veteran who had seen many grisly occurrences could, of her handsome young husband's fate. "From what I saw and judge," he said to her, "one fell and the other plunged while trying to rescue him. No man can be greater than this. . . ."

People who live near the Mountain never cease to marvel at the diversity of those who respond to its Lorelei-like quality. They might have thought that a folksinging and recording star, such as Dolan Ellis, nightclub owner and a member of the New Christy, Minstrels singing group, had already made enough money so he couldn't care less about whatever in the way of monetary rewards the Mountain might hold. If so, they were understandably amazed when on March 25, 1965, Ellis suffered severe cuts and broken ribs when he fell one hundred fifty feet down a defile near Weaver's Needle. He was lifted out by an Air Force helicopter, after a companion, Dale Wright, went for help.

The Apaches are coming to believe more strongly than ever, as do an impressive number of other people, that it is indeed the curse of the Apache Thunder God on those who defile His sacred abode that causes many of the unpremeditated murders as well as other kinds of killings and tragedies on the Mountain.

But the writer's years of searching out its history and affairs convinces him that at least some of the tragedies stem from the pervasive atmosphere of fear that seems to grip many once they are in its inner maze—the frightening aspect it impinges on those who approach its deadly interior for any purpose. Perhaps they look at their companion and think how many times in similar circumstances there one has murdered the other, or they reflect on the countless people who found death lying in wait for them around the bend in the barranca, or from behind a boulder, and soon become so jumpy and distrustful that fear causes them to do things that would be inconceivable under any other circumstances.

Perhaps a little cabin fever gets into it, too. Everyone has heard how it works on partners who make a gold strike, but are caught in the winter snows before they can get out to civilization and have to winter together under conditions that make for morbid thinking, until finally one, or both, imagines the other is out to kill him for his share of their stake. The result is almost inevitable.

Below is an exact copy of a news story that appeared in the *Arizona Republic* of May 19, 1966.

Apache Junction—An attempt to stifle a yawn resulted in the accidental shooting of a 20-year-old Californian while on a trip into the Superstition Mountains, Sheriff Coy deArman said yesterday.

The victim, Dale Vandeman of San Bernadino, was rushed to Mesa Southside Hospital for emergency surgery late Saturday after a bullet from a .357 magnum revolver tore through his body.

Officers said Vandeman was visiting Jack Rogers, a prospector, in the Superstitions, and dozed off while holding the revolver with his left thumb hooked in the trigger guard.

In waking, he told officers, he raised his hand as he yawned, and squeezed the trigger.

Chapter 17

It was only natural that the lure of possible, even probable, quick riches attached to Superstition Mountain would attract some honest characters—those who would come in good faith to prowl the heights, canyons, lofty plateaus and mesas behind the Mountain, legitimately looking for the legendary gold mine.

It is even more to be expected that its infamy would beckon to blacklegs, tinhorns, and sharpers of all sorts—such as the bush league con men who peddle maps for what the traffic will bear—but fakers all, down to the sorry barflies who for a drink at the nearest bar will offer to reveal the "real story" of the Old Dutchman.

Among the thieving gentry mentioned above, there will always be some who are steel-nerved—the aristocrats among thieves, who lend spice to their noisome professions. These do not cavil, of course, at trimming an easy mark, but much prefer, when the stakes are high enough, to engage in one of the most dangerous ventures known to man: preying on killers, desperadoes, sadists and psychotics, and the latter, when attracted to the Mountain for any one of several nefarious purposes that might be their individual bent, were often victimized by those artists among con men who like their knavery to be dangerous. The con men then took to living abroad, one presumes.

But within the past decade or so, the spreading and enormously lucrative industry of tourism has discovered Superstition Mountain's potentiality as a tourist attraction, and legitimate promoters and entrepreneurs of all sorts and shades interested in catering to tourists have also been drawn to its vicinity, in ever increasing numbers. Mostly they settle in and around Apache Junction and begin besieging prospects far and near by mail with brochures and long-distance telephone calls boosting real estate opportunities near the Mountain, or with prospectuses extolling the enriching potentialities of stocks or partnership shares in enterprises that the Mountain would shill for, so to speak.

These printed appeals invariably feature beautiful pictures of the Mountain, usually in color and contain glowing prose. They are aimed at romantics all over the world—people who might like to settle down where they can see the Mountain every day and, if they have a dash of adventure in them, stroll in the shadow of its awesome crags, sort of nibble around the edges of adventure as it were. Appeals were also directed to those who might want to pay only a temporary visit to a vantage point near the Mountain and who could afford air-conditioned hotels, motels, and amusements. If they were potential investors, they were urged to consider becoming a canny business type and financing some of these conveniences for visitors.

The Mountain does have a considerable appeal for tourists, curiosity seekers, the unabashedly morbid, the on-the-level prospectors, and people just wanting to linger in the vicinity, drawn by the tantalizing nearness of the lost mine and the noisomely blossoming reputation the area that cradles it has for evil happenings.

Most of the promoters had the hard practicality indigenous to financiers who know that dreamers can be made into good customers by convincing them they are "canny business types," and playing on their hope of acquiring a lot of money which can be used to pay off the mortgage on the house, get personal debts off their backs and rid them of all financial needs—needs that sit heavily on their minds and wake them in the still of the night, when they only want to sleep and perchance to dream of the exotic things that money—big money —can buy.

Along with them came unscrupulous promoters—quite a few of them, really—who adopted various shortcuts to wealth while using the lure of the lost mine as bait. Their favorite gambit was to produce a piece of rich gold ore and claim they had discovered the Lost Dutchman Mine and had got the

piece of ore there. They would then brandish an assay of this
ore that seemed to prove their "mine" was enormously rich
and, it usually turned out, they had already organized a
company to exploit their discovery and were offering to sell
stock in it to the public.

One larcenous trio of recent note got up one of these stock
ventures, and their stock sold like hot cakes on a frosty morning. They even stung some people in Apache Junction with
this stock, and they are known to be the hardest to sell of anybody in the world in regard to get-rich-quick schemes connected in some way with the Mountain. But, alas, the tricky
entrepreneurs in question overlooked some detail or other and
brought the FBI into the situation, who threw 'em into jail.
Then came the sad, but wholly expected, denouement that
they had *not* discovered a rich gold mine. They had not even
found the chunk of rich ore. An uncle of one of them could
testify that it was rich in gold all right enough, and he could
further testify that they'd stolen it from a gewgaw cabinet in
his parlor.

All in all, only a small percentage of the promoters who
tried to use Superstition Mountain as a shill had a streak of
larceny of undue proportions in them. Most of the promo-
tional-minded gentry who showed up were naive. They had in
mind making an honest buck. They also had small amounts of
money to invest in such things as sandwich shops, laundro-
mats, filling stations, barber and beauty shops, and appliance
repair shops. But they quickly learned that there were already
enough—and more than enough, few though they were, of
such facilities in Apache Junction and its immediate vicinity.
The crying need was for some dreamer-promoters who could
promote new business ventures for the area, and at one and
the same time create a market—customers, in other words—
for these new ventures.

Looking back it seems inevitable that one day an honest
dreamer of heroic stature *would* show up in the vicinity of the
Mountain, equipped by training and experience to take advantage of the business opportunities inherent in a situation
where transient people were being brought, literally in droves,
from all over the world by the mystery, drama, and challenge
in the stories about the potential riches waiting for the one
who could find the lost gold mine that was within a half-day's

walking distance of Apache Junction, and all of whom had *some* money.

Such a dreamer was W. Winfield Creighton—a man highly skilled in smoothness and persuasion who had acquired considerable experience in ramrodding large promotions.

When he stopped at the Junction's dusty little crossroads filling station one day in 1955, he was on his way, with his wife, Phyllis, to Houston, Texas, he afterwards told the writer, to consider taking part in promoting the new Champions Golf Course there which was then in process of being launched by famed professional golfers Jimmy Demaret and Jackie Burke, who have since been made multimillionaires by this already famous golf course and real estate venture.

"At that time this tiny community," Creighton said, "consisted, believe it or not, mostly of an old saloon, a restaurant, a few scattered houses, and a small roadside zoo that had a complement of little desert animals. Superstition Mountain was about three miles away, but in the clear desert air it appeared so close to the filling station that it almost seemed I could put my hand out and lean up against it.

"Of course I had often heard about the so-called Lost Dutchman Mine, and its supposed location in the Mountain, and the countless murders that had occurred on that mysterious-looking mass of high crags and cliffs, but the stories had failed to fascinate me to the extent they had so many others. However, as I stood there that day I could suddenly feel the pull of the Mountain, as I still do to this day. An overpowering conviction came to me then and there that I could never be satisfied until I had explored it. I figured I'd need about a week, but soon months slipped by and I found myself firmly hooked by its mystique as so many others have, and the deal in Houston forgotten insofar as I was concerned. I realized by this time that I wanted to *live* in its vicinity and I began to look for a convenient business opportunity.

"Checking into local history a little, I found that at the turn of the century the area around the base of the Mountain was barren desert land for many miles in every direction, crisscrossed by two dusty roads. With the building of Roosevelt Dam in 1906, Apache Junction came into being where the two roads crossed, one an old Indian path known as the Apache Trail which led to and from the Dam, about thirty miles away, and the other the main road from Tucson and

Florence, to Mesa and Phoenix. In February of 1923, George Curtis, a native of Logan, Utah, came to the area with his wife and three small daughters and filed for title on the site. Two weeks later he pitched a tent under a large ironwood tree and became the Junction's first entrepreneur as well as its owner.

"I learned that some two hundred acres of land embraced this whole little town, and that all of it was now held in a forty-nine-year leasehold by Hugh Evans, a Phoenix real estate developer, and was available for purchase. The idea of buying this leasehold and developing the area to take advantage of the flood of tourists I felt could be attracted by the Mountain was a powerful stimulant to the promoter in me, and I agreed to buy it after only briefly considering its seemingly limitless possibilities.

"In effect I now had ownership of an entire town, such as it was, and my main project was to develop facilities so that all those attracted to the vicinity by the fame of the Mountain would tarry and spend money on the various types of accommodations I planned to build for them. The former junction of two narrow dirt roads smack dab in the center of my newly acquired property, now had grown to *four* federal highways, 60, 70, 80, and 89 and one state highway, 88. It seemed to me the most ideal spot for a promotion that I had ever seen."

Creighton knew that most of those who came to find the Lost Dutchman Mine, or to dream over it, did not come to exploit or hurt anyone; nor were they merely dreamers. Deep down they had a practical streak that made them realize that while a dream could be a starter, it took work and initiative to get practical results. They were ripe for any kind of opportunity that would support them and let them live near enough to occasionally prospect the Mountain. What mostly made them tick was that they were the kind who are never satisfied until they know for themselves what is over the sea, or where the horizon meets the plain, or around the bend in the river, or on the other side of the mountain—any mountain.

They came from the farms and the hamlets and the teeming streets where the residents and their burgeoning broods are continually boiling onto the sidewalks to add to the yeasty ferment that is producing the bold leaders of tomorrow; and they came, too, from the expensively quiet streets in the cities where some of the residents only have distinction inherited

rom those long dead, and what pallid life there is goes on
ehind heavy drapes.

The world is full of people who would like to flee their lives
f quiet desperation, and most of them are cradling a dream
—a dream in which they are not mere spectators, if even that.
ather they see themselves walking and laughing and loving
hrough scenes of gaiety. They do not crave to look into
ored eyes that have seen the whole of it, or fondle one whom
nuch past experience has made a jaded critic. Instead they see
hemselves lighting faces hungry for laughter, and foregather-
ng with those who, like themselves, are eager to know the
eautiful and the glamorous and stroll untouched meadows,
nd surmount unvisited peaks, which the plentiful possession
f gold makes so easy.

Behind their desks, machines, social duties, and over their
inks and farmland, they dream of Monte Carlo, Las Vegas,
unken treasures—and the Lost Dutchman Mine, and the car-
ival and excitement that gold can bring them, if only for a
ay or a week.

The factory worker's whirring machine may dissolve to a vi-
ion of kaleidoscopic lights in an infamously gay theater
here young, beautiful, bare-breasted girls emerge before the
iewer as casually as a flower unfolds from a bud. Gold can
o easily make this vision a reality.

The social worker, revolting against the unrelieved diet of
irges, slatterns, and drunks that are his daily fare, dreams of
orld-famous comedians who can make him laugh and laugh
nd forget all but the moment.

The tractor pulling the gang plow can be daydreamed into a
indswept convertible, its engine singing a song of power, and
1e tires humming vagabond counterpoint over the long,
nooth roads toward shining cities in the distance, while seat-
d beside the driver is a laughing girl, her hair blowing in the
ame wind that molds her thin dress to the delights of her
ender body, projecting a vision that is the wellspring of all
1at makes man what he is.

How many haven't dreamed of an evening when Lady
uck was making them her darling at a green baize-covered
ible with the wondrous designs painted on it, and in its
enter the magical, glittering, delicately balanced wheel that has
ore power than Aladdin's fabled genie to produce the gold
1at makes dreams come true.

Or while the dice are obeying one's every exhortation, a
one's elbow a beautiful young girl crowds close. Maybe she'
the wife of some decrepit old count who is at the momen
doddering about his moldering castle several thousand mile
away, while the frustrated young countess, toying with th
idea of seduction, might turn and say: "Oh, Monsieur, you s
prodigieux wiz ze dice. Pairhaps you would be so kind as to
show me how I too can win so much monee?"

Daydreams are everyman's defense against the frustration
and despair that must come to all who hew the wood, draw
the water, nurse the machines and till the crops of the land
How many men are there who haven't longed to climb th
Matterhorn, or spend an afternoon dominating the brav
bulls, or to gun a jet plane through the sound barrier, or per
haps punch the heavyweight champion square on the butto
and see him sink slowly down, or bet on the wheel, the dice o
the cards and let his winnings ride and ride until the pile o
chips before him is high enough to make his most extravagan
dreams come true? Who hasn't cornered in his dreams a stoc
on Wall Street? Or found a vein of gold in a far, wild place
say Superstition Mountain?

Luck coupled with daring can bring gold in great quantitie
—it has happened, often in Las Vegas and Monte Carlo, o
Wall Street, at Sutter's Mill, Virginia City, and from a ticke
on the Irish Sweepstakes. The beautiful, desirable, titillatin
things of stone and brick and mortar and diamonds and ru
bies and emeralds and precious furs, and things wondrousl
fashioned of gold and steel can come from the impetus o
dreams. Dreams furnish the seed for actions that bring thing
that are different and put people in places where longings ar
fulfilled, where glamor and excitement and gaiety permeat
the air. But always the dream must come first.

"I have always loved to dream, but never before Supersti
tion Mountain and its Lost Dutchman Gold Mine did I fin
the reality to match them," Creighton told the writer. "Bac
in the days when I was wandering from job to job, promotio
to promotion, trying to find the one that held the promise
dreamed about, I don't know what I would have done withou
dreams. They were my shield against often disheartening cir
cumstances. In large part the dream is the best thing, or a
least it often has been for me. Often—very often it was th
only satisfaction or profit I gained from some best-forgotte

venture or other. Without a dream to gloss things over for us, or to lend at least some lure to what so often turn out to be humdrum necessities, the lives of even the most accomplished or luckiest of us would be much poorer; indeed some of us would hardly have a bearable life at all.

"*Now* I had a dream about exploiting the Mountain and it was utterly consuming me."

To handle the various deals he envisaged to exploit the fascination of the Mountain, Creighton organized a stock corporation called "Superstition Mountain Enterprises, Inc." In time, such were his remarkable powers, there came to be associated with him in this corporation and others he organized to develop the Junction, many resplendent financial figures in Arizona and Texas, including John Mills, Robert Foehl, George Wolf, Lewis Himmelstein, all wealthy, most of them multimillionaires. They are men whose very names are bywords in Arizona, and most other places in the United States, for solidity and financial success and probity in their dealings.

Men like these are not easy to "sell" on the stuff of dreams, but it was as easy as eating Mom's apple pie for Creighton to sell his dreams to these men of wealth and accomplishments, because he had first sold them on himself. He was a master beguiler at any time, and his own deep conviction regarding the potentialities of the Junction increased his entrancing powers many times over. Part of the proof of this are the millions of dollars his money men soon invested in his grand design.

With his dreams serving as a sort of blueprint, Creighton and his backers began working wonders with that once "dusty little crossroads."

"Our first break," Bill said, "was in getting a contract to build a U.S. Post Office there. Then I began bulldozing down all of the nondescript buildings."

One of Creighton's most notable—almost incredible—accomplishments was getting federal highway 70 renamed "The Lost Dutchman Gold Route." It begins on the Atlantic Ocean at Morehead City, North Carolina, and runs clear across the United States to Los Angeles. It officially received its new name in October 1961, during an impressive dedication ceremony that was held at Apache Junction. Among the notables on hand was Wesley Bolin, Secretary of State of Arizona, Dr. Werner Leinz of Baden Württemburg,

West Germany, as official representative from the German state where Walz was born in 1808, and Dr. Edward Schneider, West German Counsel General in Los Angeles. Representing the U.S. 70 Highway Association was its president, J. J. Di-Paolo and Joe Dubois, association vice president.

When Creighton heard that the Houston Colts might be interested in doing their spring training in the vicinity of Phoenix, as the Giants and Boston Red Sox were doing, he approached Paul Richards, general manager of the Colts, on the proposition that his team train at Apache Junction. He was told that Richards might consider it if the Colts had a baseball park, a grandstand and all the other things that go with it for exhibition games for people who would pay to see them practice. "We'll build one," Creighton said, "one of the very finest and according to any reasonable specifications you may advance."

Organizing the Lost Dutchman's Baseball Corporation to be run by a nonprofit committee, and raising $150,000 to build a beautiful ball park, which was called Geronimo Stadium, and another $24,000 as a guarantee to the Colts against gate receipts, seemed to be a breeze for Creighton, who had by now convinced many that before long a metropolis would rise at Apache Junction, over which Superstition would brood, somewhat like the Acropolis over ancient Athens in Greece.

The grandstand, though surrounded by barren desert, nevertheless has the advantage of facing the Mountain, and when the fans found the action slow on the base paths they could shift their eyes to the towering ramparts of Superstition and speculate on all the goodies that could be bought with what it was hiding, and have shuddery thoughts of what might be going on up there that very minute!

Since then the Colts have moved out, but the San Francisco Giants replaced them at the Junction, and train there every winter and spring.

Next, to the utter amazement of the people who had been living in rather inconvenient circumstances in the vicinity of the Mountain, Creighton induced one of the largest chain grocers in the West, A. J. Bayless, to build in his little town a modern supermarket with 24,000 square feet of floor space— a market that rose literally in a sea of cactus. As a matter of fact there's a great deal of cactus surrounding it today.

A gift shop and a modern restaurant were soon opened, followed by a typical old western-type saloon, a barber shop, a beauty shop and many other business facilities needed to make a community complete.

Then came a bank, and the post office increased its floor space from 1,280 square feet to a total of 8,000 square feet. Several gasoline stations soon followed, and many more stores.

"One day," says Creighton, "I was standing in the middle of *my* town and looking at all of these beautiful new business buildings that were up and operating or in the process of being built, and houses being built in every direction from the crossroads, and I glanced over to a large vacant lot across from the junction of the five great highways and envisioned a beautiful modern hotel standing on it. Suddenly it seemed perfectly natural to me that there should be one there."

Soon, his momentum was such, he had organized the Superstition Mountain Hotel Company, and in a matter of a year and a half there was a hotel, the Superstition Ho, on the site—a two-and-one-half-million-dollar structure second to none in beauty, convenience, and construction, with 146 rooms and several large public rooms for convention and entertainment facilities. It opened in September 1960. The convention hall will seat and feed 350 people at a banquet comfortably.

A championship golf course came into being just up the road on the newly organized Apache Country Club Estates, with Lorne Greene, star of "Bonanza" beating the propaganda drums for it. They made him a vice president and director of the company. In a letter signed by him under the company letterhead, he said in part, ". . . Apache Country Club Estates, as we see it, is for those who can sense the differentness as they enter Pueblo Drive and face the world-renowned Superstition Mountain." They built him a home on the property that is supposed to be an exact replica of the famous ranch house he and his TV sons use in the filming of "Bonanza."

Along with the great material growth of the area its spiritual growth kept pace. A new Catholic church was built, as well as one for the Latter Day Saints, and the Baptists built one there, too. Others followed.

Today any town worthy of the name has various service

clubs, such as Rotary, Lions, Kiwanis, and a Chamber of Commerce, and now Apache Junction has these also.

Smack dab up against Superstition Mountain, with no other dwellings within miles of it in any direction, Creighton promoted an amusement project called Apacheland. Apacheland is a replica of the Old West of around the 1880s. Over $400,000 was invested in it. Among its other facilities for attracting tourists are complete western streets upon which to shoot western movies. He bought the land for it from Mrs. Gertrude Barkley.

A mile or so away Creighton had caused to be built a sound stage, also on former Barkley land, in the most modern manner and with all the latest technical equipment to shoot the indoor scenes. A number of Hollywood movie companies used both facilities to make many films there, and segments of quite a few TV shows, including "Have Gun Will Travel" and Dick Powell's "Stage Coach West" were made there, and today there is a waiting list for the facilities.

To get the fullest use from Apacheland's appeal, Wild West shows are staged there daily in season, admission one dollar. Scenes, supposedly from life as it was in the Old West, are enacted in the main street, such as shootouts, bank robberies, and the comeuppance badmen receive who come to terrorize the good people of a town, fondle the saloon girls without paying, and drink at the bars for free. Always the badmen ride black horses and are dressed in black, complete to the inevitable black hat, black holster and black waist-type bandolier belt. As they emerge from the bank carrying their sacks of swag, presumably the savings of honest cattlemen, good guys gallop up on white horses, arrayed in white, like angels, and mow the varmints down with their white-handled six-guns, all but one varmint that is: the leader who, his gun shot out of his hand, perforce must use his fists to fight it out man-to-man with the leader of the good guys whose gun is now empty. It was wondrous to behold how popular these shows have become, with the tourists flocking there from every point of the compass. Over fifteen hundred of them have come to a single afternoon show.

One of Creighton's favorite stories, with which he regaled newcomers, tells about the girl who runs a gift shop in Italy.

t seems that a vacationing schoolteacher who taught at the
Junction went into the gift shop and was waited on by this
pretty girl who spoke English. After making a purchase the
teacher said: "I'd like them shipped to Apache Junction,
Arizona, U.S.A." "Do you live in Apache Junction?" asked
the girl. "Yes, do you know where it is?" "Certainly I do," she
replied, "everyone who reads does. It is right at the base of
Superstition Mountain where the Lost Dutchman Gold Mine
was been lost, and where my Uncle Angelo is going some day
and find it. His cousin, Guiseppe, whom he once helped get
out of jail, has gone to America where Providence gave him
an opportunity to buy for a large sum a wondrous map. Uncle
Angelo has sent him the money to buy it and it will lead them
straight to the whole mountain of gold!"

Ken, Jack, and Tom Cordalis figured that a restaurant
under the tallest and most vertical cliff on the Mountain
might be a good thing for all those pilgrims who would be pow-
erfully attracted by the prospect of dining well that far up
its slopes. They selected a truly spectacular spot from every
standpoint. Calling their courageous venture the Superstition
Mining Camp Restaurant, they managed to haul enough material up to their site to build a large rough building with a
plank floor. They furnished it with long unpainted "scrubbed
white" plank tables, and benches for the customers to sit on.
They had a dirt road scraped in from several miles away, and
advertised that they were open to serve customers "Just like in
the old mining days . . . when cook shanties were an important part of the mining camps throughout Arizona territory.
'Come and get it," said the ad. What would be waiting for
you, it promised, was mouth-watering, such as, "all you can
eat from heaping platters of roast chicken, and big juicy slices
of sirloin roast beef . . . daily specials include baked ham, wall-
eyed pike, prime ribs of beef, or charbroiled steak . . . coleslaw
in big bowls, big tureens of oven-hot baked beans, and large
baskets of sourdough rolls, blueberry muffins, homemade raisin
bread, with huge pitchers of milk and coffee—and everything
set on the table at the same time."

The thought of getting all these succulent viands in a setting
incomparable for wildness and danger proved irresistible, not
only for countless tourists, but residents of Phoenix and envi-
rons, too. The venture was a huge success and rapidly became

nationally famous and the "in" place for Phoenix and vicinity
—a fabulous place for Phoenix residents to take their relatives and guests from back East.

Chapter 18

During the years that the appearance of the Mountain's
neighborhood was being changed by Creighton, et al.,
modern methods in murder and sadism in regard to the killings, deaths, and disappearances on and near the Mountain
were more than keeping pace. The manner of some of them
paled by comparison the most grisly of those that had in
years past become settled Superstition Mountain legends.

Anno Domini 1964 in particular, proved this by the
number of murders and deaths that occurred on the Mountain
during its span of twelve months. Also, it demonstrated that
the one-hundred-year-old lure of the gold the Mountain was
supposed to be hiding on its blood-soaked heights had not di-
minished for honest prospectors and adventurers, any more
than it had for those who have always figured that the Mountain is a safe place to prey—those to whom murder and pil-
lage are what working for wages is to others. Herbert LeRoy
Shockey, thirty-one, was eminently of this latter breed.

He earned the revolting distinction of producing the most
hideous of the dark deeds that have made the name of Superstition Mountain almost a synonym for deadly ambush and
bushwhacking, the number and ferocity of which have no
parallel in connection with any other locality where man has
searched for lost treasure.

Herbert evidently fancied himself as somewhat of a reader
and a thinker despite an almost perfect record of failure in
benefitting from what formal schooling he had been exposed
to. When he read in a newspaper article about the number of
murders that have occurred, and were occurring on the "Mur-
dering Mountain," and that no one had ever been tried for
them, with the sole exception of the trial in the case of Ferreira that produced a slap-on-the-wrist manslaughter verdict,
he thought that here was a territory made to order for the

methods he had in mind to finance goodies for himself without having to work for them as do squares.

Picking up his seventeen-year-old girl friend in California, he motored straight for this Mountain of opportunity for killers. He planned as his first project there to obtain by robbery the best equipped housekeeping trailer he could find—an equipage he particularly longed for. He noted in several articles about the Mountain that some of the people who were attracted by the Mountain came to it outfitted with expensive gear, and traveled in trailers and buses marvelously equipped for keeping house in its foothills.

Judging by subsequent events one wonders if he believed that murder would be the most convenient and least toilsome way for him to obtain one of these trailers. Who, he might have reasoned, would pay much attention to another murder or two in *that* locality. And now that he and his juvenile girl friend were traveling together, the first order of business was a pad, preferably one on wheels, and bread for same, with a few luxury items, like, man, imported threads (expensive suits) and kangaroos (Italian shoes) for both her and himself that would flip the squares.

Herbert was no humble apprentice in regard to his chosen way of life. He was a fully qualified journeyman when he headed for Arizona and its infamous Mountain where killings really are so common as to excite little more than cursory regional interest. For one thing, he was wearing a gold watch that had not long before adorned the wrist of Fred McSwain, a motorist who had been so injudicious as to offer a hitchhiker a ride. Herbert, as he tooled contentedly along highway 60-70 to Phoenix, would occasionally glance at this watch and be grateful for the impeccable taste which caused that good Samaritan, McSwain, to buy such an expensive watch—a watch that had been unbuckled from McSwain's limp arm scarcely a minute after he had been strangled in a motel room he had hired for the night on the California shore of beautiful Lake Tahoe. Herbert also had a camera, a 30-30 rifle, and a wallet of McSwain's and what money he'd had on him. As he drove along he had this rifle leaning against the front seat between the girl and himself. He would alternately pat the girl and the rifle; he expected great things from both once he reached his destination.

When he arrived in Phoenix he rented a motel room. The

next morning bright and early he made for the Mountain. Once he made the scene he wasted no time prospecting for gold mines in the conventional sense. Herbert was a boy who, even if he found a vein of rich gold ore, would have scorned the plebian task of extracting it from its rocky embrace with the customary pick and shovel.

His eyes must have glistened when on that sunshiny morning of February 24, 1964, he gazed at the wildly brushed and deeply cut slopes that fell gently away from the precipitous cliffs towering up to five thousand feet on the northwest end of Superstition Mountain, and noted the occasional truck camper and auto trailer that could barely be glimpsed among the fierce desert verdure of the area. He finally settled on making a choice between two impressive truck campers, one a Ford and the other a Chevrolet, each parked in separate and remote glades. He drove up to where the Ford was parked and called out a greeting. A man came out and he struck up a conversation with him. Soon he managed to peer inside the camper enough to apparently convince him that it wasn't furnished as completely as he would like, whereupon he politely excused himself and bumped his car over the tortured ground to the Chevrolet camper.

There he introduced himself to the owner, who in turn announced that he was John Bertella of Sherrill, New York, and asked his sweet-faced wife, Margaret, to come and meet the nice young gentleman, who had told John he would like something to eat.

Her sons, John, Jr., and Ted, who were at home back East, were to say afterwards that their sixty-four-year-old mother was entirely too good-hearted and would invite in and feed literally anyone who came to her back door. On at least one occasion (involving a couple of delinquent and depraved teenagers) she and her sixty-two-year-old husband had had a very bad experience, and her continuance of the practice worried her sons. But during all her long, hard-working, decent life, nothing had ever swerved her from her belief in the essential goodness of humanity, nor lessened her desire to be always hospitable and to do everything in her power to help those who had come upon misfortune.

She didn't hesitate on this occasion—she welcomed the opportunity to be hospitable, as she always had. "Come in, come in," she urged Herbert, "and have a bite with us." Once inside, Herbert saw the most completely equipped pad on wheels he had ever encountered. It was all and more than he was looking for. Margaret busied herself at the ingenious trailer stove, and John began to tell Herbert how he had been a farmer, but had retired to become a construction worker, and that now they were on a five-month vacation in order to fulfill an ambition of many years standing: to prowl the area where Jacob Walz had found an immensely rich gold mine. "At this very moment," he told Herbert, "we are almost in the middle of the Peralta Massacre Ground, as shown on this U.S. map I have for the area." (U.S. Army Corps of Engineers Map Service, Goldfield Quadrangle, N3322.5-W11122.5/7.5, Arizona)

After a few moments the impatient Herbert suddenly excused himself and stepped out to his car, which was parked only a few feet back of the Bertella rig, and got McSwain's rifle. When he turned around John was standing in his doorway hospitably waiting for his return, so he instantly and with practiced smoothness shot from the hip and brought John to ground, as they say in the West. Not wishing to waste ammunition, and probably also having in mind that more shooting might attract attention, he stunned Margaret with the rifle butt as she collapsed in grief over her wounded husband. Then he cut both of their throats, thoroughly, with the hunting knife he carried in a sheath on his belt.

Dragging them to a small wash nearby, he pocketed John's wallet and their watches (John's was an old-fashioned gold railroad-type pocket watch that had been handed down in the family). He hid their bodies with a couple of small rugs he took from the camper, on which he also piled some brush. Soon he and his teen-age girl were on their way in Bertella's camper to a hideout—a large, deep cave he knew of near Blanding, Utah. He had once hidden out there after a previous brush with the fuzz. On the way, one of them practiced Margaret's signature, imitating it so well that they were able to cash some of the traveler's checks they found in the trailer, a real windfall for the devoted couple.

But the weather turned unusually cold around Blanding after a few days, and they didn't want to light a fire in the cave for fear it might attract attention, so they rassled the camper off the truck and pushed it into the cave. But even then it wasn't warm enough. They decided to skid the camper back upon the truck and drive down to Furnace Creek in Death Valley where they knew it was practically always warm. It was warm, as advertised, but, man, was it Squaresville! Absolutely Endsville. Besides, Herbert was bugged by the number of people who seemed to be staring at the truck-camper rig, which was still carrying the Bertella license plates —he had not yet figured out a way to secure new ones—and he made up his mind to hightail it back to the cave in Utah. Another of Margaret's traveler's checks was cashed and they wheeled for their cave again.

But Herbert was to experience, as Robert Burns so succinctly put it, that, "now a' is done that men can do, and a' is done in vain," because the bodies had been discovered back on Superstition Mountain somewhat sooner than Herbert had evidently expected, and a sharp-eyed tourist had been alerted by a story he had read about it in the *Phoenix Gazette*. As a matter of fact, he had cut the piece out of the paper and had it in his pocket. His unusual interest in the story was aroused by the fact that it told of a nationwide police search going on for a stolen truck-camper almost identical to his own, presumably driven by a murderer, and giving its license number. Observing that he was getting low on gasoline as he approached Tonopah, Nevada, this tourist pulled into a gas station, and noticed almost immediately that a truck-camper like his own was being serviced in front of him. It reminded him of the clipping he had in his pocket and he quietly took it out and, as he had a strong feeling it would be, the license given in the police alert was the same as the one he was staring at on the back of the Chevrolet before him. He quietly notified the station proprietor, who called the sheriff's office.

By this time Herbert Shockey and his companion were back on the highway, but the sheriff radioed ahead to have roadblocks set up. When Shockey saw the first roadblock, he instantly wheeled the camper off the road into the desert, but it soon stalled in a wash and he leaped out to take to his heels and find cover in the brush, carrying the rifle and leaving the girl in the camper. "It's what's happening, baby, good luck," he probably said to her. But when those down kiddies, the police, ordered him to come out with his hands up, or be rushed and, like shot, he chickened out—meekly surrendered, as the squares say, plainly showing that while he got a charge out of inflicting savage wounds on other peoples' bodies, he didn't want any of that sort of thing for himself.

When they searched him they found John's treasured keepsake, the gold railroad pocket watch. It had served John well through many years, and it served him well then and there, because it really nailed his killer. Herbert had goofed, and the faithful old watch made it for keeps.

In jig time his girl friend was handcuffed to him and they were on their way back from Utah to Phoenix for trial, but she was subsequently turned over to the juvenile authorities, and Herbert was brought to trial for murder. Several impassive Apaches came to that trial; perhaps they wanted to see how their Thunder God would handle such desecration of His abode as Shockey had perpetrated.

Never in connection with even the most bloodcurdling tales of Apache raids in Arizona had an Apache been described as a killer on the order of Herbert as they heard the witnesses at that trial testify as to what Herbert had done—killed a couple who were being hospitable to him. An Apache is your friend for life if you are genuinely kind and hospitable to him.

With pale-set faces the jury suffered through the evidence against Herbert, and shuddered, some becoming nauseated, when they were handed the pictures of the bodies of the gentle Bertellas—pictures that showed only too graphically their ghastly wounds. On Friday, August 27, 1964, they adjudged Herbert guilty of double murder.

September 9, 1964, was a warm, sunshiny day in Arizona —a day when all outdoors seemed to call to those indoors to come out and walk or play or picnic, or just to lie in an upland meadow. But for Herbert it was the day he was brought before Superior Court Judge Irwin Cantor to be sentenced. He was given two life sentences to run consecutively in order that he might be shut away forever from the temptation to rob, strangle, and cut throats.

"The Court," Judge Cantor said to him, "strongly recommends to future parole boards and governors of this state, or any persons empowered by law to commute sentences, or grant paroles or pardons, that you should not receive parole or pardon, nor should your sentence ever be commuted."

That afternoon an automobile marked with the insignia of the Maricopa County sheriff's office left the county jail with

Herbert sitting handcuffed to a burly deputy sheriff. Another deputy, Charles Tweedy, drove the car through the outskirts of Phoenix and, as they neared Apache Junction, midway to Florence where the state prison is located, passing close to brooding Superstition Mountain and the place in the lee of its towering, perpendicular cliffs where he had ferociously butchered his victims, Herbert kept his eyes straight to the front. Unlike the killers of the animal world, the weasel, hawk, and mountain lion that almost invariably return to their kill, Herbert could not face the scene of his kill even the second time.

Over him, as he passed, the Mountain stood grandly and impassively as it has for billions of years—it has seen countless killers and listened to the pitiful, hopeless pleas for mercy of many victims as their murderers poised the death thrust, shot, or blow.

To the Thunder God of the Apaches it may have been a different matter. He might have permitted Himself a sardonic smile when He noted the averted eyes of the worst of the defilers of His abode as he was passing on to a life that is the closest approximation to the grave's eternal stygian embrace—life imprisonment without possibility of parole!

Chapter 19

The man who finally discovered the source of the Old Dutchman's gold was Alfred Strong Lewis, a mining engineer who was prospecting the Goldfield mining property where Charles Hall had taken out his millions. Here is the story, as told to the writer by Ted Sliger and three of his business associates who now own the mine.

Ted, a wealthy businessman, is the owner of the Buckhorn Mineral Wells, nationally known as the Buckhorn Baths, which is located a few miles from the Mountain. Thousands come each year from all over to refresh and heal themselves in its restorative waters. Among them, the San Francisco Giants baseball team. The team comes each spring to train nearby, and the members invariably bathe regularly in the waters from the hot mineral wells and sing their praises of its magical qualities. For more than twenty years they have been coming there to restore vigor, sapped by their long winter layoff.

"Alfred Lewis also used to come to my place for the baths," Ted said. "One day he approached me in quite a bit of excitement. 'Ted,' he said, 'I've found a hidden mine shaft up near Goldfield and it looks like the old Peralta Mine.' He then went on to describe how he had uncovered an ancient Spanish shaft that had been cleverly hidden under a monstrously large boulder. Various little signs near the base of the boulder had caused him to suspect that there might be something interesting under the boulder, and finally he had toppled it over with a few sticks of dynamite, and there was the shaft, expertly timbered Spanish-fashion, descending into the earth. 'This shaft,' he said, 'is very near Goldfield and only a short distance west from the northwest end of Superstition Mountain, a mile or so from where Miguel Peralta and his men were massacred. The mine shaft that the boulder covered is on the part of the old Goldfield property now owned by Ernest and Dow Shumway of Mesa.'

"He went on to tell me how, after Hall died, his two daughters who inherited the flood-ruined Goldfield Mine immediately offered it for sale because mining engineers told them that it would be impossible to drain or pump out the mine. Besides, their father had left them well off. George Young, once mayor of Phoenix, bought the property from them.

" 'I understand that Young and some associates put over one million dollars into an effort to find an access to the vein other than the shaft that was forever flooded out. I do know for sure that one of their efforts involved sinking a shaft straight down for eleven hundred feet, and from it they ran many lateral shafts, or "drifts" as miners say, to probe the area for quite a distance in every direction. I suppose they ran out of hope, and probably money too in time. Anyway, they sold their holdings in the area to the Shumway brothers, who have been holding it as an investment for several years. I have a deal with them to prospect the whole area and buy them out if I found anything and could raise the money. Now I'd sure like to do that because I think this old Spanish shaft I've discovered is probably the original vein. Would you like to throw in with me?'

"I immediately called a friend of mine in California, C. C. 'Doc' Waterbury," Ted Sliger said, "who is wealthy and knowledgeable in business. He agreed to come over immediately to see what could be done in a practical way about exploiting Mr. Lewis' discovery. While I was waiting for him to arrive on a plane that night, I decided to call another good and well-experienced mining man I knew, Tom Russell, from up in the Payson area of northern Arizona, as well as another friend, Hugh Nichols, who owns and lives on a large ranch just up the road a piece from me. He is also a wealthy man who has had quite a bit of mining, oil, and business experience."

Nichols tells about what happened next. "The four of us, Ted, Waterbury, Russell, and myself," he said, "had Lewis show us the old shaft. We went down the entrance which the boulder had hidden, down to where the shaft hit bottom sixty feet below, then there was a lateral shaft that inclined downward and westward on about a forty-five-degree angle for about thirty feet until it came to a vein of ore. It was a vein, or lode, as hard-rock miners say, of very rich ore—fairly festooned with wire gold.

"The group of us, Lewis, Waterbury, Nichols, Russell and I, then and there decided to buy it if we could, on an equal partnership basis for all."

Late that night, Russell, Waterbury, and Sliger went into Phoenix and contacted the Shumway brothers. While Waterbury and Sliger waited in the car outside, Russell bought the property from them for about twenty-five thousand dollars, paying five thousand down that night, to bind the deal. This purchase consisted entirely of eighty miners' claims, as there were no deeds to the land available then. A few months ago they finally obtained a patent from the federal government [the legal instrument by which the U.S. conveys legal fee-simple titles to public land] on the claims on which the old Spanish shaft is located.

"The reason we knew it was an old Spanish working, and almost certainly the Peralta Mine," Russell told the writer, "is that it was timbered by ironwood, some of which had been cut by an axe, and some burned apart—none of it being sawed. In those days the Spanish didn't have saws good enough to cut ironwood; as a matter of fact it takes a hell of a good saw to do the trick right today. Another thing was that the timbers were so old that they were going through the process of being petrified. The wood cells were filling with iron pyrites [fool's gold]. The sapwood on the outside of these timbers was rotted and gone, but the hearts were sound. Under normal circumstances ironwood heart is almost jet black, whereas these old timbers had taken in so much iron pyrites they aged to a yellow cast. When you put one of them in the bright sunlight and look at it through a magnifying glass its pyrites glitter brilliantly. In addition I sent some of this old ironwood to a professor I know at the University of Arizona and he confirmed that it had been cut over a hundred years ago, and had been underground for at least that long. That was conclusive proof that it was a very ancient Spanish shaft and because of the extreme richness of the vein it could only be the Peralta working. Besides, geologists and mining engineers, some of them world-famous, who have come to the Mountain, attracted in their turn, as so many others have been by the tales of the Old Dutchman's gold find nearly a century ago, have almost without exception declared that the formation of the Mountain itself was contrary to all that is known from scientific studies about where gold is found. Most of them had concluded that the Peralta Mine was undoubtedly very near the Mountain, but not on it or its companion peaks.

"When you consider the fact that the vein of gold found by Peralta, Walz, the three Mormons, and Mr. Lewis—a rich vein from which chunks could easily be broken off by one man and enough of these carried away by him alone if necessary, or on a burro or two, that would be worth thousands of dollars for each load, and that it was the *only* vein, or deposit, of gold that was ever discovered even *near* the Mountain—there can be no doubt as to the identity of Lewis' discovery."

As an example, Hugh Nichols then showed the writer a chunk of rough ore, about half the size of an ordinary male fist, that he had picked up with his own hands at the end of the lateral shaft. "As you can see," he said, "this fragment of ore is extremely rich with what is known as free gold. With the naked eye you can see there is much gold in there. I estimate there is at least fifty to sixty dollars' worth of it in this one piece. The other stuff which you see around the gold is principally silica quartz impregnated with a great deal of manganese.

"There was much evidence," Hugh said, "to show that someone [and almost certainly it was the Old Dutchman], had found the hidden mine before Alfred Strong Lewis blasted the boulder off the entrance to it."

"Lewis showed me the cleverly constructed and concealed little passage," said Russell, "that someone had used to get under the boulder. You could see where the ironwood timbers had been cut in order to permit this passage into the old shaft. This mysterious little entrance under the boulder, and other evidence, showed that it was Walz who had dug that neat little passage. The Indian girl *had* to have shown him, for instance, how Peralta had hidden the shaft, or he could not have known exactly where and how to dig it. Everything about his ingress showed he knew exactly what to expect when he got there. He had cut his way past the ironwood timbering, found the rich ore and covered up the marks around the boulder each time he left so carefully that even the sharpest eyes could detect nothing unusual there. All these things made it clear beyond the shadow of a doubt that someone had taken the intruder there and showed him exactly where to start his little shaft. That person could only have been Ken-tee."

Russell believed, as all the partners did, that the elaborate precautions Walz took to elude his trackers when he visited his mine also extended to the hints he occasionally dropped as to its whereabouts, and were deliberately contradictory, to throw off searchers, and no doubt designed to be mischievously misleading as well. As evidence toward this conclusion Russell pointed to the fact that Walz became increasingly bitter, and he grew irascible with almost everyone except children, and toward the last liked no adults who hadn't been treated badly by someone or by fate. Everything about his later years, Russell believed, showed that the last thing he would ever have done was tell *anyone* how to find the source of his gold, and that it is more than likely, then, that *if* he told Julia about it being in the path of the shadow of Weaver's Needle at 4 PM he was just trying to put her off for the time being. In the first place, as Russell saw it, he could hardly have believed he was actually dying—few people ever do, or he was being plain sadistic, not at all an unlikely theory when his experiences and his last years are taken into account.

In any event, the partners feel that the Old Dutchman, provided he can know in his present celestial abode what is going on, would take a great deal of sardonic amusement from knowing that people to this day—and more of them than ever—are still fruitlessly searching for the mine miles from where it is. He would be as one with the Thunder God in this.

Russell believed that Peralta for protection against surprise attacks from the Indians, and for other good reasons, such as plentiful grass and water and game, sought out as a matter of absolute necessity the site for the camp discovered by Tom Daly up in Superstition Mountain. "It is as certain as almost anything can be in this world," said Russell, "that he needed just such a place for his miners to retreat to during weekends, and to serve as a rest camp for those who were ill, or exhausted, or needed recreation, as witness the little racetrack they built for themselves up there. Mules, horses, and burros also needed good care, feed and rest, especially in view of the brutally hard work both men and animals had to do while mining under such primitive conditions. It was also a place where he could, as he did, securely store supplies, build a large blacksmith shop, make charcoal, and construct his *arrastres* for reducing the ore right where there was an abundance of feed and water [a rare thing up on Superstition] for the mules who powered the *arrastres*. The area around the mine itself for a mile to a mile and a half in every direction was wide open to an Indian-type attack, unless extensive and, under the circumstances, almost wholly impracticable fortifications were constructed, whereas the Mountain camp was almost a perfect spot to defend, because its topography is such that it prohibitively favored the defender. And being mostly on a mesa, attackers could hardly gain the element of surprise— the very element Mangas Coloradas and his combined force of braves used to fatal effect against Peralta and his men when they came down out of this natural fortress to flee back to Mexico."

"We began to take the gold out of the shaft as fast as we could," says Nichols, "and after we had taken about forty-two thousand dollars' worth of it, we broke through into another abandoned shaft—a much bigger and more modern one this time, but only an extremely short stretch of it. This turned out, we believe, to be a part of the old shaft of Charles Hall's Mammoth Mine, the one that the flood had cut and covered and no one had been able to find since! This was the vein from which Hall had taken gold worth nearly three million dollars. The great difficulty, as we soon learned, was the landslide not only had cut off the vein at that point, and shifted it somewhere else, but had mixed almost everything else underground like it had been churned by a gigantic food blender.

"We brought in several large pieces of dirt-moving machinery and began scraping off the surface all around the area where the two shafts, Hall's and the Peraltas', had penetrated the earth. We built a mill and ran this surface ore through it. From assays we had made there was gold in every foot of ground up there—just enough at the present price of gold—to pay for the work of extracting it. But finally, after we had moved an awful lot of earth, and still hadn't found the vein again, though we knew that it must be down there *somewhere* and that it was bound to be enormously big and rich, at least as rich as the lode the Peraltas, Walz, and Hall had worked, we held a meeting at which we decided that we were just taking money out of one pocket to put it into another by taking the gold from the ore in the dust we were mining, and though, as I said, it was only enough to pay us for the work we were doing, yet it was ore that would be very profitable if the price of gold ever goes up.

"As long as we hoped that any moment we might find the old vein again, any amount of work, trouble and expense was all right with us, and it was no more than reasonable that we keep trying, but sober second thoughts told us that while that vein might be somewhere right close to the surface, as were the portions the others had been lucky enough to find, it also might now be a half mile away, or a half mile deep. Also, Alfred Lewis had died since discovering the boulder's secret and that disheartened us quite a bit, because we had been depending on him a great deal. Then Tom Russell died, and that was a devastating personal loss, as well as business loss to us. The three of us who remain are no longer as interested as we once were in making money, and that, too, makes a whole lot of difference."

Chapter 20

We sat one evening, Beatrice, widow of Alfred Strong Lewis, and the writer, in beguilingly comfortable canvas chairs in front of her little house, located on the very top of Goldfield Hill, my omnipresent tape recorder listening to us, the sun setting over our left shoulders and casting its rays —rays that were becoming a flaming glory as the sun neared the horizon—on the northwest face of the Mountain about a mile away, while she told how she happened to be where she was, and about the period she has been guarding the mine area against vandals and predators of all sorts.

After Alfred had died the four partners had hired her as the only remaining paid employee of the operation to continue living in the comfortable cottage (the reconstructed former mine office) on the property as a watchman-guard. In the wild terrain that surrounds it there is only one road on which anyone could approach the hilltop site of the mine except by foot—a rough dirt road closed by a stout gate at its lower end.

A quick, alert-minded, vigorous, ninety-pound woman in her late sixties, she had taught herself to be a crack shot many years before, and since accepting her present job always kept a loaded double-barreled shotgun nearby at all times. She now had her husband's interest in the mining company, Goldfield Mines, Inc., that was set up by Nichols, Sliger, Waterbury, and Russell to buy and mine the property.

She was born in Indiana, she said, and her father, Jerry Woodward, was a peppermint farmer near Maquoketa. Peppermint, as she went on to describe it, is of the same family as spearmint, with only a very little difference in flavor. It is grown in fields, much like hay is, harvested the same way, then cut and stacked to dry. "I used to help at this all my young life," she said, "and I loved every minute of it. I can close my eyes right now and smell the delicious fragrance as plainly as if I was back in one of my father's fields in peppermint harvest time.

"You get the pure oil of peppermint by running the stalks through a still, consisting of a furnace, a boiler, and a series of steam pipes, which lead to a condenser where the vapor off the mash is turned into the oil or essence that then runs into a vat.

"I always keep a little bottle of it here. It means a lot to me," she said.

She left the farm to study nursing and in due course became a registered nurse. In 1941, while on a vacation in Arizona, she met Alfred, who was then working as a mining engineer at Cave Creek, Arizona. She had fallen in love with Arizona years before when she came out there to nurse her sister through a bout of crippling arthritis. "Alfred was the second love affair of my life—Arizona was the first," she said with a smile. "We were married in 1944 after a three-year courtship, and never were a man and woman happier together than we were.

"We were especially happy and content after Alfred retired and got permission from the Shumway brothers to move up here and have this house for us to live in while he prospected the whole Shumway holdings. The agreement was that he would evaluate the claim in his capacity as a mining engineer and propsect all of it to try and find where the old vein was, and try to sell the property, or, if he found something that he thought was worth buying for himself, he could do so at a price they set in advance. But I honestly hoped, at least at times I did, that he would never find the vein, because I was so happy just as we were.

"I can remember so well how excited he was," she said, "when he found the old mine entrance under that boulder. Why did he check around that boulder so minutely? He never knew that himself for sure. Call it a hunch, maybe, but he felt afterwards that some faint signs around its base happened to catch his eye and made him think someone or something had been under it at one time."

" 'I'll find some fellows with money to go in with me and we'll buy out the Shumways ourselves,' he said to me. Then he contacted Ted Sliger and the rest you know about.

"My husband never had any doubt," she said, "but that the little entrance to the mine he found under that boulder was done by one person—one who had discovered the secret of how Peralta had hid his mine. That and other conclusive indications he found, such as some tools that were of a manufacture unknown in Peralta's time, made it seem that it *had* to be the place where Jacob Walz got his rich concentrate. Besides, it had to be someone like Walz who died before carting off all the concentrate, because if anyone else had known about it they would certainly have at least carted off the rest of it."

The little house sits within a stone's throw of where the boulder once stood. In that now peaceful, wildly beautiful, but unimaginably lonely setting where not a sound was to be heard except the calling to each other by the birds, including a large flock of quail she had tamed and fed and were constantly around her, it was hard to imagine that on a morning only a little over a century ago, so many men had died on the Massacre Ground over yonder a little to the left of the Mountain, and so plainly to be seen from where we were sitting.

Much less could one visualize the war whoops, the crashing of musketry, the flashing sabers, the twang of the terrible swift arrows of the Apaches, the screams of the wounded and dying men and horses, and the slaughter that was taking place on that long-ago morning as the deadly struggle raged that was not to end until the Mexicans were dead to the last man.

"Alfred had a regular passion for prowling around over there and trying to reconstruct the battle in his mind, and picking up relics and souvenirs, though he never found any of the gold concentrate," Beatrice said. "By the time he died he had became an authority on the subject of the Massacre. Through examining old Spanish, Mexican, and Arizona mining records he learned quite a bit about the area, too, and had written the history of the battle as he imagined it. Wait, I'll get you the manuscript," she said, jumping up to go inside. When she came back she laid a thick sheaf of neatly typed script in the writer's lap. "If you can get any helpful information out of it, you are welcome to it," she said. "Alfred would have liked for you to, I'm sure."

Then she showed him a glass jar of gold nuggets Alfred had picked up at the bottom of the old shaft after he first discovered it.

As he sat there listening and gazing over toward that macabre but magnificent Mountain which in the now crimson light of the fast sinking sun looked startlingly like a vast cathedral, he was suddenly struck by the thought that he hadn't uncovered a single pleasant story about it.

Many writers besides this writer soon began finding their way up to the aerie on the hill where once Peralta, the Old Dutchman, and Charles Hall found fortunes, to interview the "little Old Lady with the every-ready shotgun" who was guarding the "hill of gold." Almost daily she also faced down some of the toughest characters who ever stabbed anyone in the back, cut off a head, or bushwhacked some unsuspecting prospector, who came as jackals, vultures and hyenas came.

There began to be open speculation as to how long it would be before she was found up there savaged to death by some of the many of life's rejects who, having read the myriad of newspaper articles, magazine pieces and books about Super-

stition Mountain, Goldfield and the Lost Dutchman Gold
Mine, found their way to the area where it was easy for arrant
cowards to rob and murder and get away with it.

"Are you ever afraid up here?" this writer asked her while
stretched out on one of the comfortable old canvas ship's deck
chairs that were strewn around the little yard on the northeast
end of her house, from where there was a spectacular view of
the Mountain's towering parapets. As a matter of fact, the
writer found his way up there so often to talk to this indomitable and wonderful lady that one day the canvas on one of
these chairs collapsed under him and his conscience dictated
that he haul it and a companion one down to a ship's chandler
in Phoenix and have them completely outfitted with the best
new canvas to be had.

"Yes," she said in answer to the question, "I am at times
but only in the still watches of the night when I come awake
suddenly and imagine I hear all sorts of stealthy sounds, but
as soon as I'm wide awake, I know it was just night fears and
I go back to sleep again. During the days and evenings I certainly have nothing to worry about because I have my mockingbirds and boss quail to look out for me."

"Mockingbirds, boss quail . . .?"

"Why sure," she explained, "neither man, beast, nor bird of
prey can get within a half mile of here without the boss quail
of any one of a dozen large flocks I feed sounding off loud
and clear—then the mockingbirds immediately gravitate toward where the old he-quail is steadily sounding his tocsin,
and by that time I am moving up to that little spot on the very
top of the rise back of us where one can best see in all directions. As soon as the mockingbirds see that I am in position,
they start dive-bombing whatever it is that has the quail concerned. If it is a coyote, or a mountain lion or wildcat, all of
which are scared of humans, they run when I walk down toward them, but if I reach a certain closeness and something
hasn't run out of the bushes where the mockingbirds are
pointing to, then I know it is a human varmint they are
fingering, and I squat down and say loudly, 'I have a double
00 buckshot shell in one of the barrels of this here shotgun
and I'm firing into those bushes by the count of five if someone doesn't stand up: one-two-three—,' and by at least that
count of three someone stands up out of there. Then I march
'em right up the hill and around back of the house and on

down to the gate where you came in, and no matter what they say, or try to ask me, I never answer 'em, except if they get a little nasty and think maybe they can mean-mouth me and get away with it. I say, 'I have birdshot in the other barrel, and you're a-fixin' to be able to say truthfully for the rest of your life that it *was* in there.' So far none of them have called my hand, and for that I'm right thankful, except, maybe, in the cases of two or three who were that contemptible and said such filthy words, that I'm not sure I would have minded planting a charge of birdshot in the seat of their pants.

"One time a year or so ago I heard my feathered friends yelling for help, and when I got there I flushed four of the ugliest looking and acting characters out from behind a big clump of Texas sage you or anyone ever saw. They looked like the pictures you see in the papers of those outlaw motorcycle riders over in California, where they were tearing up a town, or scaring good citizens, or other nice playful capers like that. As a matter of fact I wouldn't be surprised if that was where these fellows came from with their shoulder-length hair and mustaches and beards, and unearthly looking clothes. They hardly looked human. I gave 'em the usual directions, but instead of doing what they were told, the orneriest looking of these human critters said: 'Why should we take orders from you, Old Woman? After all, there are four of us and only one of you, 'an we got guns, too. Now look here,' he said, 'we've heard you're guarding a lot of gold up there. Let us have some of it and we won't hurt you none, but if you don't we might, like, rush you right here and now, and if we do we'll have to, like, kill you.'

"Just at that moment I heard the high-pitched scream of one of those big red-tailed hawks—a scream you'll never forget once you've heard it, and when I glanced up there he was coming straight down in one of their tremendous hunting dives, seemingly right at us. Then as I threw up my twelve-gauge, I heard a 'take cover' cry from the boss quail and I knew Mr. Red Tail was after the quail who always move in close to me, because, as you know, I feed them grain every day. Well, I hit that hawk plum center and that was all for him.

" 'Now!' taunted the leader of that sorry-looking quartet, 'you've only got one shell left.'

"Each time I leave the house I always throw a half-dozen

live shells in a pocket I've sewed into every dress I have, and I've practiced by the hour ejecting old empty practice shells from my shotgun, grabbing two live ones from my pocket, shoving them into the barrels and snapping the gun closed. I don't want to sound like I'm bragging, but I'll bet I got my time down to somewhere near to what Matt Dillon would have to take.

" 'Watch!' I told them. 'See those blossoms on top of that tall cactus over there?' and I pointed to a Giant Sahuaro about seventy-five feet away—watch those blossoms!' Then I clipped them off with that last shell, and quicker almost than their eyes could see I had two more shells in my gun.

" 'Now what were you sayin' a moment ago?' I asked that head punk.

" 'Why we were just kiddin' around, ma'am,' he said, and they backed away from there like a fox leaves off from prowling around the henhouse when he hears the farmer coming."

"What would you have done if they tried to rush you?" the writer asked.

"I would have tried to kill as many of them as I could before any of them could get to me," she said without hesitation, "and there is a very good chance I would have got them all. While Al was a champion skeet shot (he hated to kill anything, as I do, unless they're killers themselves), he won quite a few trophies in his time, and he taught me to be a pretty good one, too. Still, if they'd rushed me it wouldn't have been that kind of shootin'—for accuracy, I mean. It would have been more like those shootouts they used to have in the Old West: the kind that were won by those who practiced the most, and learned to shoot accurately at close range from the hip, and that's what I've done.

"I've been to several of those quick-draw contests they are always having here in Arizona, and I seen fellows at those meets who were so fast at getting their six-gun out and getting off a shot into a prescribed target, that it had to be seen by a person experienced with guns to be believed.

"It is my firm opinion that all those fellows who became famous as quick draws in the old days out here must have practiced for years at the art, because that some of them were almost unearthly fast is beyond dispute. At those meets I went to they had electronic timing devices. The world's record with a single-action revolver is a small fraction of a second!

"A fellow named Ed McGivern, who has since died I understand, holds all the records there are. Once he fired five electrically timed shots in two-fifths of a second and put all five bullets in an area no bigger than a playing card at fifteen feet! The average time of those movie and TV star fellows in Hollywood who can undoubtedly draw and fire in fantastically quick time, is about half a second, which takes literally years of practice, but even that is far from championship time. On top of the practicing, they have famous teachers out there for those who for professional reasons need, or for personal reasons want, a lightning fast draw, fellows like Charley Heard, Rod Redwing, and Arvo Ojala.

"A few years ago," she said, "I went to a meet down at Tombstone and saw a fellow by the name of Charles Reed get off a shot in .35 of a second to win the fast draw championship at Tombstone's Helldorado historical pageant. Can you even imagine that! Among the top ten shooters was a lady, Marlene McElhaney. I would have liked to got to know her.

"The fellow who was second there that day, Roy Guthrie of Tucson, needed only .36 of a second. A man by the name of Ed Beurrier was fourth with an old-time *cap* and *ball* revolver!

"Wyatt Earp is credited with saying something that made a deep impression on me. When asked what in his opinion made him so successful in helping fill Boothill at Tombstone, as well as at other places, he said, 'It wasn't the draw; it was the drop.' And I have been guided up here by the philosophy in the remark."

Beatrice kept on guarding the mine and the property adjacent to it year after year, and becoming famous for it, while the might of the U.S. government held the price of gold down to thirty-five dollars an ounce. Meanwhile the cost of mining, especially union wages, climbed into the financial stratosphere, keeping not only their mine from being worked, but practically all other gold mines in the United States.

That is where the situation rests today, with one exception: Beatrice and her omnipresent shotgun aren't guarding the fabulous mine anymore. When she didn't answer her telephone one morning in April this spring (1970), her nephew, John W. Gould, went up there to check and found her still asleep—asleep forever. She had had a heart attack in the night. But the much-publicized shotgun was still on guard, standing against the head of the bed within easy reach of her right hand.

Her death was a great shock to her partners, Sliger, Nichols, and Waterbury; they had all thought highly of her, trusted her implicitly and were great admirers of the way she guarded the hilltop and reveled in the vast respect it created for her far and wide. All three of them, sometimes together and sometimes separately, liked to drop in on her for a chat, as so many other friends did at her little house in its wildly beautiful setting.

Now that Mrs. Lewis has died, all three surviving partners are more than ever in agreement that it is not financially feasible to make any further efforts to mine and smelt the ore of their gold mine until the price of gold goes up, or the U.S. raises its restrictions on its citizens trading in the world gold market. Until then, South Africa and Russia, to name only two countries, can, because their labor is incomparably cheaper than in the U.S., keep on profitably mining ore that is much poorer in gold content than Goldfield ore, unless the partners find the mother lode.

Chapter 21

On the very day, almost exactly to the hour that the last words of this book were typed (11 September 1970), they were bringing the body of Al Morrow by pack train from Superstition Mountain where he had prospected for nineteen years. He died two days before in a tunnel he'd dug during his search for the "golden ledge," crushed by a boulder described by Pinal County sheriff, Coy deArman, as being as "big as a large bedroom."

He had moved his bunk and a few simple cooking utensils into a wide place in the tunnel to escape the August heat that beat down on the small tent across from his shaft in Needle Canyon, seven miles into Superstition by horseback trail from First Water at the foot of Bluff Springs Mountain.

On the front of this tent was a note in Morrow's handwriting, left there for a friend he expected would visit him that day. It read: "I am across in the mine. If you need me holler, and I'll come out."

The friend came, found the note and soon discovered the huge boulder that had fallen *through* the Mountain above the shaft and landed right on top of Al, who at the moment had been on his feet holding a flashlight in his hand, evidently inspecting the roof to determine where the rumble was coming from that the boulder no doubt made as it slid ponderously at first and then came down with lightning speed.

When the sheriff's office contacted Al's nephew, Rodney Morrow of Minden, North Dakota, he advised that the body be buried where it was. "I know it is where Uncle Al would rather rest than anywhere else on earth," he said.

Like many other honest prospectors who have come by the hundreds, even thousands, to prospect the Mountain, Al had saved money all his working life to have a go at discovering the hidden mine of the Old Dutchman. Nineteen years was a long time to devote to the quest without discovering an ounce of gold, or a trace of "color," as hard-rock miners say, but Al never thought so.

Morrow, fifty-seven, was a kind and friendly man who befriended all who dared to explore near the rugged spots where he drilled the heartbreaking number of exploratory shafts with which he pocked that Mountain during those nineteen years.

A writer sought out Al's camp one day and, while having a bite of grub with him and a few cups of the superb coffee he was noted for brewing, asked him: "Isn't nineteen years a little long to pursue a dream without some encouragement, especially under such unimaginably lonely, desperately primitive conditions as this?"

"Primitive, yes, but as for lonely," said Al, whose eyes crinkled like a seafaring man's when he smiled, "you could hardly call it that out here; nearly fifty people have stopped by here during those nineteen years—prospectors headed further into the Mountain, and others, just daredevil types I guess, and two or three writer fellas like yourself came by. Also, I have hundreds of friends among all the little animals and birds who live in these mountains. They *know* I won't harm them. I've never carried a gun in my life," he said, "or killed anything on purpose. I'm not against killin' when it comes to varmints, such as coyotes, hawks, cats of any size or description, and particularly the human kind of varmint, but I just don't want to do any of it myself.

"When my little friends smell smoke, they know I'm getting ready to eat something and they crowd around me for the crumbs and scraps. The quail, squirrels, chipmunks and sparrows climb all over me. They are for all the world like children and, like children, they love to make a lot of noise just for noise sake. But do you notice," he asked the writer, "that you didn't hear a sound from them while you were arriving—except for the mockingbirds who warned me you were coming? They know for miles around that a stranger is here with me; fifteen minutes after you've gone they'll all be making so much racket that one will hardly hear my sledge hitting the rock drill. But I love them all and I've learned to understand a lot of the things they say to each other.

"Most of the honest prospectors here in the Mountain are dreamers, and not just dreamers about what they'll do with the money from the gold they all expect to find. Like me, they dream about a lot of things. The dreams help with the hard work—the drilling by hand, blasting, wheelbarrowing the rubble out after the blast, checking it out for color, and then starting all over again. Also, I have to walk the seven miles each way once and sometimes twice a month to Apache Junction for blasting powder and grub and carry it here on my back."

Morrow then sat for a while without moving or saying anything. The writer was also glad to rest quietly after the long jolting climb up there by muleback. That ride made the ground he was sitting on feel cushiony and the rock wall he was leaning against seem soft, while he catalogued and wondered about the stupefyingly meager setup that was all the home and working facilities this apparently intelligent man had, or had had for so many years. Across the way was the entrance to the shaft where the monstrous boulder was even then loosening from its womb in the Mountain. Was it, the writer wondered afterward, used, as many who live in the shadow of the Mountain think it was, as an instrument of the Thunder God's vengeance?

"You know," he continued, "having a place to live and work where big dreams seem possible has a lot more to it than a bunch of folks ever think about. Take me, f'r instance: you might call me a fugitive from dreariness. Did you ever stop to think how many millions of people work at jobs in which there's no future for them? There rarely is for this kind, even if they have an unmarried rich uncle, because most such loaded relatives leave their money to something that they think will make a big shot of them, even after they're dead. Here I'm immune from most of the things that tantalize, agonize, thwart, disappoint, frustrate and use up the majority of people's lives.

"Sometimes, too, I wonder," he said, "what I would really do if I actually found a bonanza of gold up here. Like most others, I used to think that if I ever became a multimillionaire I would buy a yacht, a big house or two, get a young girl for a wife and, well, things like that. But more often than not there's a big ulcer connected with those things—the one the owner gets to go with his shattered nerves. And you can't enjoy *anything* then. I know; I had an ulcer once.

"The cute young showgirl wives a lot of those rich old coots acquire are just hanging around for the things money will buy, and sufferin' the gaffer, and such old men know it, too, and if they don't those wives let 'em know about it quick enough. Of course I only learned what I know about these things from reading magazines and newspapers.

"It was the thousands of little things connected with fighting for a livin' that wore me out and makes this out here seem much better. Here there is always peace in my little spot and a far better than average feeling of contentment, *and* there is hope.

"This old Mountain has been mean-mouthed a lot—they say that it is the home of the Apaches' Thunder God, and that sooner or later He takes vengeance on all who come pokin' around here, but all I can say is that I'm beginning to think that the Mountain has been good to me."

Castenada would have understood Al Morrow.

EPILOGUE

This book ends, but the mystery goes on; now it is the mystery of *exactly* where the rest of the vein or lode is hiding, the lode that rode upwards from the bowels of the earth on a great volcanic upheaval eons ago, and produced the precious metal which brought Peralta and his men to their deaths; made Jacob Walz immortal; enriched Charles Hall, and caused the deaths of scores not so lucky as he—this fabulous lode that was copiously tapped by Peralta and Hall, nibbled at by Walz, provided great riches three times and, though lost again for the time being, will in all likelihood someday, somehow be found again.

It is a mystery upon which facts have had little or no effect, any more than they probably will in the future. The dream is still the thing: the dream that somewhere near or on a Mountain hard by Apache Junction, Arizona, is a great mass of gold—the mother lode here, there, somewhere—awaiting someone to discover it. It is a dream that millions of people will never let fade away; they couldn't endure their lives if they did. They will forever nourish it. Perhaps it will nourish itself on its own vitality, but go on it will, eternally.